T0376141

Unfolding Power

Documents in 20th Century Canadian Women's History

Pat Staton
Rose Fine-Meyer
Stephanie Kim Gibson

Rose Budding

(A short monologue on the feminine aspect of power)

*This force that unfolds
a rose bud
is more potent than
     nuclear brutality,
more dramatic
than your resistance to
     change—
or mine.*

*This raw, soft passion
wastes nothing,
wants nothing, is never
     defeated.*

*This power unfolding
is not to inspire guilt,
but justice.*

Judith Boel, 1979.
- reprinted with permission

Unfolding Power
Documents in 20th Century Canadian Women's History

Pat Staton
Rose Fine-Meyer
Stephanie Kim Gibson

©Green Dragon Press &
The Ontario Women's History Network
2267 Lake Shore Blvd. West, #1009
Toronto, ON M8V 3X2

Tel: 416-251-6366

Cover design: Pat Staton
Cover art: "Bounty of the Land" Watercolour monoprint 1/1 by Pat Staton.

Text design: m3marketing

Canadian Cataloguing in Publication Data

Staton, Pat, 1933-
Unfolding power : documents in 20th century Canadian women's history / Pat Staton, Rose Fine-Meyer, Stephanie Kim Gibson.

Includes bibliographical references.
ISBN 1-896781-20-9

1. Women--Canada--History--20th century--Sources.
2. Sex role--Canada--History--20th century--Sources.
I. Fine-Meyer, Rose II. Gibson, Stephanie K. III. Title.

HQ1453.S72 2004   305.42'0971   C2004-904072-3

Acknowledgements

We acknowledge the support for the initial stages of the research by Terezia Zoric and the Equity Studies Department of the Toronto District School Board, and thank Myra Novogrodsky and Beth Atcheson for encouraging us to expand on the stories of Canadian women contained in an earlier work by one of the authors - *Claiming Women's Lives*.

Table of Contents

Introduction

GREEN DRAGON PRESS

GREEN DRAGON PRESS

Introduction

"From listening to the stories of others, we learn to tell our own."
Margaret Atwood

Creating a learning environment that promotes knowledge and fosters awareness and understanding of women's history is of particular importance in the 21st century. Students often lack a true understanding of the term "feminist", and may therefore misinterpret both its historical and modern day meaning. Some young women and men disassociate themselves from the feminist movement, and hold the belief that there is no longer a need for the struggle towards a more equal and inclusive society. The assumption of achieved equality is incorrect. While it is true that the status of women in Canada changed at an amazing pace during the 20th century - only one hundred years ago Canadian women had significantly limited political and civil rights - not all women's status improved. The greatest improvement was experienced by middle and upper class women. Poor women, women from minority groups and working women in particular fields of labour, have not seen the same level of improvement. Therefore there is a vital role to be played by educators who seek to create and deliver an inclusive history curriculum.

The objective of *Unfolding Power: Documents in 20th Century Canadian Women's History* is to provide a much needed resource for use in the classroom. Although some recently published textbooks do provide important information about women, none of them are either inclusive or comprehensive when examining the role of women. Key issues have not been adequately addressed and in many cases women are presented in an extremely limited or role-specific way.

The history of women in Canada is of crucial importance because it is integral to all major events and issues. Therefore, it is essential that their diverse voices be heard. *Unfolding Power* celebrates the role of women in many fields throughout the 20th century. This collection of primary documents, along with the suggested activities will allow the instructor to supplement and enrich any Canadian history curriculum, as well as provide a springboard for further historical examination and research.

We recognize that each classroom is unique in its makeup, as well as in the needs of its students. For that reason, *Unfolding Power: Documents in 20th Century Canadian Women's History* is organized to accommodate any teaching classroom environment, as the focus is on providing materials and activities that can easily be adapted to a variety of academic levels and classroom situations. The documents have been chosen with the goal of encouraging students and teachers to further their knowledge of women's history. The documents cover various themes: work, fashion and beauty, politics, myths of womanhood, domesticity, organizing for change and leisure and sports.

Not all themes are present in every decade. Some decades, especially those of the war years, have a particular focus. Each decade includes an introduction to provide context, primary documents, and short biographical notes about significant women, important milestones for women, and selected resources to support further research. Where possible, articles and documents are accompanied by full citations, in order to encourage further research. For example, if the article is from a particular newspaper or magazine, perhaps the students could investigate the position of other contemporary publications. As well, decades can be examined as individual case studies or be studied in relation to other decades. For example, it would be useful to compare and contrast the treatment of a particular topic throughout the century. Culminating activities, listed at the end of the book, suggest ways to approach this:

GREEN DRAGON PRESS

• Has the representation of women's advertisements changed over the decades?
• Does the message communicated through media images demonstrate a changing role with society?
• How has the concept of work changed or remained constant for women throughout this century?

These are vital lessons in history that challenge the students to analyze and interpret the historical material, in place of role-learning facts and dates. Students at all levels find exploring history much more enjoyable when they can see historical issues and events reflected in their individual experience.

Throughout, we have shared key strategies that will bring history alive to students and help stimulate historical inquiry. The documents themselves are easily reproduced as overheads or as class handouts to accompany the activities. The material is primarily intended to inspire students to come to their own conclusions. Background knowledge is necessary, yet these documents are best used as a springboard for further discussion, debate, or research. They are also a wonderful way to generate interest at the beginning of a unit. It is suggested that non-traditional lessons such as skits, debates, and the creation of movie/radio shows be the central focus of any history program for junior levels. This helps students actively participate in historical narratives and creates a closer link to past events. These documents and activities aim to provide stimulation and enjoyment so that students are encouraged to study history in their senior years and perhaps throughout their lives.

It is the authors' hope that we will reach a point where women's voices are naturally integrated. To achieve this goal, we strongly suggest these documents be used in conjunction with other material presented in the course so that women become directly integrated into the curriculum. If the voices of Canadian women are heard right next to the voices of Canadian men then we will achieve a more equitable teaching environment for our students. The gains that women made were hard-won; not a single one was given as a matter of right. It is important to recognize the struggles and commitment of Canadian women who fought to achieve equity in the workplace and at home. Therefore it is not acceptable to teach the history of Canadian women by isolating women from other events and issues, or assigning special classes to examine women's history. Doing so continues to marginalize the important role women have played in the shaping of this country. Women's voices and achievements are an integral part of our history and we proudly share their stories.

Dedication

This book is dedicated to June Callwood – journalist, author of 30 books, TV and radio host, and recipient of the Order of Canada. A life long human rights campaigner, she was a founder of Nellie's hostel for abused women, Jessie's center for teen mothers, Casey House AIDS hospice, the Writers' Union of Canada, the Writers' Development Trust, Canadian PEN, Canadian Association for the Repeal of Abortion Laws and the Canadian Civil Liberties Association. June Callwood has triumphed over life's challenges with courage and humour.

GREEN DRAGON PRESS

Turn of the Century to 1909

What do women want? The question of the proper sphere.

What makes a happy marriage? A century ago, many felt the answer lay in an utterly submissive, sweetly devoted wife.

The following story appeared on Dec. 12, 1895 in the *Toronto Star*.

☞ **HINTS FOR BRIDES** ☜

The Wife's Duty to her Husband Briefly Told

Three Things for Every Woman to Consider

Here are three things, which every woman ought to consider and learn before marriage:

"1. A determination which is to possess all the characteristics of a Christian resolution to realize the change in her position from that of a queen on a throne, who has voluntarily abdicated in favor of another sovereign, with whom she is indeed to have the most intimate relations, but so far as her power is concerned, as an influence by her life and example, and her wisdom, which she should instinctively know is different from the wisdom of man.

"2. A happy resignation, without stint or reserve of herself and all that she has to her lord – for so she is to regard him, or no marriage should be contracted – should surround her like an atmosphere, so that her husband may never catch a breath of self-will. And, in deporting herself thus, she is never to assume the manner of injured innocence or that of surprise and disappointment at the change in their relations after as compared with before marriage, when the lover was ever at her beck and ready to do her bidding. Her life in her new position must be cheerily, all the day, and even if dark clouds should lower she must make it appear that the sun still shines. In a word she should live for her husband, for he either literally toils for her, or under any circumstances, bears the brunt of life's burden, and ought to do so.

"3. Lastly, a sweet devotion which does not manifest itself as though it expected something in return, but full hearty and spontaneous, should be the key-note, of her soul. Such a course will compel, if the man is heavy and wanting in magnanimity of soul; and if not, if he is of noble nature, there will burst forth a torrent of devotion and tender care on his part, even stronger than her own, and whether amiable or not, will brook no control nor cease while life lasts. Thus will their lives blend –"The twain shall be one flesh," and the glory of all we conceive, as truly womanly, will envelop her sweet life as with a halo."

GREEN DRAGON PRESS

1900 - 1909 Introduction

"What is this fascination with women? Why don't they ask about the proper sphere of men?" Wendy Mitchinson

In the late 19th and early 20th centuries, the status of women in Canada was strongly influenced by the conservatism of Queen Victoria who ruled the British Empire for more than 60 years until her death in 1901. The Victorians believed that women belonged at home caring for their husbands and children. Of course this applied only to middle and upper class women. Poor women, as well as immigrant, Black and Aboriginal women were excluded from these notions of women's proper sphere.

With the advent of industrialization and urbanization in the second half of the 19th century, many more women entered the workforce, especially in the manufacturing industries. Up to that time women had worked mainly as domestics, labourers, seamstresses or, in the case of those more educated, as teachers. Women married or not, were still restricted from a huge range of vocations. They could not work in mines, the army or the religious ministries. They were not allowed to sit as aldermen, councilors, mayors or members of Parliament. Women were prohibited from being barristers except in the province of Ontario, where there was only one female barrister (Clara Brett Martin).

When women were employed, their jobs were often considered to be less important, less well trained and more transitory than men's and consequently worth less. The average woman's life in the work force was short and her pay was approximately half that of an average man.

Secretarial work had assumed great importance by the turn of the century and because of the opportunities it offered, was dominated by men. The National Council of Women's report of 1901 mentions proudly that "24 (female) secretaries) have been heard of in Ontario and eight in Quebec." The Report also noted that 782 women were employed in Canada's civil service. By contrast, the new jobs of stenographer and typist, less powerful, were thought to be ideally suited to women, as were shop clerk and telephone operator. Steno pools sprang up in great numbers.

At the turn of the century, 16 per cent of women over the age of 13 were in the paid labour force, compared to 88 per cent of men (Statistics Canada, 1901.) Virtually all those women were unmarried, barred both by law and custom from the paid work force after they married. By far the biggest category of women who "worked out" at the beginning of the 20th century was domestic servants. In 1901, roughly four in 10 of working women were servants. Those numbers decreased as other occupations opened to women.

At the same time, there were increasing demands on middle and upper class women to become more involved in community issues. Decrease in the number of Canadian women willing to enter domestic service led to the call for immigrant women to fill the demand.

GREEN DRAGON PRESS

This advice (spelling as in the original) was written for a bride more than a century ago. Practical advice about the correct placement of wash tubs to avoid smoke in the eyes, reminders to sort clothes and directions for making starch are accompanied by suggestions about how to recycle wash water. *Mountain Life and Work*, author and publisher unknown.

☞ **COUNT BLESSINS** ☜

1. bild a fire in back yard to heat kettle of rain water.

2. set tubs so smoke won't blow in eyes if wind is pert.

3. shave one hole cake soap in bilin water.

4. sort things, make three piles, one pile white, one cullord, one work britches and rags.

5. stur flour in cold water to smooth then thin down with bilin water.

6. rub dirty spots on bord, scrub hard, then bile, rub cullord but don't bile just rench and starch.

7. take white things out of kettle with broomstick handle, then rench, blew and starch.

8. spred tee towels on grass; hang old rags on fence; pore rench water in flower bed; scrub porch with soapy water.

9. turn tubs upside down.

10. go put on clean dress, smooth hair with side combs, brew cup of tee, set and rest and rock a spell and count blessins.

GREEN DRAGON PRESS

Household Work and the "Servant Problem"

"Without electricity or many labour-saving devices, household work was both strenuous and time-consuming. A servant could greatly ease the burden of laundry day with its tubs of boiling water to be heated early and tended by hand, of ironing day with the heavy flat irons, and of cleaning, baking, and cooking. Especially was a servant a necessity rather than a luxury in homes with a young family where the wife might well be expecting another child, or in farm homes where the wife helped with outside chores - the dairy, the poultry, and the garden - in addition to coping with her inside housework. Improved technology, which came earlier to middle-class city homes than to rural districts, eased some of the physical drudgery of housework but did not reduce the demand for domestic servants.

The growth in affluence of the middle class with industrialization meant that more families could afford to hire domestic help. In addition, any decrease in physical labour through technological assistance was offset by higher standards of home and child care and by the increasing activity of women in affairs outside the home, often through the churches or organizations such as the WCTU, the Local Councils of Women, or the farm women's associations. Women were told that it was their responsibility to be concerned with issues such as prohibition, child welfare, or farm co-operation, and that they must organize their work to allow themselves time for these activities. Therefore, the demand for domestic servants, whether as status symbols or as essential assistance, constantly exceeded the supply in Ontario, as in the rest of the country, throughout the period from 1870 to 1930.

The servant girl problem existed because women in Canada entering the labour force shunned domestic service if possible. Thus, while the proportion of women in the paid labour force relative to the female population increased in the twentieth century, the percentage of the female labour force in domestic service decreased." Marilyn Barber, The Women Ontario welcomed: Immigrant domestics for Ontario Homes, 1870 - 1930, in *The Neglected Majority*, 103, 104.

- 1898 Kit Coleman, Canadian journalist, becomes the world first woman war correspondent. She is also one of the first Canadian women to hold a regular job at a newspaper and the first syndicated columnist in Canada.

- 1900 Teaching is the only career open to women in Canada that leads to a pension.

GREEN DRAGON PRESS

The poem "No Occupation," *Farmer's Advocate and Home Journal*, June 10, 1910, satirized the census classification of wives and mothers, particularly women such as Ada Nayler Butwell, who in addition to the regular work of caring for a family, looked after chickens and other farm animals, grew vegetables and cooked for hired hands on farms and small business operations such as the Butwell family brickyard.

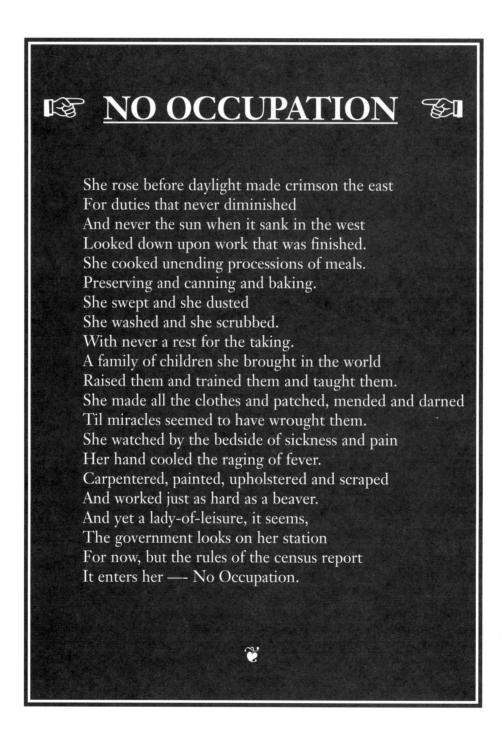

NO OCCUPATION

She rose before daylight made crimson the east
For duties that never diminished
And never the sun when it sank in the west
Looked down upon work that was finished.
She cooked unending processions of meals.
Preserving and canning and baking.
She swept and she dusted
She washed and she scrubbed.
With never a rest for the taking.
A family of children she brought in the world
Raised them and trained them and taught them.
She made all the clothes and patched, mended and darned
Til miracles seemed to have wrought them.
She watched by the bedside of sickness and pain
Her hand cooled the raging of fever.
Carpentered, painted, upholstered and scraped
And worked just as hard as a beaver.
And yet a lady-of-leisure, it seems,
The government looks on her station
For now, but the rules of the census report
It enters her —- No Occupation.

Most women accepted the lack of recognition of their critical contribution, and it would be many years before women's rights in this area were recognized in law.

GREEN DRAGON PRESS

Ada Butwell Forsythe

When the census taker called at Ada's house in 1891 and asked her occupation, she said "none, I'm just a housewife."

Ada Nayler was born in the village of Penge in Surrey, England on January 12, 1868. Her father was a brick moulder. When she was three years old, her family emigrated to Canada. They were among thousands of immigrants from England, Ireland, Scotland and Europe who endured terrible hardships on cross-Atlantic voyages. They settled in the small settlement of Madoc, near Belleville, Ontario. When her father died, Ada was apprenticed at the age of nine as a maidservant to a local family. Her work included cleaning fireplaces, carrying firewood, cleaning boots, sweeping and dusting, and feeding the chickens. She married the son of another brick-maker in 1888 and moved to Toronto where her father-in-law had a brick-yard near Bloor and Clinton Streets. For the next thirty years, Ada cooked, cleaned, and sewed for her family. She had four children who survived: Laura 1892, Arthur 1894, Ross, 1906 and Doris 1908. In addition to child-care, housework, the care of chickens, two dairy cows and a horse, she also prepared a hot noon meal six days a week for the five men who worked in the brickyard. Ada also made butter which she sold to the T. Eaton Company. Each Saturday afternoon, she hitched up the horse and buggy for the drive to the Eaton store in downtown Toronto. There she sold her butter to Mr. Timothy Eaton. When Ada was an old woman, she liked to tell her grandchildren that Mr. Eaton always said she made the best butter and he always gave her the best price. Her tremendous work load was taken for granted and she also endured illness, family conflict and financial problems. Her later life, however was filled with great happiness.

For more information about Ada, log on to www.coolwomen.org.

GREEN DRAGON PRESS

"...very many young women of the present day fail to recognize homemaking as an art, and...regard it only in the light of drudgery of housework. This we believe to be largely the result of a lack of scientific knowledge on the subject, and for the remedy of which we look largely to the study of the subject in a scientific manner by our girls in the public schools."

Letter from the Corresponding Secretary of the Local Council of Women to the editor of the Victoria BC *Daily Colonist* in March 1903.

Household Furnishings.

FOR ILLUSTRATIONS SEE OPPOSITE PAGE.

1. Canadian washer, $3.50 ; reacting, $5.00.
2. Self-wringing mop, 25c ; diamond mop stick, 10c ; mop cloths, 10c.
3. Wooden wash tubs, 50c, 60c, 70c, 80c ; fibre tubs, 80c, 95c, $1.15, 1.30 ; fibre pails, 32c, 40c ; wooden pails, 15c, 17c.
4. Folding tub stands, $1.00 ; folding ironing boards, $1.25 ; linen covered and varnished, $1.75.
5. Clothes lines, cotton or hemp, 50 ft, 15c ; 75 ft, 20c ; 100 ft, 25c ; manilla, 5c, 10c ; wire, 50 ft, 20c ; 100 ft, 35c.
6. Clothes pegs, 5 doz for 5c.
7. The Dowswell washer, $3.50.
8. Leader churn, No. 1, 9 gals, $3.75 ; No. 2, 15 gals. $4.00 ; No. 3, 20 gals, $4.75.
9. Queen mangle, three maple rollers, casters, folding table, best English steel springs, $15.00.
10. Wash board, Globe, 15c ; solid back, 20c ; toy wash boards, 10c ; pastry boards, 25c ; bosom boards, shaped neck, 25c ; sleeve boards, 10c ; skirt boards, 25c, 35c, 50c ; bosom and sleeve boards, 35c.
11. Wringers, Royal Dominion, $2.50 ; Leader, $3.00 ; Paragon, with ball bearings, $3.45.
12. Clothes horse, folding, 4 ft, 35c ; 5 ft, 45c ; extension, 4 ft, 75c ; 5 ft, 90c ; 6 ft, $1.00.
13. Butter ladles, 5c, 8c.
14. Table mangles, $7.00.
15. Salt boxes, 10c.
16. Butter moulds, ½ and 1-lb, 20c.
17. Clothes arm, 5 arms, 15c ; towel arm, 3 arms, 10c, 15c.
18. Coffee mill, 25c, 50c, 75c.
19. Butter moulds, oblong. ; and 1-lb, 25c.

20. Maple bowls, 10c, 20c, 35c, 50c.
21. Carved bread boards, 35c, 45c, 65c, 75c, $1.25, 1.50.
22. Leader churn, steel frame. No. 1, 9 gals, $4.00 ; No. 2, 15 gals, $4.25.
23. Dash churns, 5 gallons. $1.25 ; 7 gallons. $1.50 ; 10 gallons, $1.65.
24. Knife trays, 10c ; lined and varnished, 15c.
25. Butter spades, 5c each.
26. Window cleaners, 9-inch, 25c ; 12-inch, 35c.
27. Step ladder with pail rack, 5 ft, 50c ; 6 ft, 60c ; 7 ft, 75c ; pine, extra strong, with pail rack and extra spreader, 5 ft, 90c ; 6 ft, $1.10 ; 7 ft, $1.35.
28. Knife board, 15c.
29. Wood spoons, 4c, 5c, 6c, 8c.
30. Hunter's axe handle, 7c ; axe handles, 10c, 15c ; adze handles, 15c ; pick handles, 15c ; broad axe handles, 15c ; D spade and fork handles, curved and straight, 25c ; hammer handles, 5c. All made of second growth hickory.
31. Platform scales, weighing to 600 lbs, $12.00 ; to 1,200 lbs, $14.75.
32. Butter spades, 5c.
33. Grocers' or household scales, weighing 4 lbs, $2.50 ; weighing 10 lbs, $3.75.
34. Happy medium bucksaws, 40c.
35. Wooden knives, 5c.
36. Spice cabinets, glass jars, $1.50 ; with drawers, $1.25.
37. Folding coat and hat rack, 10 pegs, 15c ; 13 pegs, 30c.
38. Champion scales, weighing from 1 oz to 240 lbs, $5.00.
39. Stable brooms, best quality cane, hardwood

handles, 50c, 60c, 70c ; split cane, 50c, 60c ; bass, 85c.
40. Shoe brush, 15c, 25c.
41. Hat and coat hooks, 4 pegs, 25c ; 6 pegs, 35c.
42. Towel rollers, 15c, 20c, 25c.
43. Bamboo hat and coat hooks, 15c, 20c ; white enamelled, 25c.
44. Sink brush, 10c.
45. Stove mit. with dauber, 15c.
46. Stove dauber, 5c, 7c, 12c.
47. Crumb brush, 15c, 35c, 45c.
48. Banister brushes, bristle and fibre, 20c, 25c, 35c, 40c ; whisk root, 25c.
49. Shoe daubers, 5c, 10c, 15c, 20c.
50. Window brushes, grey bristles, 25c, 35c, 45c ; 10 ft handles for above, 15c.
51. Wool dusters, 20c.
52. Stove brushes, 10c, 15c, 30c ; best quality bristles, 25c, 50c.
53. Double banister brushes, 35c, 45c, 50c.
54. Scrub brushes, green corn, 6c ; whisk root, 8c, 10c, 15c, 20c, 25c ; white fibre, 10c, 25c.
55. Bottle brush, 5c.
56. Shoe brush, plain, with top-knot dauber, 15c ; handled, with top-knot dauber, 10c, 15c, 20c, 25c, 30c, 35c, 50c.
57. Heather sink scrubs, 5c.
58. Hearth dusters, japanned handles, 25c.
59. Wool wall dusters, with handle, 50c.
60. Dish mop, 5c.
61. Feather dusters, turkey, 25c, 35c, 45c, 50c, 65c ; ostrich feathers, large size, $1.00, 1.15, 1.35.
62. Silver brushes, 20c, 25c.
63. Silver brushes, 25c, 35c. [$1.00, 1.25.
64. Hair brooms, handles included, 55c, 75c, 90c,
65. Table scrub fibre, 5c.

- 1900 Women are included on the program of the modern Olympic Games competing in golf and tennis.

For those who could afford it, one way out of the drudgery of housework was to hire someone else to do it. Domestic service, a predominantly female occupation, was the most common paid employment for Canadian women before 1900.

Finnish domestic servants. Ontario Archives/FIN 6886-13.

When other, less onerous and better paid, occupations became available, the call went out to Europe for domestic servants.

- 1901 In a bid for fame and fortune, Annie Taylor climbed into a padded barrel with her "good luck" cat and became the first person to go over Niagara Falls. Annie survived, but the cat did not, taking all its (and Annie's) luck with it-she died penniless.

GREEN DRAGON PRESS

Many women rejected domestic work and sought paid employment in offices and factories. But often working conditions were no better than domestic service and could even be dangerous. A number of inquiries were instituted such as the Royal Commission to Inquire into the Dispute between Bell Telephone Company and Its Employees at Toronto. The commissions' mandates were to examine strike issues but often seemed less interested in the employees' grievances than on the possible effect of women's work outside the home having an adverse effect on their future child-bearing and child-caring roles.

- 1905 The Edmonton Grads begin a 35-year winning streak: 502 of 522 basketball games and four world championships.

The Strain on Operators

It is to be remembered in the first place that the class of persons employed as operators is composed mostly of girls and young women between the ages of 17 and 23, that persons of these years are preferred to others because of the greater facility with which they learn the work and acquire dexterity, that these are years during which the nervous and physical system of a woman is peculiarly sensitive to strain and susceptible to injury, and that harm done to, or impairment of the system sustained at that time of life is apt to be more far reaching in its consequences than would be the effects received from similar causes in maturer years. The effects moreover upon posterity occasioned the undermining or weakening of the female constitution cannot receive too serious consideration.

The work of telephone operating does not appear to be of a kind to fit a woman for any other occupation or calling; additional significance is therefore to be given to the fact that the average time spent by operators in the service in from two to three years....

Secondly, the work of telphone operating under any conditions involves a considerable strain upon the nervous system. Some of the doctors maintained that it was not a fit work for woman even where carried on at a moderate rate. The faculties are kept constantly on the alert, there is a high tension on the special senses, and a certain amount of mental worry...

The special senses of sight, hearing and speech are called into operation not only continuously but constantly in a concerted manner, when not actually employed they are not resting because necessarily on the alert. The physical strain save for the obligation of sitting continuously in one postion over a considerable period time, and the reaching and stretching entailed where switchboards are large in size, or operators expected to assist with the work on boards adjoining their own is not considerable, and, to a degree, helps, to offset the effect of the nervous strain; on the other hand where there is not a proper regard for these matters the strain may be increased rather than diminished. The liability to injury from shocks, the harsh words and abuse of subscribers, the irritation caused by the intermittent glowing of lights reflecting the impatience of subscribers, the occasional buzzing and snapping of instruments in the ear, the sense of crowding where work accumulates and the inevitable anxiety occasioned by seeking to make the necessary connections when a rush takes place, all combine to accentuate the strain upon an operator, and they are all factors more or less absent from others callings in which women are engaged....

Royal Commission Appointed to Inquire into the Dispute between Bell Telephone Company and Its Employees at Toronto. Report. Canada. Department of Labour. Sessional Paper No. 36, 1909: 129-131

GREEN DRAGON PRESS

☞ THE MOCK PARLIAMENT ☜

A Large and Well-Pleased Audience at the Pavilion Last Night -- Bill to Enfranchise
Men Rejected.

A large number were present at the women's mock Parliament held last night at the
Pavilion for the benefit of the W.C.T.U. building fund. Ald. Hallam and Hon. S.C.
Biggs had charge of the proceedings. On the floor of the Pavilion desks were arranged
for the members on a raised platform. Dr. E.H. Stowe was leader of the Government
and Mrs. McDonald and Mrs. Brown of the Opposition and Patrons, respectively.
Mrs. Rutherford acted as Speaker.

After a deputation of the Men's Enfranchisement Association and Men's
Temperance Union, headed by Mr. J. S. Robertson had been received, and questions
put by members had been answered an Act proposing "to extend the franchise to men
on the same conditions as to women" was taken into consideration. Interceding
speeches were made both for and against the bill, the majority of which contained
many well-taken points. One astute argument was that as women came last in the
ascending scale of creation she was certainly superior to man. The bill was finally
rejected. Those speaking in favour of it were its mover, Miss Laing, Miss Jackson,
Miss Smith, Mrs. F.S. Spence, Mrs. Campbell and Mrs. Riches, whilst those who
opposed it were Dr. Gullen, Miss Wiggins, Mrs. Stevens, Mrs. McDonnell and Mrs.
Hughes.

A telegram was received in the course of the evening from Mayor Fleming , who
is in Ottawa, congratulating the Parliament on its success, and hoping that it would
not nominate one of its members for the civic centre.

After the adjournment D'Alesandro's Orchestra played a number of selections and
the Verdi Quartette sang. Refreshments were sold "on the European plan."

The Globe. February 18, 1896

❧

• 1907 Women operators strike the
Bell Telephone Company.

GREEN DRAGON PRESS

Women Organizing for Change

It has been estimated that during the period just prior to and after the turn of the century, nine out of every ten women in Canada belonged to some kind of organization. It was the main way they had to access political power, in some cases through the men they knew. The large number of national voluntary philanthropic and religious organizations, which had developed since the 1870s, included inter-denominational groups like the Women's Christian Temperance Union (WCTU), cultural organizations like the Women's Art Association of Canada, and purely charitable societies. Now they began to organize as women for women's issues.

Women organized for the vote, for prohibition, which they felt would solve social problems of poverty and disease, and for justice for women in the workplace. They learned these skills in their church organizations and in the collective sharing of work in the early days of the country. The events they organized ranged from small endeavours such as carrying suffrage banners in Labour Day and Dominion Day parades, organizing local meetings such as the 1896 gathering of seven women teachers that launched the Toronto Women Teachers' Association, a founding association of the Federation of Women Teachers' Associations of Ontario (FWTAO), all the way to impressive, well organized demonstrations like that organized in 1909 by the Canadian Suffrage Association, the powerful Women's Christian Temperance Union and hundreds of members from 14 suffrage societies. One thousand women marched to the Ontario Legislature. A petition of 100,000 names of people supporting suffrage was presented. It was ignored.

Women organizers understood how to organize entertainment and use humour to make a point. One such endeavour, repeated with good effect several times was the Mock Parliament. The first, staged in Winnipeg in 1893 by Dr. Amelia Yeomans, journalist E. Cora Hind and Mrs. J. A. McClung, a temperance advocate who was the future mother-in-law of Nellie McClung, featured women taking roles for and against suffrage. It got excellent media coverage. Three years later in 1896 a similar event organized in Toronto's Allen Gardens by the Dominion Women's Enfranchisement Association in co-operation with the Ontario W.C.T.U. attracted attention to the suffrage cause. Later, in 1914, the day after Manitoba Premier Roblin once again stated his opposition to votes for women, Nellie McClung and the Political Equality League staged a mock "Women's Parliament" in the Walker Theater in Winnipeg. It was such a success it was repeated twice to sold-out audiences. The proceeds from the ticket sales financed the rest of the Manitoba "Votes for Women" campaign.

By this time, men supporters were well represented in the audience and some took part in the play. Women played the parts of the premier and MPPs and debated the pros and cons of granting men the vote, exposing the sanctimonious and contradictory arguments used by male politicians to deny female suffrage.

GREEN DRAGON PRESS

Women playing the part of legislators received a deputation of vote-seeking men pushing a wheelbarrow full of petitions. The Premier, played by Nellie McClung, congratulated the men on their "splendid appearance," but told them "man is made for something higher and better than voting."

"Men were made to support families. What is a home without a bank account? In this agricultural province, the man's place is the farm. Shall I call man away from the useful plough and barrow to talk loud on street corners about things which do not concern him? Politics unsettles men, and unsettled men mean unsettled bills - broken furniture, and broken vows-and divorce.... When you ask for the vote you are asking me to break up peaceful happy homes-to wreck innocent lives...

It may be that I am old-fashioned," she concluded. "I may be wrong. After all, men may be human. Perhaps the time will come when men may vote with women." And she assured them solemnly that "The man who pays the grocer rules the world." McClung was faithfully echoing the words and tone of Premier Roblin speaking to the suffragists the day before, and the crowd applauded wildly.

MOCK PARLIAMENT

... AND ...

PROMENADE CONCERT

FOR THE BENEFIT OF THE

W C. T. U. Building Fund

PAVILION

Tuesday February 18th, '96

*

ASSISTED BY THE

- VERDI QUARTETTE -

MISS NORMA REYNOLDS, Directress

*

-- D'ALESANDRO ORCHESTRA --

PROGRAMME AT 7.45

*

REFRESHMENTS ON THE EUROPEAN PLAN

NORTH-ELDER PRINT.

Programme

1 Overture .... "Vendetta." .... Orchestra
2 Deputation from Men's Enfranchisement Association and Men's Christian Temperance Union
3 March .... "Oriental Echo," .... Orchestra
4 Evening Sitting, Mock Parliament
5 Waltz Song .... "Se Seran Rose," .... Ardiff
                    Miss Gertie Black.
            Violin Obligato by Miss Hilda Davis.
6 Polka .... "Trilby" .... Urchestra
7 Quartette ... {(a) "Lady Mine Thy Casement Open ... Barmby
              {(b) "Robin Adair," ... Arranged by Macy
                    The Verdi Quartette.
                         Miss Mima Lund, Contralto.
Miss Elda Idle, Soprano.   Mr. H. C. Scatsbury, Baritone.
Mr. H. C. Johnson, Tenor.

PROMENADE

1 March .... "The Honeymoon," .... Rosey
2 Valse Di Concert ... "Lune de Miel," .... Waldteufel
3 Gavotte .... "Heart's Delight," .... Warren
4 Grand Selection ... "Il Trovatore," .... Verai
5 Russian Mazurka ... "La Czarina," .... Ganne
6 March .... "King Cotton," .... Sousa
7 Gavotte .... "La Parisienne," .... Wanmer
8 Spanish Serenade ... "La Paloma," .... Balfour
9 Galop Di Concert ... "High Tide," .... Armstrong
1 ....
2 ....
3 ....
4 ....

The "Plan of Members' Seats" included in the programme for the event identified the women who participated as "members of Parliament." A number of well-known women activists and educators participated, including Dr. Emily Howard Stowe, her daughter, Dr. Augusta Stowe Gullen, Ada Marean Hughes, and Leticia Youmans.

- - - Plan of Members' Seats - - -

			Center			
Noxon, A. / Brant	Abercrombie, W. / Welland.		SPEAKER, HON. A. O. RUTHERFORD	McDonell, M. / Toronto, N.	Forster, M C. / Perth	Allen,, B. / Lanark
Savigny, A. G. / Victoria, W.	Burwash, M. / Ottawa.	Stowe, Hon. Dr. E. H. / Oxford.	Clerk, H. Johnston	McDonell, M. / Toronto, N.	Riches, S. / Lennox	Harrington, L.C. / Stormont
Redmond, M. A. / Peterboro.	Stevens, Hon. H. / Kingston.	Gullen, Hon. Dr. A S / Brant.	Asst. Clerk, M. J. Luke.	Hunter, G. / Dundas	Rose, C. M. / Grenville	Brown, A. / Muskoka
Vance, A. / Nipissing.	Ford, Hon. E. A. / Monck.	Hughes, Hon. A. M. / Middlesex, W.		Parker A. / Halton	Jackson, M. M. / Addington	Henderson, O. / Victoria, E.
Lelean, E. / Waterloo.	Teskey, S. Ray. / Northumberland.	Sims, Hon. A. / Hamilton.		Biggs, S. E. / Norfolk	Smith, M., B.E. / Lincoln	Hilborn, S. / Parry Sound
Summerfeldt, J. / Simcoe.	Campbell, F. R. / Huron.	Wiggins, Hon. L. E. / Ontario.		Spence, S F. / Prince Edward	Walker, H. / Cardwell	Bowbeer, C. / Carleton
Duff, A. J. / Peel.	Yeigh, E. / Algoma.	Doane, S. A. / N. York.		Brown, M. A. / Frontenac	Youmans, L. / Lambton	Wrigley, G. / Dufferin
Cook, C. / Wellington	Forest, I. / Glengarry.	Laing, M. R. / N. Middlesex.		Sanderson, A. / Bruce, N.	Chamberlain, A. J. / Elgin	Faircloth, L. S. / Bruce S.
Cowan, A. M. / Kent.	Ward, F. C. / S. York.	Rose, J. M. / Essex.	J. Semple, Sergt.-at-Arms	Orr, W. H. / Stormont	Coad, E. / Wentworth	Mason, W. / Leeds

Illustrations courtesy Moira Armour.

• 1908 Lucy Maud Montgomery's first novel became an instant bestseller, *Anne of Green Gables* is now a world-renowned Canadian classic, translated into 30 languages.

GREEN DRAGON PRESS

The Eureka Club

"The Eureka Club was founded in 1910. I always remembered that mother said that they had twenty members, and my mother was president of it for one year. They sent out mail and things like that, did little kindnesses. They were a social club when they first were formed, and they were very proud of the fact it wasn't too long before they all sat back and said we ought to be doing something worthwhile and there were many things they did. For instance, they sent Christmas baskets to the needy, and that grew into quite a thing...."
Bee Allen in *No Burden to Carry: Narratives of Black Working Women in Ontario 1920s to 1950s*, 123.

THE CLUB WOMAN
'Mid a clatter of tea-cups and spoons
And an atmosphere suited for swoons,
The President hen
Rails at the men,
And talks of prisms and prunes.

A club is all right in its place. Find the place.

Coloured Women's Club of Montreal

Wives of Black railroad workers founded the Coloured Women's Club of Montreal in 1902. The aim of the club was to bring attention to the problems faced by Blacks in Montreal, especially racial discrimination. They also assisted newly arrived Black immigrants.

Fédération Nationale Saint Jean Baptiste

The Fédération Nationale Saint Jean Baptiste was established in 1907 in Montreal as a distinctly Catholic, francophone women's organization. Their mandate was to help girls and women through education and to work toward improving working conditions. One of the founding members, Marie Gerin Lajoie was a leader in the suffrage movement in Quebec.

As women became more highly organized, their opponents began to use satire as a weapon, a sign that their power was beginning to be felt and could no longer be ignored.

An example of a contemporary post card satirizing women's organizations. Note that the handwritten comment "A club is all right in its place. Find the place." indicates the sender's approval.

Canadian Women's Movement Archives, University of Ottawa.

GREEN DRAGON PRESS

New Fashion Freedom

One area where women's lives were changing for the better was dress. The introduction of the bicycle in the late 1880s and its increasing popularity led to a visible social change. A relatively inexpensive form of entertainment and exercise, bicycles enabled women to travel independently, at least for short distances. The bicycle has been credited with increasing the movement toward dress reform as female cyclists sought clothing that allowed greater freedom of movement than the current fashion and concerns for modesty allowed.
In 1895, the popular *Evening Star* columnist "Portia" described the difficulties encountered when trying to ride a bicycle wearing a skirt:

"...in learning to ride, a skirt is a terrible obstacle. The novice continually steps on it in trying to place the foot on the pedals. She topples over much more frequently on account of catching her skirt than because she can't balance herself...

Then when the beginner is fairly under way, and taking, it may be, her first ride alone, her exaltation is cruelly modified by the knowledge that her skirt is "all on one side," or flying up to her knees in front- and she dare not let go of the handle bars long enough to adjust it."

Quoting an unnamed "English statesman" in support of the importance of dress reform, Portia concluded the column with his statement that:

"...if women could be at once placed on a perfect political equality with men and continued to dress as detrimentally to their mental and physical health as at present, they could not hold their newly-acquired prerogatives two years. Certain it is that women have handicapped themselves in every way by yielding to a false standard of requirements in dress. The best opportunity that has ever been offered of throwing off this one particular tyranny is with us at present."

Eatons Catalogue, 1901.

GREEN DRAGON PRESS

In the next decade women's entry into many new kinds of work as they replaced men called to war, required practical clothing and led to major changes in women's fashion. Restricting corsets and hobble skirts were clearly unsuitable for work in factories and on the farm.

The Liberation of Women

There is one direction in which women are gradually becoming emancipated which can only lead to good. I mean the direction of actual bodily freedom in the matter of dress and activity. Women's progress in this direction is surprisingly small as yet, but it is encouraging. That women should so passionately demand freedom of action in the world, and at the same time cling so decidedly to the fetters of conventional dress, which render freedom impossible, is one of those instances of unreason which leave the masculine mind in hopeless amazement. There are women who would welcome martyrdom for what they believe to be the cause of personal freedom, who would not accept the freedom of their own natural bodies as a gift.

Bliss Carman, circa 1910

The poet Bliss Carman spoke out in favour of dress reform, albeit in somewhat patronizing tones, citing women's demands for freedom of action while clinging to the "fetters of conventional dress..."
Bliss Carman, quoted in Ramsay Cook and Wendy Mitchinson, *The Proper Sphere: Women's Place in Canadian Society*, 80, 81.

GREEN DRAGON PRESS

Notable Women

Nellie McClung

Born in 1873, McClung was a teacher, best-selling author and noted speechmaker, famous for her quotable remarks. In 1914 she helped defeat the Manitoba Conservative government which had opposed giving women the vote. In 1916, women won the vote in Manitoba, Saskatchewan and Alberta and in 1921 Nellie was elected to the Alberta legislature. Eight years later, she was one of five women who successfully petitioned the British Privy Council for the right of Canadian women to be regarded as "persons."

"Never apologize, never explain. Get the job done and let them howl."
Nellie McClung

Clara Brett Martin

Women encountered considerable resistance in their efforts to gain admission to the legal profession in Canada. Clara Brett Martin was admitted as a lawyer in 1897, the first woman in Canada and the British Commonwealth. Martin showed great courage and determination in her six-year fight to become a lawyer, but after discovery in the 1990s of anti-Semitic remarks in her correspondence, she became the subject of controversy. Martin was a product of the dominant white Anglo-Saxon society of her time which had strong prejudices against groups such as Jews, Blacks, immigrants and Aboriginal people. But her personal experience of sex discrimination (she encountered hostility and harassment at law school and as an articling student) did not, apparently, alert her to the evils of other forms of discrimination such as anti-Semitism.

Sara Mallabar 1861-1958

Mallabar came to Winnipeg from Rivière du-Loup, Quebec, when she was a small child. She worked as a clerk, married John Mallabar in 1889 and moved to Mexico where together they managed a dry goods shop. John died in 1901, leaving Sara with four children. She moved back to Winnipeg and opened her own business, first in beauty treatments and by 1906 as a "Consumer and Hair Goods" business. After providing costumes for numerous Gilbert and Sullivan productions, Sara obtained a contract with Eaton's to provide costumes for their Santa Claus Parade. Eventually her business grew and she opened shops in Toronto and Montreal where she provided costumes for opera companies.

EMILY PAULINE JOHNSON (1861-1913)

Born in 1861 on the Six Nations Reserve near Brantford, Ontario, Pauline Johnson was the youngest child of Mohawk Chief George Henry Martin Johnson (Tekahionwake) and an English mother, Emily Susanna Howells. Her literary career began early with the publication of her poetry. Her poem "The song my paddle sings" was featured in *Toronto Saturday Night* in 1892, the same year that she began a performing career. Throughout her lifetime she traveled extensively as a "platform performer" where she recited her poetry, told stories and sang, often in Native costume. She performed across Canada and in England, the United States, Europe and Australia. Pauline Johnson was loved and admired by her fans and when she died in 1913 dozens of tributes appeared in newspapers and magazines around the world recognizing her remarkable career.

"There are those who think they pay me a compliment in saying that I am just like a white woman. My aim, my joy, my pride is to sing the glories of my own people. Ours is the race that taught the world that avarice veiled by any name is crime. Ours are the people of the blue air and the green woods, and ours the faith that taught men and women to live without greed and die without fear." Pauline: A Biography of Pauline Johnson, by Betty Keller, Vancouver: Douglas & McIntyre, 1981, 5.

GREEN DRAGON PRESS

Activities
1900 - 1909

HINTS FOR BRIDES

In your own words, briefly summarize the three things a woman "ought to consider and learn before marriage." Form small groups, and write a modern version of the document entitled "Three Hints for the Modern Bride of the New Millennium" and "Three Hints for the Modern Husband."

HOUSEHOLD FURNISHINGS

Ask students to examine ONLY the illustrations on p15, and try to guess the use of each item.

Draw conclusions: Lead the class in a discussion on the labour intensive chores required in a household at the turn of the century.

THE MOCK PARLIAMENT

Re-enact the mock parliament, using the *Globe* article and the seating plan/program.

THE VALUE OF HOUSEWORK

What constitutes housework now, compared to the turn of the century? Make a comparative list of the type of labour involved in working in the home at the turn of the century and now. Imagine you owned a company like Molly Maid at the turn of the century. Make a list of services, and how much you would charge. Now, look at the document where the woman claims she has "no occupation," and Ada's story, p13. What defines occupation? How were these women primarily occupied?

Resources

Coburn, Judi. *The Shacklands*, Toronto: Sumach Press, 2002.
Grey, Charlotte. *Flint and Feather: the life and times of E. Pauline Johnson Tekahionwake,* Toronto: Harper Collins Canada, 2002.
Glazebrook, G. de T, Brett, Katharine B. and Judith McErvel. *A Shopper's View of Canada's Past: Pages from Eaton's Catalogues 1886-1930,* Toronto: University of Toronto Press, 1969.
Hallett, Mary and Marilyn Davis. *Firing the Heather: The Life and Times of Nellie McClung,* Saskatoon: Fifth House, 1993.
Merritt, Susan E. *Her Story: Women from Canada's Past,* 1993, *Her Story II: Women from Canada's Past,* 1996, and *Her Story III: Women from Canada's Past,* 1999, St. Catharines, Vanwell Publishing Limited.
Savage, Candace. *Our Nell: A Scrapbook Biography of Nellie McClung,* Saskatoon: Western Producer Prairie Book, 1979.

GREEN DRAGON PRESS

1910 – 1919

Should women be in civic life?

Presentation of a petition from
the Manitoba Political Equality
League, 23 December, 1915.
Front L to R: Dr. Mary Crawford,
Mrs. Amelia Burritt, Back L to R:
Lillian Thomas, Mrs. Fred Dixon.
Provincial Archives of
Manitoba/W9905.

One strategy used by the suffragists to bring their cause into the public eye, or to the attention of legislators was the petition. In 1915, two petitions were presented by the Manitoba Political Equality League to the newly elected Liberal government of Premier J.C. Norris.

One petition contained 39,584 names; the second contained 4,250 names all collected by 94-year-old Amelia Burritt.
Provincial Archives of Manitoba/9907.

GREEN DRAGON PRESS

1910 – 1919 Introduction

"Women who believe in woman suffrage seem to think that we men want to deprive them of their liberties; but we wish to do no such thing. All men who are worthy of the name of men, place woman upon a very high pedestal, to which no man in his sphere, could ever hope to attain: and we want her to remain there, where she can command our respect and esteem and use the powers that God has given her for the good of humanity....Why should she besmear herself with the rottenness of politics?"
Letter to the editor, *Toronto Globe*, 1912.

Since the late 1870s, North America had been experiencing the birth of a reform movement – the first stage of feminism.

Thousands of middle-class women became involved as volunteers with the creation of parks and recreation programs for children and improving public health. Women also became involved with the "temperance movement" which advocated the prohibition of alcohol, because it was seen as a threat to the stability of the family. While their main objective was not votes for women, they soon realized this was a way to achieve the desired changes by making their voices heard through the democratic process. Across the country, women mobilized to advocate for the right to vote. But discussion about women's proper sphere continued into the decade. A 1914 headline in the *Albertan*, asked rhetorically "Should women interfere in Civic Life?" The article led with this line. "What is woman's sphere and woman's work? Should woman take any part in the outside world?"

It went on to report on a debate of the local council executive, where a councillor warned that: "The women of today were shirking their proper responsibilities and the day would come when the men would have to cook the meals, while the women were out legislating."

In any event women were not "out legislating" but they *were* taking on new roles.

World War 1 changed forever the role of women in the labour market. After 1915 when thousands of young men were called up for military duty, their jobs had to be filled. Keeping up production in factories was crucial so women, especially single women, were called on to fill the jobs. There was also a huge increase in the number of women working in offices and in sales, as they replaced men transferred to the war industries. Women were an essential component of the Canadian workforce during wartime. Black women, however, were excluded from most of these jobs. They did find ways to help the war effort and a Black woman, Hattie Rhue-Hatchett from North Buxton, Ontario wrote a song "The Sacred Spot" that was adopted as a marching song by soldiers

Most, though not all, suffragists supported the war effort and even as they worked to support it, they continued to struggle for the vote. Women finally won the right to vote in provincial elections for the first time in 1916 in Manitoba, Alberta and Saskatchewan. In each of the other provinces, women fought and won the right to vote in the following years.

GREEN DRAGON PRESS

Quebec was the last province to grant women the right to vote, in 1940. At the federal level, most women, providing they were British subjects, obtained the right to vote in May 1918, shortly after the end of World War 1. Aboriginal women obtained this right only in 1960. When women were finally granted the federal vote, it was as much due to the conviction of the Prime Minister, Sir Robert Borden, that they would support his party in the conscription crisis, as it was to their acknowledged major contributions to the war effort. The Military Voters Act was passed in September 1917, and provided that all British subjects, male or female who had participated actively in any branch of the Canadian armed services were to vote in any general election prior to demobilization. A large number of nurses were enfranchised by this act.

The Wartime Elections Act, also passed in September 1917, gave the vote to every woman who was a British subject by birth and had a relation serving in the forces. At the same time as many women were enfranchised, all conscientious objectors and naturalized British subjects who had been born in an enemy country lost their vote, and Dr. Augusta Stowe-Gullen, pioneer feminist, had the pleasure of observing anti-suffragists making speeches on the necessity and importance of women voting and even helping them get to the polls.

☞ RIGHT TO VOTE IN PROVINCIAL ELECTIONS ☜

Province	Right to Vote Provincially	Right to Stand for Provincial Office
Manitoba	January 28, 1916	January 28, 1916
Saskatchewan	March 14, 1916	March 14, 1916
Alberta	April 19, 1916	April 19, 1916
British Columbia	April 5, 1917	April 5, 1917
Ontario	April 12, 1917	April 24, 1919
Nova Scotia	April 26, 1918	April 26, 1918
New Brunswick	April 17, 1919	March 9, 1934
Prince Edward Island	May 3, 1922	May 3, 1922
Newfoundland	April 13, 1925	April 13, 1925
Quebec	April 25, 1940	April 25, 1940

GREEN DRAGON PRESS

The Fight for the Vote Continues

*"For too long we have believed it our duty to sit down and be resigned.
Now we know it is our duty to rise up and be indignant."* Nellie McClung.

Premier Duff Roblin of Manitoba, Nellie McClung's long time opponent in the battle for suffrage made the following statement to a suffrage delegation in 1914.

"Does the franchise for women make the home better? My wife is bitterly opposed to woman suffrage. I have respect for my wife; more than that, I love her; I am not ashamed to say so. Will anyone say that she would be better as a wife and mother because she could go and talk on the streets about local or dominion politics? I disagree. The mother that is worthy of the name and of the good affection of a good man has a hundredfold more influence in molding and shaping public opinion round her dinner table than she would have in the marketplace, hurling her eloquent phrases to the multitude. It is in the home that her influence is exercised and felt."

Maternal Feminism

Like Premier Roblin, opponents of female suffrage believed that women should devote themselves to their home and family and predicted disaster if women entered public life. In the catalogue for the Public Archives of Canada exhibit (*The Widening Sphere: Women in Canada 1870-1940)*, Jeanne L'Esperance described this view of women's role and the strategy devised by women suffrage leaders to counteract it:

Traditionally, woman's sphere was the home, and the commonly accepted role for the adult woman was that of wife, mother and homemaker. With monotonous regularity those who debated this question throughout the nineteen and early twentieth century came up with the same answer. The family was the fundamental building block of society and woman was its centre. Yet technological innovation and industrial growth were inevitably impinging upon the home in this period. Mass production removed certain household tasks from the home to the factory, while labour-saving devices and ready-made food and clothing meant that domestic tasks consumed less and less time. Although new theories on infant care made mothering a more time-consuming task than it had been, the falling birthrate and increased life expectancy meant that parenting was not a lifetime task. At the same time disquietude at social changes made critics see any attempt by women to lead an independent life as an attack upon the family, and therefore upon the stable basis of society. On the other hand women had to prepare their children for the trials of the contemporary world. How could they do this if they were weak, helpless and uninformed and confined within their narrow sphere, the home? The answer, which women thinkers formulated, was the concept of "maternal feminism," or widening their influence by taking out into the world the very qualities which made them so valuable within the family. Women were traditionally the culture bearers who passed on to their children the values and ideals of their society.

GREEN DRAGON PRESS

Nellie McClung suggested, with her usual biting wit, that there were hidden reasons for opposing votes for women.

VALENTINE GREETINGS

BACK TO THE BACKGROUND

Be careful, men, of the advocate
Of woman's rights in the single state.
    If you marry one,
    Your trouble's begun—
You'll count for less than half your weight!

COPYRIGHT 1908 BY RAPHAEL TUCK & SONS CO LTD

Satirical valentine post card: Canadian Women's Movement archives/archives canadiennes du mouvement des femmes.

"… This deep-rooted fear, that any change may bring personal inconvenience, lies at the root of much of the opposition to all reform.

Men held to slavery for long years, condoning and justifying it, because they were afraid that without slave labour life would not be comfortable. Certain men have opposed the advancement of women for the same reason; their hearts have been beset with the old black fear that, if women were allowed equal rights with men, some day some man would go home and find the dinner not ready, and the potatoes not even peeled! But not many give expression to this fear, as a reason for their opposition. They say they oppose the enfranchisement of women because they are too frail, weak and sweet to mingle in the hurly-burly of life; that women have far more influence now than if they could vote, and besides, God never intended them to vote, and it would break up the home, and make life a howling wilderness; the world would be full of neglected children (or none at all) and the homely joys of the fireside would vanish from the earth.

I remember once hearing an eloquent speaker cry out in alarm, "If women ever get the vote, who will teach us to say our prayers?"

Surely his experience of the franchised class had been an unfortunate one when he could not believe that anyone could not vote and pray." Nellie L. McClung. 'Speaking of Women,' *Maclean's Magazine*, May 1916.

• January 28, 1916: women in Manitoba ceased to be disqualified from voting and holding office solely because they were women. But most women of colour were prohibited from voting at the provincial and federal level until the late 1940s.

GREEN DRAGON PRESS

World War 1: 1914-18

"In Europe, Canadian women volunteers organized hospitals, clubs and nursing homes for soldiers and nurses, and many joined the British women's services. War provided Canadian women with many opportunities to prove their worth as citizens. However, many feminists were not wholehearted, uncritical patriots. To some, war was a cruel and useless waste of human life and they did not hesitate to criticize it, as the inevitable result of the patriarchal values of Canadian society."

Nellie McClung. *In Times Like These*. Toronto: McLeod and Allen, 1915.

Francis Beynon was one feminist who was certainly not a "wholehearted, uncritical patriot." The daughter of Methodist farmers who moved from Ontario to southwestern Manitoba and then to Winnipeg, the strong-minded and eloquent young woman saw Winnipeg as a place to found a new social order. She wanted to make Christianity relevant to the modern world, but was wary of the notion of a socialist utopia. She was hired as women's editor of the *Grain Growers Guide*. At first she was popular though her columns dealt more with women's rights and pacifism than household questions. With the onset of the war, Beynon assumed that feminists would lead the fight to end the war. This, and her commitment to the immigrants in the north end of Winnipeg, set her against Nellie McClung and the majority of women in the suffrage movement, most of whom were upper class and British in origin, and many of whom had sons in the trenches (as did McClung.) McClung actually argued that only women born in Canada or Britain should be given the vote and in fact she would urge women to use their vote to support conscription.

Prior to the war, prejudice against the foreign born certainly existed, but the war provided an excuse to openly express distrust of people who had come from countries Canada was fighting. Beynon continued her outspoken opposition to the war and was finally forced out of her job at the paper and moved to New York in 1917 to join her sister and brother-in-law, the journalist Vernon Thomas, who had himself been fired from the *Winnipeg Free Press* for publicly supporting left-wing MPP F.J. Dixon's antiwar speech in the provincial legislature. In her farewell column, Francis explained that she was going to "that Mecca for all writers …the city of New York."

She later published a novel, *Aleta Dey*. The heroine was a Winnipeg farm journalist, feminist, and Christian pacifist, and many viewed the book as non-fiction. Beynon worked at a mission and wrote a few articles for American reform journals but little else is known about her years in New York. She returned only once to Winnipeg just before her death in 1951.

GREEN DRAGON PRESS

Women were the subject matter of propaganda posters aimed at encouraging men to enlist, and were also encouraged to contribute to the war effort in a wide variety of ways.

Right: Patent medicine advertisement called on women to help win the war, stressing the value of "Dr. Pierce's Favourite Prescription" to make them strong and healthy. Courtesy Moira Armour

WOMEN ARE NEEDED

TO

HELP WIN THE WAR

WOMEN CAN be usefully employed in nursing the wounded, in making up the soldiers' kits and a thousand other ways—BUT

THEY MUST BE STRONG and HEALTHY

DR. PIERCE'S FAVORITE PRESCRIPTION MAKES WEAK WOMEN STRONG.

It can now be had in Tablet form at all Druggists.

fight for her

COME WITH THE IRISH CANADIAN RANGERS OVERSEAS BATTALION MONTREAL

Lt.Col. H.J.TRIHEY - O.C.

Left: Whistler's Mother Propaganda poster. Hal Ross Perrigard, Lithographer, after Whistler. Poster, 87 x 55 cm. Harris Lithographing Co. Ltd. Toronto, ca 1917. Picture Division, National Archives C-95738.

GREEN DRAGON PRESS

Keeping the Home Fires Burning

Canadian women did many kinds of work for the war effort. Unemployed women or those who had previously held jobs as clerks, domestics or factory workers, moved into better-paying factory jobs. They made uniforms, army boots and

On the home front – City of Toronto James Collection 2439.

munitions, among other things. In Kingston, Ontario, women became 'conductorettes' on the Kingston, Portsmouth and Cataraqui Electric Railway Company. Housewives and well-to-do women formed knitting and sewing clubs. Knitting even became acceptable in church. Besides making garments for the men stationed overseas, women rolled bandages and raised money for hospitals and canteens near the battlefront.

In Vancouver, women of the Garvey Movement organized a branch of the Universal Black Cross Nurses and Negro societies in Toronto, Montreal, and Halifax solicited funds and distributed propaganda leaflets, occasionally in cooperation with larger white fraternal organizations. (Robin Winks, *The Blacks in Canada*, 319) At least one Black woman trained as a nurse in New York, and is believed to be the first Black nurse to practice in Canada during WW1, though not overseas. However, the better paying jobs in munitions factories were closed to Black women.

Women's group met regularly to pack Red Cross parcels. The *Labour Gazette* reported in July 1915 "the efforts of the various women's organizations of the city have been for the last months in the direction of patriotic work. During the month of June 12 tons of linen was collected by the Daughters of the Empire and forwarded to the headquarters of the Red Cross Society in England, while socks to the number of 1,800 pairs were collected on Empire Day and sent to England to be distributed among the soldiers." And in Dufferin County, Ontario women met to hear musical entertainment, a paper about cereals and their value as breakfast foods, and a reading – "Waterloo." They sang "It's a Long, Long Way to Tipperary" as they sorted and recorded the articles made by the group to be sent to England. A roll call was held, each woman giving her place of birth and the meeting ended with the singing of the National Anthem. As the war neared its end, Black women formed the Women's Charitable Benevolent Association to look after the poor and sick, to run soup kitchens and to provide temporary homes for returning soldiers.

GREEN DRAGON PRESS

The following article in a local newspaper reported on the federal government's response to requests for free or reduced postage.

"Ottawa, Nov. 30. —The Post Office department is in receipt of applications to have parcels addressed to soldiers in France sent free or at reduced rates of postage, there evidently being an impression that the department has control of these rates and could do as it wished. This is not so, as the question of postage is fixed by international agreement. Under international law, provision is made for the free transmission of parcels for prisoners of war, but this privilege does not extend to parcels for troops engaged in active service, nor it is within the power of the department to so extend it." Dufferin County Archives.

an Instrumental Solo. A Paper was read by
Mrs Duke. Cereals and their value as break fast
foods. All sang Tipperary then a Reading by Mrs
George Rawn "Waterloo". Roll was called and members
gave the place of their birth. Meeting closed
with singing of the National Anthem.

Jan 28.
    A Special meeting was held at Mrs. Ira
Stirks to pack a bale for the Red Cross
Society. The following articles were sent:
1 pair pillows & 1 pair Socks. Mrs Haffey.
1 " pillows & 1 pair pillow cases. Mrs Lemon
1 " pillows & pair " cases Mrs. D.N. Potter
1 " pillows & " pillow cases.
8 handkerchiefs 1 chest Protector. Mrs Jas. Armstrong
1 day Shirt. Mrs. Wesley Kee.
1 pair of pillows, 1 pair pillow cases
1 night dress, & 10 bandages. Mrs. J. Mason.
2 pair socks. Miss Lizzie Mills
1 " Socks & 1 night dress. Mrs. W. Atkinson
2 " Socks - Mrs Alex Jackson
1 " Socks & 1 night shirt. Mrs. Wm Leggett
1 " Socks & bandages. Mrs Lewis
2 " Socks - Mrs. Jas. Taylor
1 " Socks - Mrs. Wilson Duke
1 " Socks - Mrs Do. Potter
1 " Socks - 1 Shirt. Mrs. A. R Mills

GREEN DRAGON PRESS

Women on the Farm

The need to send inexperienced women from the cities to work on farms arose because the demands of war had created a shortage of labour in many Ontario industries; agriculture was no exception. Farmers, desperate for workers, although skeptical of the plan, finally agreed to listen to a government scheme to use "city girls" to harvest small fruits and vegetables such as strawberries, apples, tomatoes and beans.(Report of the Trades and Labour Branch for 1917, Vol I., Part IV, 1918, 47.)

Actually, it was not unusual for Ontario farmers to use working-class and Native girls and women during the harvest. However, the increased opportunities for such women to work in urban factories during the war and the overwhelming demand for food created by the war effort forced farmers to consider new sources of labour. Many middle-class women students did not work for pay during the summer months and these were seen as a potential new labour source.

At twenty-three Erskine Keys had just graduated from the University of Toronto. She was one of many women from urban centers who went to Ontario's Niagara Peninsula during the summers of 1917 and 1918 to harvest fruit.

While she was there Keys wrote home almost every day. In her first week in the countryside she complained of the lack of work due to bad weather in this letter to her mother.

"I'd give anything to come home...this is not a paying job...only 3 1/2 hours work all week...It's too expensive to stay here doing nothing [never mind] the agony. I Can't stand it...the fields are full of water.... I'll come home and work, at least there will be no board to pay....I told one man that I had left a perfectly good job in the city and he told me to go back to it."

Before going to Beamsville, Keys worked at the T. Eaton Company and at the Maclean Publishing Company for $7.35 and $7.50 per week respectively.

Excerpt from: "...this is not a paying job": the Farmerette Movement in Ontario during the Great War" by Margaret Kechnie. (unpublished.)

GREEN DRAGON PRESS

Teacher Winnifred Cassel and three friends working on the farm: In: *Speak With Their Own Voices: a documentary history of the Federation of Women Teachers' Associations of Ontario,* by Pat Staton and Beth Light. Photo courtesy Winnifred Cassel.

Denny House, Bramsville, Ont.
Sunday, July 1st '17.

Dear darling wee Beadie,

Thanks ever so much for the letter I got yesterday. Lady, I was glad to get it. Poor wee Beadie, Teenie's so sorry her wee Beadie is lonely. I'd give simply anything to come home. Certainly this is not a paying job. Just fancy! Only 3½ hrs. work all week. I think if we don't get work before Tues. I'll come home. It's too expensive to live here doing nothing — to say nothing of the agony. I can't stand it. I simply must come home if we don't get work. Of course I don't think it's the farmers' fault — it's the weather. They say they've never had so much rain before. Half the fields are buried under water so I expect half the crops of fruit are ruined. Just this morning Spedie & I passed a field of green onions completely covered with water all except their tops. I wouldn't be a farmer for anything. And guess what! That fool Miss Harris has sent for the other 40 (forty!) girls to come up to-morrow. I call it a crime. Four girls in the bunch have had work for the last three days & made $3.10. Rita & I & Spedie & about six others are the only others who have made anything. So I think I might as well come home & get a job in the city — where at least I don't have to pay my board. I'm sure we won't get any work to-morrow because it's pelting rain now & the farmers don't seem to need us either until August & they don't say anything when we say we wonder if 75 girls will get work. So what's the use of staying this month. This weather is proving fatal to the fruit. Last year they needed workers awfully badly, but I don't see that they'll need us this year. I think it would pay to come home until they find out for sure that they need us. Don't you think so? Please tell me in your next letter darleen, what you really think, & if we don't have work before then, I'll come home. One man whom I told I'd left a perfectly good job in the city to come here, advised me to go back so I think I will

Women in a munitions factory.
Public Archives
Canada.
PA 24639.

City of Toronto James
Collection/981.

GREEN DRAGON PRESS

Overseas

A total of 3,141 nursing sisters served in the Canadian Army Medical corps in the Great War; 2,504 in England, France and the Eastern Mediterranean. Forty-six died during the Great War from drowning, disease and from shrapnel wounds suffered during air raids that struck field hospitals. Nursing Sister Margaret Lowe of Binscarth, Manitoba died of shrapnel wounds received during a German raid in France in May 1918. On June 6, 1998, her great-niece Arlene Hill wrote an eloquent letter to the Toronto Star, excerpt below.

Nursing Sister Margaret Lowe. Photo courtesy Arlene Hill

Eighty years ago, my great-aunt, Margaret Lowe, was one of the four Canadian nurses killed at Canada's 1st General Hospital in France near the end of World War I. Another three died at the 3rd Stationary Hospital in unprecedented bombing raids on hospitals that previously had been considered exempt from attack.

Although I never knew her, I came upon her unexpectedly from time to time. In childhood, I discovered her service medals in the top drawer of my mother's dresser, next to her own nursing pins. I wanted those medals to enlarge on the slim story of how she had run from safety of tents and huts into the open area to help someone who was injured and, in doing so was fatally wounded herself....I am left to imagine if my great-aunt was one of the two volunteers selected to help the injured (every nurse volunteered but the matron chose the nearest two). Or, possibly, she ran to help the two doctors caught by a bomb while tending the injured (one killed, one wounded)....ultimately it doesn't matter. What does matter is that those women died the very month Canadian women received the right to vote. The major factor in granting that privilege was recognition of the contribution of women to Canada's war effort during World War I....Above all, our voting privilege is a gift from those nurses who died, whether on board a ship that was sunk, from illnesses contracted or, like those who died near the end of May, 1918, as direct casualties.

Surely we owe it to those who paid so dearly for our freedoms, to be constantly vigilant, to listen with discernment, and to exercise our franchise at each opportunity with care and gratitude.

ARLEEN HILL
Peterborough

GREEN DRAGON PRESS

Casualty Form—Active Service.

Fill in Only.—Unit, Number, Rank and Name.

M. F. W. 54. (A. F. B. 103.)
250M.—1-16.
H. Q. 1772-39-920.

Unit, Regiment or Corps.......... A M C T D No 10

Regimental No. Nurse   Rank Lieut   Name Lowe Margaret

Enlisted (a)..........   Terms of Service (a).......... C.E.F. Depot   Service reckons from (a)..........

Date of promotion to present rank..........   Date of appointment to lance rank..........   Numerical position on roll of N.C.Os...........

Extended..........   Re-engaged..........   Qualification (b) Prof. Nurse

Report		Record of promotions, reductions, transfers, casualties, etc., during active service, as reported on Army Form B 213, Army Form A. 36, or in other official documents. The authority to be quoted in each case.	Place	Date	Remarks taken from Army Form B. 213, Army Form A. 36, or other official documents.
Date	From whom received				
		Embarked	Halifax	29.5.17	
		Disembarked	Liverpool	8-6-17	
25.6.17	C.A.M.C.	TAKEN ON STRENGTH	Westenhanger	29.5.17	Gen. D.O. 176
25.6.17	"	Posted to Ont Mil Hosp Orpington	Westenhanger	8.6.14	Pt II D.O. 176. W. Webster COMMANDING C.A.M.C. DEPOT
23.6.17.	O.M.H.	Taken on strength	Orpington	8.6.17.	Pt.11.D.O.149.
5-12-17	16th Can St.	Struck off strength to No.16 Can Gen Hosp	Orpington	28-11-17	Pt. I Do 290 W.M. Crawford Major Camc

---

Forms R. 150   E.T.
3232. 15 M.

Surname **LOWE**   Christian Names **Margaret**

Rank Nursing Sister

Promotion N/S. 29.3.17

Unit Reinf.C.A.M.C.Nursing Sisters.

Place of birth Ma̶y̶ Ayrshire.Scotland.

Married (Yes or No)

Appointments 29.5.17

Date of leaving Canada 29.5.17

Name and Address of Next-of-Kin   Father.
Thomas Lowe.
Binscarth.Manitoba.Canada

Date and Cause of Resignation

Report		Record of Promotions, reductions, transfers, casualties, etc., during active service. The authority to be quoted in each case	Place	Date	REMARKS Taken from Official Documents
Date	From whom received				
		T.O.S. Camc. CEF on arr. f. Can.			
22.6.17	Dms.	posted to Camc Dep.		29.5.17	Co 799
"	"	Posted to Ontario M.H.		8.6.17	Co 802
8-10-17	DMS	Posted to No16 Can Gen	Orpington	5-10-17	CO 1310
4.12.17	do	Posted to No.16 Can Stat Hosp.		29.11.17	CO 1579
4.12.17	16 Can St H	S.O.S. remaining for temp duty in England on Proc o/seas		8.12.17	A.F.B.103
13.12.17	4.C.G.Hp	Att temp duty cease to be attd		5.12.17 / 26.1.18	
29.1.18	Dms	Proc o/seas		26.1.18	C.O.130
23.2.18	10.C.M.Hp	arr in France 26.1.18 / Joined 10.C.M.Hp 28.1.18			
16.3.18	do	SOS on returning to No.1 B.G.Hp		8.3.18	
23.5.18	A.M.S.	Reported from Base wounded		19.5.18	Q 989 8316 R Chest Penet. pen
27.5.18	do	Adm 24 Gen Hosp	Etables	21-5-18	Q992 "
29.5.18	do	Died of Wounds (Enemy Air Raid)		28.5.18	Q 994

1537

(Some) women win the vote

- When the government was returned to power it recognized its debt to women by convening a Women's War Conference at Ottawa from February 28 to March 2, 1918. Delegates from all women's organizations in Canada were addressed by the Governor General and prominent Cabinet members on such topics as child welfare and national health. Finally, March 1919, a bill was passed giving the vote to Canadian women, though many women of colour and Aboriginal women were still excluded.

On December 17, 1917, women with close relatives in the Canadian or British armed forces voted for the first time in a federal election. The next day, a Toronto woman, Janie Smythe, wrote the following letter to suffragist Flora Denison expressing her feelings about the experience of voting.

Toronto, 1917

22 Glengrove Ave. W
Toronto Dec. 18,1917.

My Dear Mrs. Denison.

It is befitting that you should be the first one I should write to since I recorded my first vote. It was a proud day yesterday for me and an hour which you and others have by unceasing devotion to the cause, made possible. I may not be recognized by humanity at large, as having a complete number of organs and faculties with more or less average mental ability to use them! In a word, am equal of my husband, at least technically speaking. I have my vote owing to my sister nursing soldiers. Stepmothers are not fully qualified for such a high honour as voting. I trust that when next we shall meet that I shall bear myself with true and becoming dignity in my new state of equality....

Janie Smythe

Mrs. Flora M. Denison Papers, Thomas Fisher Rare Books, University of Toronto. Library. Mss Coll.

Although the government did provide financial support to the families of World War I soldiers, they often found themselves in financial need. Mrs. R.D. Farquharson wrote to explain her circumstances in a letter to the Prime Minister, Robert Borden. As the wife of a soldier, Mrs. Farquharson had been granted the franchise. Her request for advice on how she should vote in the forthcoming December federal election was not very subtle.

Kamloops, B.C.
Nov. 27th, 1917

Dear Sir—

I write to ask your opinion on which way a Soldier's wife with a family of seven should vote. As far back as I can remember we have upheld the Borden Gov. This year my husband is in France. When he enlisted (Feb. 1916) it was with the understanding that the C.P.F. [Canadian Patriotic Fund] were to make up what the Gov. lacked in providing as a living, since that time the price cost of living has gone up at least double and our allowance remains the same as it was when the C.P.F was started. My oldest child is a girl eleven years old my youngest 15 months, the price of fuel and clothing is awful as well as the price of the plainest food-stuffs. It is impossible to keep the family on $75.00 per month. I have asked the C.P. Society also the City for help and can't even get an investigation. I am ashamed to ask from the returned men who have done so much for us. Where there is being so much money wasted and spent on Election and such, surely it is not necessary that any little one's should suffer when a small cheque of perhaps 75.00 would meet extra expenses for winter and make us comfortable...

I remain yours,

To Win-the-War
Mrs. R.D. Farquharson
460 Columbia

Robert Laird Borden Papers, MG26 H, Vol. 61, 30683
Public Archives of Canada.

GREEN DRAGON PRESS

Ada Kelly

Ada Kelly was the first Black woman hired to teach in the in public school system in an Ontario School Board, (Windsor, Ontario.) Her Normal School principal wrote her a glowing letter of recommendation, although to our contemporary eyes it seems patronizing and even racist. (see following pages)

In 1916, her salary for the year was $650. Inspectors' reports speak of her excellent teaching and organizational skills. In later life she was a strong community leader and served as a mentor and example to many younger members of her extended family.

Photo: courtesy Christine Kelly.

- 1918 – Founding of the Federation of Women Teachers' Associations of Ontario. Over the next eight decades FWTAO would make tremendous contributions to the fight for women's equality.

GREEN DRAGON PRESS

F. P. Gavin, B.A.
Principal.

Windsor, Ont., Aug 17th 1913

W. J. Shrene Esq.
        Sec - Treas. Trustee Board,
            SS. U= 4 Raleigh.

Dear Sir - I understand Miss Ada Kelly (colored) of Windsor is an applica for a position in your school. Permit me to say a word on her behalf. I had her in Windsor Coll. Inst all through her High School course and know well her attainments and abilities.

        She was one of our best students throughout her course and graduated with an unusually broad and thorough training. She is a young woman of good ability, studious hab

F. P. Gavin, B.A.
Principal.

Windsor, Ont.,..................................191

and smith a very fine character.

If I could afford a private teacher or governess for my own children I know of no one whom I would sooner have.

If you can give a coloured girl the position I feel sure you will not regret trying Miss Kelly if you should do so. She is a much better teacher than many a white girl. She is an attractive looking young woman, well mannered and always neatly dre

Yours truly,

F. P. Gavin

Aftermath

The experiences of 70 years of grassroots organization, speaking, writing, cooperating had created a pool of experienced women reformers ready to cope with the aftermath of the Great War. Though they had deep concerns about the human cost of the war and strong commitment to preventing another, as expressed in the poem *In Flanders Now* by journalist and author Edna Jacques, still they had high hopes for the future. But even though women had proven their worth as citizens during the war, when it was over they were expected to step back into the home and give up their hard-won jobs to returning veterans.

Below is one of the many propaganda bulletins that were issued by the Ontario Government. Some, like this one, were directed to female employees, others to their employers.

☞ TO WOMEN WORKERS ☜

Are you working for love
Or for Money?

Are you holding a job you do not need?
Perhaps you have a husband well able to support you
And a comfortable home?
You took a job during the war to help meet the shortage of labour.
You have "made good" and you want to go on working.
But the war is over and conditions have changed.
There is no longer a shortage of labour. On the contrary
Ontario is faced by a serious situation due to the number of men unemployed.
This number is being increased daily by returning soldiers.
They must have work. The pains and dangers they have endured in our defence give them the right to expect it.
Do you feel justified in holding a job which could be filled by a man who has not only himself to support, but a wife and family as well?

Think it over

Department of Labour Archives of the Ontario Government. *Women at Work: Ontario 1850-1930.*

GREEN DRAGON PRESS

✝ IN FLANDERS NOW ✝

We have kept faith ye Flanders dead,
Sleep well beneath the poppies red
That mark your place,
The torch your dying hands did throw
We held it high before the foe
And answered bitter blow for blow
In Flanders fields.

And where your hero's blood was spilled
The guns are now forever stilled
And silent grown.
There is no cry of tortured pain
And blood will never flow again
In Flanders fields.

Forever held in our sight
Will be those crosses gleaming white
That guard your sleep
Rest you to peace the task is done
The fight you left us we have won
And peace on earth had just begun
In Flanders now.

Edna Jacques, *Uphill All the Way*, **p.129**

For all the changes and increased opportunities for women, emphasis still remained on the importance of women's role as homemaker.

"The life of the average woman is divided, generally, into two periods of work, that of paid employment and that of homemaking…. Happily, it appears from an investigation of the conditions affecting girls as wage earners that the knowledge which helps them to be good homemakers is necessary to their well being in paid employment… Lack of training in home making is probably the greatest drawback, which a girl in paid employment can have."

Marjory MacMurchy, *The Canadian Girl at Work*. Ontario, Ministry of Eduction, 1919, preface.

GREEN DRAGON PRESS

The social ideology that restricted white women to narrowly defined roles, was doubly strong for Black women. As Carrie Best recalls in her autobiography her mother demonstrated throughout her life the tenacity and will power that challenged the stereotype of Black womanhood.

New Glasgow, Nova Scotia, ca 1917

Compared to our present life style, we would I suppose be classified as 'respectable…' If we were poor, we as children were never conscious of it, for we were never lacking in food, clothing or home comforts.

My mother was a meticulous homemaker and cook often catering for social gatherings in the town. Although kind, loving and generous she was none the less a disciplinarian guarding the sanctity of the home and the family's safety like a lioness with her cubs. Black womanhood was held in low esteem during the early part of the twentieth century and only the home afforded the protection needed to ensure security from outside influences.

An incident that occurred at the close of the First World War tells its own story. A race riot erupted in the town of New Glasgow as the result of an altercation between a black and a white youth. Bands of roving white men armed with clubs had stationed themselves at different intersections allowing no Blacks to go beyond that point. We had learned of the riot from our father when he came home from work. My oldest brother was at work at the Norfolk House and my mother who had been driven home by the chauffeur of the family for whom she had been working knew nothing of the situation.

Finding my younger brother my father and myself at home and my older brother missing my mother inquired as to why he was not home. It was dusk.

In all the years she lived and until she passed away at the age of eighty-one my mother was never known to utter an unkind blasphemous or obscene word, nor did I ever see her angry. This evening was no exception. She told us to get our meal, stating that she was going into town to get my brother. It was a fifteen-minute walk.

At the corner of East River Road and Marsh Street the crowd was waiting and as my mother drew near they hurled insults at her and threateningly ordered her to turn back. She continued to walk toward the hotel about a block away when one of the young men recognized her and asked her where she was going. "I am going to the Norfolk House for my son," she answered calmly. (My mother was six feet tall and as straight as a ramrod.) The young man ordered the crowd back and my mother continued on her way to the hotel. At that time there was a livery stable at the rear entrance to the hotel and it as there my mother found my frightened older brother and brought him safely home.

Carrie Best, *The Lonesome Road: The Autobiography of Carrie M. Best*, New Glasgow, NS, Clarion Publishing, 1979, 43,44.

GREEN DRAGON PRESS

Notable Women

Dr. Maud Leonora Menten

Maud Menten graduated in medicine from the University of Toronto in 1907, earned a PhD, and in 1913 in Germany, collaborated with Dr. Leonor Michaelis to develop the Michaelis-Menten equation, a basic biochemical concept, fundamental to enzyme research. A gifted linguist and artist, she was also an enthusiastic mountain climber. Her research and teaching career lasted for 50 years.

Matilda Casselman Ness 1864-1932

Ness was the postmistress of Kirkfield Park, Manitoba for 21 years. She was a voracious reader and loved the theater, music and movies. She was an accomplished horsewoman as well as a driver of early automobiles. Oh yes, and she raised 10 children. When her son was reported missing the First World War, Matilda enlisted in the Winnipeg Women's Volunteer reserve intending to make her way to Europe as a member of the reserve, with the intention of finding her son. She never did travel to Europe but instead she hired a pilot to drop leaflets over Belgium and France, with her son's photograph and her address in Manitoba. She died before her son's fate was discovered. He had died after a gas attack in 1915.

Helen Armstrong

Helen Armstrong was a labour activist who sought to build a fair social system in Canada. She took an active role in the Winnipeg general strike and was described in the press at the time as "dangerous" and the "wild woman from the west..." The wife of a Winnipeg streetcar conductor and strike leader, Helen spoke out for better pay, shorter working hours and safer conditions for the thousands of women working in oppressive conditions in factories and sweatshops. President of the Women's Labour League and a member of the Social Democrat society, Helen was at the centre of the strike action, helping those in need, especially single women, with no one to support them. Helen was arrested a number of times during the strike for her activities. She demanded a "family wage" for women who were single, widowed or divorced and who made a dollar a day or less. The role that Helen played in openly challenging the plight of workingwomen, helped to eventually create better labour conditions in Canada.

GREEN DRAGON PRESS

Activities
1910 – 1919

PETITIONS

As a class decide on a social/equity issue that you feel should be addressed at your school. Create a petition and circulate it within the school. Research where to send the petition.

ARGUMENTS AGAINST WOMEN'S SUFFRAGE

Using the documents in this chapter such as Premier Duff's speech, p31, and the Valentine's card p32, create a chart with two columns. In column one, list the arguments against women's suffrage. In column two, in your own words comment on the logic of the arguments.

VALENTINE'S GREETINGS

Create a satirical post card. Instead of an anti-suffrage message, make it pro-suffrage.

AFTERMATH

"To Women Workers" p46. Do you believe is was fair that women were pressured to give up their jobs and return to the home to make room for returning veterans ? Was there a more just solution? Organize a debate, as it might have taken place at the time. Students may choose to dress in historical costume.

ADA KELLY

Read and discuss the letter of recommendation, page 44. The principal implies that there might be a problem hiring a Black woman to teach for the Board. Do you think his concern was justified? Why? Do you think the principal placed undue emphasis on Ada's personal appearance? How would this be related to her teaching ability? How do you react to his statement that if he could afford to hire a private teacher for his own children, he would have no hesitation in hiring Ada?

Resources

Acton, Janice, Penny Goldsmith & Bonnie Shepard, eds. *Women at Work, 1850 – 1930*, Toronto: Canadian Women's Educational Press, 199974.
Alfred, Marguerite & Pat Staton eds. *Black Women in Canada: Past and Present,* Toronto: Green Dragon Press, 2004 (revised.)
Letters of Frederick Stanley Albright and Elnora Evelyn Kelly Albright.
http://members.rogers.com/echoinmyheart.
Staton, Pat. *It Was Their War Too: Canadian Women in the Great War,* Toronto: Green Dragon Press, 2004.
The Nursing Sisters of Canada – www.vac-acc.gc.ca.
"Women Take the Right to Vote," www.coolwomen.org.

Video: *And We Knew How to Dance:* National Film Board

GREEN DRAGON PRESS

1920 – 1929

Smocks and Blouses of General Appeal

6308

6312

6313

6307

6310

6314

Everywoman's World, 1920.

GREEN DRAGON PRESS

1920 - 1929

When I hear men talk about women being the angel of the home I always, mentally at least shrug my shoulders in doubt. I do not want to be the angel of any home; I want for myself what I want for other women, absolute equality. After that is secured then men and women can take turns at being angels.
Agnes Macphail, first woman Member of Parliament.

In the 1920s, Canadian women experienced a world very different from that which their mothers and grandmothers had known. Partly through the contributions they had made to the war effort, and partly through the dedicated campaigning of the suffragists, Canadian women had made some substantial gains in their struggle for equality of status. Agnes Campbell Macphail of Ontario became the first woman elected to the House of Commons in 1921. Nellie McClung won a seat in Alberta the same year, becoming the third woman to sit in that province's legislature. At the 1928 Olympics, great female athletes like Ethel Catherwood and Bobby Rosenfeld won gold medals for Canada. In what has become known as the "Person's Case," in August 1927, Emily Murphy and four Alberta women - Nellie McClung, Henrietta Muir Edwards, Louise McKinney and Irene Parlby, later known as the "Famous Five," - petitioned the Judicial Committee of the Privy Council of Great Britain, for clarification on women's eligibility for appointment to the Senate. On October 18, 1929, the Committee ruled Section 24 of the British North America Act should apply equally to women. With that decision women became eligible for nomination to the Senate. One year later, Cairine Reay Wilson was the first woman to take her place in the Senate of Canada. By implication this victory meant that many other fields opened to women.

But even as women gained new rights society still sought to confine them to the stereotypical view of women's place. Mass circulation magazines and advice books acknowledged the hopes raised in this new decade by featuring "the girl of the new age," creating the popular notion of the "flapper." There was, on the other hand, some doubts about the idea of "the new woman." The end of the Great War had left many Canadians feeling threatened and insecure, and they turned to traditional values and institutions for a sense of stability. Marriage remained the accepted occupation for women, and many magazines offered advice and information on the subject.

> • In 1921 2.2 per cent of married women were working for money. Statistics Canada

"We believe that the home is the natural and rightful domain of women, and therefore that home economics, the science of the home, is pre-eminently the proper and logical study for womankind; we believe that as women are largely the spenders of money, national thrift would dictate that they be taught to spend wisely; that as the keepers of the health of the nation we believe they should be taught the principles of hygiene and dietetics; we believe that in the different branches of this subject there is ample scope for the varying abilities of the most brilliant minds of the sex; we believe that much undesirable and unnecessary competition between the sexes will be avoided, and many other social problems solved when the dignity of homemaking is

GREEN DRAGON PRESS

adequately recognized and home economics given its rightful place in a national and international scheme of education. Finally, let us never forget that upon the physical stamina, the mental and moral fibre of the mother-to-be depends the character of the life, yea, the very life of tomorrow."
J.H. Putnam and G.M. Weir. *Survey of the School System* (Victoria: Province of British Columbia, 1925,) *Not Just Pin Money*, 339.

"The kitchen is the centre of the house. At meal times the centre of interest shifts to the dining room. When the work of the day is over, mother and father and children and friends sit down to enjoy the evening by the open fire in the living room, or sit down on the porch in summertime to enjoy the evening air and the colours of the sunset and the pleasant view. The centre of interest is where the people are. But the kitchen is mother's workplace and factory and laboratory. There she keeps most of her tools and does most of her work, and while she is there, that is the centre of the house."
Helen MacMurchy, "How to Make Our Canadian Home," no. 3 in *The Little Blue Books Home Series* [Ottawa: Department of Health. 1922].

" A woman's home was her castle - so the ads said - and in the twenties household conveniences made housekeeping...well a little more convenient. Almost everything could be run by electricity, refrigerators, floor polishers, sewing machines, even clothes wringers. The crank-up gramophone was on its way up to the attic. Wood and tile kitchen floors were covered over with "linoleum." Aluminum came on the market and iron skillets and pots disappeared.
The Crazy Twenties: Canada's Illustrated Heritage. Toronto: Natural Science of Canada, 1978.

Not all magazines promoted this view. One, the *Business Woman*, a Canadian magazine run entirely by women, encouraged enterprising women to pursue business and the professions, and other, more hopeful voices were raised. In an article titled "What Shall We Do With "Our Flapper?" in the June, 1927 *Maclean's* magazine, Mrs. A.N. Plumptre, described as the wife of Rev. Canon Plumptre and president of the Ontario Division of the Red Cross Society, gave her views.

"There is much criticism abroad regarding the young girls and youths of to-day; they are said to be undisciplined, reckless, extravagant and frivolous, falling far below the standard set by the preceding generation. In my opinion, our young people are not altogether to blame for these tendencies and their divergence from previous types. They only reflect the general tendencies of the times they live in, just as the Early Victorian maidens who wore crinolines, coy curls,—and fainted in any emergency calling for prompt action-lived up to the conventions and requirements of that very stilted age.

There is today a general tendency toward the loosening of restraints, and a noticeable inclination toward unconventionality which in itself need not be regarded as alarming, for, after all, conventions can be overdone. We should congratulate ourselves that the old hide-bound custom of paying calls has been dispensed with. No longer is it incumbent on all the hostesses in one neighborhood to receive on a certain day and be greeted by a succession of two-minute callers, each of whom would then rush on to the next house on her list....The War has released the present generation of girls from that convention.

GREEN DRAGON PRESS

Humberside Collegiate Year Book 1927-28.

And here let me say that one good thing about young girls of to-day it their naturalness. They are delightfully and refreshingly natural. They are not inclined to pose or affect certain mental attitudes. In other words, with all their faults-and they are superficial ones-I think our girls of to-day value sincerity and show it by their frank honesty."

Having come to the defence of the modern young women, Mrs. Plumptre then proceeds to criticize a tendency toward elaborate entertainments and demands by some young women that their escorts spend excessive amounts of money on them, which she saw as delaying marriage, and the consequent negative consequences for the birthrate.

"The girls who expect young men, who are perhaps students at college or juniors in banking houses, to provide taxis, expensive seats at theatres, flowers, candies and little suppers to wind up an evening's entertainment, very often involve these boys in temptations and hardships for which the pleasure derived from a few evenings' amusements affords no compensation. They are also fostering those conditions that lead to the postponement of marriages. Neither a young man nor a girl with this standard of expenditure is very likely to be willing to start married life on small means, therefore early marriages are being made less possible by such luxurious tastes."

Plumptre then sounded a familiar anti-immigrant warning:

"Canada needs more than anything Canadian homes and a home-born increase in population. But how can homes be established in these times of financial stringency when young people have accustomed themselves to every form of luxury? Early marriages would go far toward building up the kind of population our country needs."

GREEN DRAGON PRESS

New freedoms:

New changes in dress came for several reasons. Women working on the farm and in munitions during the war, of necessity adopted appropriate clothing, and fabric needed for the war effort took priority. The new fashions in dress and hairstyles suited the new confidence many women had gained as they explored work opportunities that been previously closed to them. Clothes were less constricting and the shorter hairstyles less time consuming.

Dress patterns: The Designer Publishing Company, 1923.

GREEN DRAGON PRESS

Opportunities for clerical work in business and the civil service increased dramatically after 1900. High schools and private business colleges offered courses in typing, shorthand and other office skills. But, in addition to technical aptitude, women had to be able to offer proof of their respectability and good character to obtain clerical positions. *The Widening Sphere: Women in Canada, 1870 - 1940, 44.*

Humberside Collegiate Year Book, 1927.

GREEN DRAGON PRESS

New Opportunities for Women in Paid Work

With the return of large numbers of men after the war, women were strongly encouraged to return to the home and give up their places in factories and offices. Many women strongly objected to these demands. The attitude toward workingwomen had changed in other ways. It was now acceptable for a young woman to work until she married, since her wages could help with the family expenses. Women's presence in the workforce was tolerated as long as they did not try to take jobs normally held by men. Women were strongly encouraged to focus on so-called "women's" jobs.

Examples of contemporary advertising

NURSES' SCHOOLS INFORMATION
FREE TUITION including even board and room to young women ages 18 to 35, learning in city institutions this dignified profession, paying $200 a month on graduation, and which is of real service to the world. Catalog on ALL schools in U.S. AMERICAN SCHOOLS ASSOCIATION 1102C Times Bldg., N.Y. or 1515C Capitol Bldg. Chicago.

Go to High School in Your Own Home!
Secure your matriculation—the gateway to the professions—or a teacher's certificate; or take Commercial training and fit yourself for private secretary. Civil Service training opens the way to a permanent Government position. Short Story Writing brings quick returns while Civil Ask for a copy of "The Efficient Mind" which outlines the world famous Pelman training. THE CANADIAN CORRESPONDENCE COLLEGE, Dept. 724 York Building, TORONTO. "Canada's Oldest Correspondence College."

"The life of the average woman is divided, generally, into two periods of work, that of paid employment and that of homemaking....Happily, it appears from an investigation of the conditions affecting girls as wage earners that the knowledge which helps them to be good home-makers is necessary to their well-being in paid employment... Lack of training in home-making is probably the greatest drawback which a girl in paid employment can have." Ontario Ministry of Education publication, 1919, reprinted in the 1996 book *The Proper Sphere: Woman's Place in Canadian Society.*

More and more women were being employed as sales help in stores, as filing clerks and stenographers in business offices and as factory workers because they could perform such duties as well as men - and at much lower wages. As late as 1929, women workers in the needle trades in Montreal were earning wages between $8.37 and $16.95 a week. And a week was 55 hours of work! The Quebec Women's Minimum Wage Commission, established in 1919, tried to do something about such wretched pay, but employers and politicians prevented much improvement. The commission did note in 1928 that a single woman's living expenses came to somewhere between $10.85 and $19.81 a week. How women earning just over $8.00 per week were expected to live was left unstated.

GREEN DRAGON PRESS

Opportunities for Black women though, were few and far between. Violet Blackman came to Toronto in 1920. She describes the city and the opportunities for Black women:

"That was 1920; then Toronto was just a village. The streetcars had no sidings to them; you could jump on and off, but they always had the motorman and a conductor on them. The Exhibition Ground and Sunnyside, that was all the lake, and the Union Station - there was nothing but the lake. You couldn't get any position, regardless who you were and how educated you were, other than housework because even if the employer would employ you, those that you had to work with would not work with you." *We're rooted here and they can't pull us up.* Dionne Brand et al., 172,173.

In her memoirs, Nova Scotia-born Carrie Best writes about the decision she made in 1923 not to do housework for anyone else but herself but to pursue a nursing career - an idea she discarded when she realized she was not cut out for the operating room. She then decided to become a teacher.

"Why not? I was of sound mind (?) and body and I could read and write, the only qualifications necessary for a Black School Teacher at the time. All that was needed was a permissive license-as easy to get then as a motor vehicle license today.
"Yes, I would be a teacher with all the rights and privileges-even being referred to as "Miss"-imagine that! So I accepted a call to Delaps Cove in Annapolis County and one bitterly cold January morning arrived in Annapolis. With all the conceit, self-assurance and ambition of Don Quixote, I set out armed with my permissive license as a weapon, to slay the windmills of ignorance, and arrived at the home of Addie Ruggles in Annapolis...Introducing myself I said "I am Carrie Prevoe the new teacher for Delaps Cove; making sure to put proper emphasis on the word teacher-for after all she was only a housewife! "Oh!" she said kindly, "Have you ever been there?" "No! I haven't," I replied, "this is my first teaching job." "Well my dear," she said kindly, "My sister is one of the six families who live there, and when she leaves down here in the fall, with her winter's provisions for up there, we never see each other until late spring."

Alarmed at the thought of the cold and isolation awaiting her, Carrie took Addie Ruggles' advice and returned home. Though she did teach for a short time elsewhere she considered that her teaching career had really ended that morning in Addie's kitchen. Her decision proved to be correct for she eventually became a well-known newspaper publisher and community organizer.

That Lonesome Road: The Autobiography of Carrie M. Best, 44-46.

• 1921 Agnes Macphail becomes the first woman Member of Parliament

GREEN DRAGON PRESS

Canadian Women and Sports

Women's right to participation in competitive sports was not easily won. They had to contend with medical concerns about their "femininity." (it was said that participating in sports would impair their reproductive ability), opposition to the idea of women performing in front of male spectators, dress restrictions, and inequities in funding and facilities. All these obstacles conspired to exclude women, especially in high performance sports. Winning the right to compete at the Olympic Games was especially difficult.

In the nineteen twenties and thirties women became more visible, and this period has been called the golden age of women's sport. In 1928, for the first time women were allowed to participate in track and field competitions at the summer Olympic Games in Amsterdam.

Photo courtesy Pat Staton

GIRLS SPORTS

No girl in sport began to play in club competition so long ago at such an early age as Doris Butwell. Doris began when she was at the Humber Bay School to play softball, and almost immediately she was snapped up for the Humber Bay district team, which played in the Major Back in 1923 she is to-day.

Doris Butwell

Sunnyside League. Doris, it seems, was as good as

She was considered a marvel then, for she was only about fourteen years old. She was one of the heaviest hitters of the Major League, and used to receive for Billy Smith. She had nice style behind the bat, and some of the spectators perhaps can remember the funny little twist of her wrist as she tossed the ball back to Billy.

Doris got her first initiation into the basketball game with the Lakeside Club. She didn't play much basketball for them in that first year, 1924-5, for she did not know anything about the game, but she did play the odd

Then Doris went to Commerce and learned to play basketball. She played for the Commerce Juniors, but was always too light for senior competition. That was in 1925-6, and in the same year she started basketball in earnest for the Lakeside intermediates. That year they were runners-up to Epiphany for the city championship, and last year they were runners-up for the Ontario title to St. Catharines.

Doris has played softball with Lakesides since the club started. Instead of catching, she has been playing second base, where she looks just about the best. She's still up there near the top in batting.

The Evening Telegram January 7, 1928.

The Canadian women's team won two gold, silver and a bronze medal. The success of the "Matchless Six," (Ethel Smith, Myrtle Cook, Jean Thompson, Bobbie Rosenfeld, Ethel Catherwood and Jane Bell) resulted in a huge outpouring of public interest, echoed recently in the response to the Canadian women Olympians' success in speed skating, rowing, ice hockey, cycling, curling, biathlon, swimming, wheelchair racing, basketball and track. Of course, women of all ages have always participated in a wide variety of non-competitive sports and found great reward in terms of physical well-being, self-confidence and friendship.

GREEN DRAGON PRESS

WE WANT TO PLAY ... WE'LL PLAY

Helen Lenskyj

Pendant les années 20 et 30 au Canada, les femmes commencèrent à pratiquer les sports d'équipe, surtout la balle-molle et le ballon-panier: toutefois, des barrières à leur participation complète dans le domaine du sport existaient encore. L'engagement de quelques femmes dans le monde des sports, dominé par les hommes, fut néanmoins exceptionnel. Cet article fait revivre les activités de trois de ces femmes: Doris Butwell Craig, Gladys Gigg Ross, et Hilda Thomas Smith.

The twenties and thirties have been called, by some historians, the "Golden Age" of women's sports in Canada. Others have written histories of sport and physical activity as if women were either invisible or incapable of participating — except perhaps as spectators. It is true that there was a remarkable growth of interest in women's team sports, especially softball and basketball, at this time, but barriers still existed to women's participation. In many respects, the experiences of Doris Butwell Craig, Gladys Gigg Ross, and Hilda Thomas Smith were exceptional. As Gladys explained, "We were into sports which weren't common for girls at that time, so we just thought, 'what do we care about what you think . . . we want to play, we'll play!' " In another sense, the lives of these women are representative of many of their female contemporaries — athletes whose achievements remain unrecorded in a literature which still retains much of its early preoccupation with male-dominated, professional sport.

Doris Butwell Craig was born in 1908 in the Humber Bay area of Toronto. One of four children, she had a sister, Laura, who was fourteen years her senior, and two brothers close to her own age. Doris attended Humber Bay Public School and Central Commerce. After completing high school, she did secretarial work until her marriage in 1932.

Doris was labelled a tomboy by family members from a young age. Quite early in life, she discovered that climbing to the top of "a great big tree" in the backyard was an effective way to avoid doing the dishes. Other escapades included scaling a windmill and hopping a freight train for a mile or so. Family reaction curbed some but not all of Doris's adventures. Reflecting on the tomboy label, Doris said, "I am and I'm not." While her athletic ability and her obvious relish for competition were labelled tomboyish, she perceived these as advantages in terms of friendship, since they allowed her to enjoy a camaraderie with the boys and men in her family and neighbourhood that was unusual for a girl in those days. "Anything the boys could do, I could do, too, and do it as well as they could . . . I didn't feel any different." Remembering ice hockey games on the Humber River, she said, "They knocked me down just the same as they knocked each other down . . . that didn't bother me." The idea of contact sports, however, did bother Laura, who did not share Doris's love of games like basketball and softball. "All that roughness, people sliding into you and hurting your shins" — this was not Laura's idea of fun. Doris attributed this to personality and age differences, noting that Laura did not have the advantage of growing up in the flapper era — the "crazy twenties"; Laura was a wife and mother by this time.

Doris began playing softball when she was about twelve. Her brother's novel training method was obviously a key factor: "He stood me in front of double garage doors that were mostly glass and he would

215

DORIS BUTWELL

CRAIG'S ATHLETIC ABILITY AND OBVIOUS RELISH FOR COMPETITION WERE ADVANTAGES IN TERMS OF FRIENDSHIP

say, 'you can't miss it now, you know!' and I didn't miss it! I never missed it! We never broke a glass on that door." These sessions, Doris claims, taught her to concentrate — "thinking down to her fingers," in her words — and she attributed her subsequent success as "a pretty good hitter" to co-ordination and agility.

During her school years Doris played in interschool basketball competition. As a participant in regional tournaments, she travelled all over Ontario and recalled that the level of play in this team was more demanding. "You really had to play . . . we played boys' rules . . . and I can remember mother counting over one hundred bruises on me!" Doris viewed the introduction of men's rules and the interest taken by male coaches as "a breakthrough" in girls' team sports in the twenties. She explained her position in terms of commitment to the game. While acknowledging that there was, of course, a place for recreational sports in women's lives, she believed that good athletes needed the opportunity for serious training and competition and should not be limited by the "girls'-rules" mentality. Critics at this time, however, were agonizing over the alleged "masculinizing" effects of serious competitive sports on the bodies and the personalities of young women. These critics emphasized the dangers of men's rules and the risks to female players when men, who did not understand women's "peculiar physiology," acted as their managers and coaches. Little of this opposition appears to have affected players like Doris, who viewed men's role in women's team sports as a positive trend.

Apart from the basketball program, the physical education offered by the school system did not leave much impression on Doris. She remarked of the gym exercises, "I used to just walk through those things." Similarly, the contest often recommended for girls — throwing the ball for distance — posed no particular challenge to a softball player: "I could always throw the ball the farthest. I always won that. I didn't think that was any great

achievement." Her other sporting successes at school included a gold medal in the Ontario high schools' competition for standing broad jump. For a short time, too, Doris was coached in diving by Olympic swimming coach Ab Shilcock, until a back injury curtailed her training in this area.

Doris first played basketball for the Lakeside Athletic Club in the 1924–25 season. The club was sponsored by Silverwood Dairies, with the company providing uniforms and equipment. In the days before the diamond was enclosed with a fence, the practice was to "pass the hat" at games; later, admission was charged. It was at the games that Doris received several job offers, presumably from employers who saw publicity opportunities in having a secretary who was a public figure. Newspaper coverage of women's sports did, in fact, make Doris and her teammates public figures; columns written by former athletes Alexandrine Gibb and Phyllis Griffiths appeared regularly in two Toronto newspapers at this time, and a third, written by Bobbie Rosenfeld, appeared in the 1930s. One offer impressed Doris more than all the others: the chance to play softball for a Chicago team, for $60 per week. At the time, Doris earned $16 per week as a secretary, and her status in softball was strictly amateur. Yet she didn't even discuss the offer with her family. "No, you just didn't do that," she explained.

Gladys Gigg Ross grew up in North Bay, one of a family of ten children. A childhood incident served to bring her athletic ability to the attention of Claude Kewley, a sports writer who also coached girls' track and field. Kewley happened to notice the nine-year-old Gladys running down the street, pursued by her sixteen-year-old brother, and was impressed with her remarkable speed. In the following years, Gladys developed an impressive record as an all-round athlete, scoring the most points in high-school field-day events for four years as well as playing basketball and softball.

A 1933 newspaper report of the North Bay collegiate field-day pro-

216

GREEN DRAGON PRESS

gram showed interesting differences between boys' and girls' events. The longest race for girls was 65 yards, compared to 880 yards for boys. Throwing events for girls were limited to the baseball and basketball throw (for distance), whereas boys had javelin and shot-put events. Gladys's best performances were in sprints and high jump. Her introduction to jumping came about when Ethel Catherwood, the 1928 Olympic gold medalist, was competing in North Bay, and Kewley urged Gladys to jump with Ethel. Her first attempts were hampered by long gym bloomers, but a switch to her brother's shorts produced considerable improvement. She continued to practise at home daily in summer and a few times weekly throughout the winter, using high-jump stands which her father had made. At a time when coaching for girls was not particularly systematic or rigorous, Gladys's self-motivation was obviously an important factor in her success.

Gladys played on the collegiate basketball team, which was coached by the girls' physical-training teacher, but she was not very enthusiastic about "P.T." classes, which offered little more than wand drills and folk dancing. Her sporting activities, however, extended outside school. The CPR sponsored a girls' basketball team, in which both Gladys and her younger sister Bernice participated. Unlike school basketball, the "Ceepees" played by boys' rules and occasionally played against boys' teams, with several impressive successes. Girls' participation, however, was not without its restrictions. On one occasion when the team appeared on the main street on Sunday morning in their CPR shirts and shorts, having missed the Saturday night train, the CPR superintendent warned them not to repeat this kind of public display — shorts were considered appropriate only at the game.

Outside of school, a small group of North Bay girls, including Gladys, trained in track and field, first with Claude Kewley and later with Leo Troy, who taught boys' P.T. at the high school. By 1930,

when the first British Empire Games were held in Hamilton, Ontario, four girls, including Gladys, were ready to compete. This was at the time when there was a movement among American and some Canadian women to eliminate competition from all levels of girls' and women's sports, on the grounds that females were not physically and emotionally capable of coping with the strain and excitement. Other concerns included women playing during menstruation and the unsuitability of male coaches for girls' and women's teams. Gladys's experiences suggest that, without male coaches, opportunities for North Bay girls would have been minimal. She did recall, however, that the menstruation issue sometimes arose. Male coaches "wouldn't ask you right out, of course, and if they did in those days, we probably wouldn't know what the word meant!" Their indirect approach was to ask, "How are you today?" or "Do you want to practise today?"

In spite of the competition controversy, the 1930 games offered track and field, swimming, and diving for women. Track and field included 60-metre, 100-metre, and 200-metre races, 4-x-100-metre relay, hurdles, discus, javelin, running high jump, running broad jump, and the inevitable baseball throw. Controversy over the so-called "gruelling" 800-metre distance for women, following the 1928 Olympics, was responsible for the omission of this race from the British Empire Games and subsequent Olympics until 1960. Gladys won medals for high jump, broad jump, and running; a few years later, in the 1932 Olympic trials, she missed out on first place in the running broad jump by one-quarter of an inch.

Softball was Gladys's major sporting interest for over thirty years. There were few school teams when she was young, but women's softball clubs, sponsored by business or industry, were flourishing throughout Ontario. At the age of twelve Gladys joined the Senators' team in North Bay and became its secretary. At fourteen she was secretary of the Northern Ontario Women's Softball Association, and **a few years** later

was appointed northern convener of the Women's Amateur Athletic Federation (WAAF), Ontario branch. At this time, too she was writing a sports column in the *North Bay Nugget* — "In the Feminine Realm of Sport." She played softball until 1944 and continued in executive roles for many years after. It was in 1953, when Gladys assumed the presidency of the provincial Women's Softball Union, that it became, as Bobbie Rosenfeld expressed it in her column, "not only a government for the women, but by the women as well." For the first time in its twenty-two-year history, the positions of advisors, traditionally held by men, were filled by women.

Hilda Thomas Smith, like Doris, was growing up in Toronto during the 1920s, a time when women's team sports were thriving. Her interest in sport began as a student at Oakwood Collegiate and as a member of the Essex Playground softball team. Her brothers did not share her sporting interests and her family rarely watched her play, but obviously enjoyment of the game was the most important factor for Hilda. On occasions when someone expressed disapproval, her response was, "That's their business. I'm doing what I want to do!"

In the early 1920s, Hilda joined the Atheneum Ladies' Athletic Club, which was sponsored by the Atheneum Bowling Alley. This club was taken over by the Lakeside Ladies' Athletic Club in 1925, and so Hilda and Doris became teammates around this time. Like Doris, Hilda played softball for the Lakesides in summer and basketball in winter. The team achieved front-page coverage in the *Evening Telegram* in 1928, when they held a fifteen-point lead in the city intermediate basketball championship. Other important events in Hilda's sporting career included being the first player to hit a ball in the first softball game under floodlights, held in Toronto in 1930. On one of the team's frequent out-of-town trips, Hilda travelled to North Bay, where she met another softball and basketball enthusiast, Gladys Gigg Ross.

All of Lakeside's executive members were women; coaches and

GREEN DRAGON PRESS

IN THE SUPREME COURT OF CANADA

TUESDAY, THE TWENTY-FOURTH DAY OF APRIL, A.D. 1928.

PRESENT:

> The Right Honourable Francis Alexander Anglin, P.C.,
> Chief Justice.
> The Right Honourable Mr. Justice Duff, P.C.
> The Honourable Mr. Justice Mignault
> The Honourable Mr. Justice Lamont
> The Honourable Mr. Justice Smith.

In the matter of a Reference with respect to the meaning to be assigned to the word "Persons" in section 24 of the British North America Act 1867.

Whereas by Order-in-Council of His Majesty's Privy Council for Canada bearing date the nineteenth day of October in the Year of Our Lord One Thousand Nine Hundred and Twenty-seven "P.C. 2034", the question hereinafter set out was referred to the Supreme Court of Canada for hearing and consideration pursuant to section 60 of the Supreme Court Act, namely, --

Does the word "Persons" in section 24 of the British North America Act 1867 include female persons?

As whereas the said question came before this Court for hearing on the fourteenth day of March in the Year of Our Lord One Thousand Nine Hundred and Twenty-eight, in the presence of Counsel for the Attorney General of Canada, the Attorney General of the Province of Quebec and Henrietta Muir Edwards, and others, petitioners.

Whereupon and upon hearing what was alleged by Counsel aforesaid, this Court was pleased to direct that the said Reference should stand over for consideration and the same having come on this day for determination, the following judgment was pronounced:-

"The question being understood to be "Are women eligible for appointment to the Senate of Canada" the question is answered in the negative."

Ent'd Fol. 133
I.B. n°9

The Persons Case

"It would be absurd to ask a woman today if she thought of herself as a person."
April 28, 1928 Supreme Court of Canada Decision. Archives of Canada.
"...and to those who ask why the word [person] should include females, the answer is,
why should it not?"
Lord Sankey, Lord Chancellor of the Privy Council, London, England October 18, 1929
Ontario Women's Directorate - Moments in History, 1992.

The 1920s ended on a note of triumph for women's rights with the winning of the Persons Case in 1929, which proved by reinterpreting the word "person" in Section 24 of the British North America Act that women were eligible for appointment to the Canadian Senate. Although the campaign started in 1927, its roots reach back to 1916 when Emily Murphy had just been created the first woman police magistrate within the British Empire. During her first day as a judge an enraged defence lawyer told her that she was not a "person" under the BNA Act and therefore had no right to be holding court anyway. In 1919 the first conference of the Federated Women's Institute of Canada sent a resolution requesting the prime minister to appoint a woman to the Senate. Other powerful women's organizations followed suit, but they were told that the nomination of a woman was impossible without an amendment to the Act. In 1927, Emily Murphy, with Nellie McClung, Irene Parlby, Louise McKinney and Henrietta Muir Edwards, petitioned to the Supreme Court asking for an interpretation on just who were "persons." Their question was

"Does the word Persons in Section 24 of the British North America Act, 1967, include female persons?" The argument was heard in the Supreme Court of Canada on March 14, 1928. The verdict came five weeks later and was a bitter disappointment for the petitioners. The court ruled against them. The five Supreme Court justices decided that the BNA Act must be construed in the light of what was intended in 1867, when no woman was enfranchised in Canada, and that therefore women were not eligible for appointment to the Senate.

"The question being understood to be 'Are Women eligible for appointment to the Senate of Canada' the question is answered in the negative."

After a year during which the five appellants hoped that the government would introduce a motion to amend the BNA Act, they decided to appeal to the Judicial Committee of the Privy Council in London. Finally, on October 18, 1929, Lord Sankey, the Lord Chancellor read the decision at Temple Bar.

Their Lordships have come to the conclusion that the word persons includes members of the male and female sex and that therefore the question propounded by the Governor General must be answered in the affirmative, and that women are eligible to be summoned and become members of the Senate of Canada.

GREEN DRAGON PRESS

Famous 5 Foundation

Emily Murphy (March 14, 1868 – Oct. 17, 1933): a prominent suffragist and social reformer; the first female magistrate in the Commonwealth; leader of the 'Persons' Case; author of books and articles under the name of Janey Canuck.

Henrietta Muir Edwards (Dec. 18, 1849 – Nov. 10, 1931): published Canada's first women's magazine; established the prototype for the Canadian YWCA; an artist as well as a legal expert; co-founder of the National Council of Women (1893) and the Victorian Order of Nurses (1897).

Louise McKinney (Sept. 22, 1868 – July 10, 1931): organizer and staunch supporter of the Women's Christian Temperance Union; first woman to serve as a Member of of the Legislative Assembly in the Commonwealth when she was elected in Alberta in 1917, the first election in which women could vote or run for office; a champion for the first Dower Act in Alberta.

Irene Parlby (Jan. 9, 1868 – July 12, 1965): an advocate for rural women in Alberta; first female cabinet minister in Alberta, the second in the Commonwealth (1921); the first president of the United Farm Women of Alberta (1916); delegate to the League of Nations in Geneva (1930).

Nellie McClung (Oct. 20, 1873 – Sept. 1, 1951): novelist, reformer, journalist and suffragist who led the fight to enfranchise North American women, beginning with western Canadian women in the early 1910's; Liberal MLA for Edmonton (1921-1926); first female Director of the Board of Governors of the CBC (1936); delegate to the League of Nations in Geneva (1938).

GREEN DRAGON PRESS

Notable Women.

Agnes Macphail

A teacher in rural Ontario before running for election, Macphail was the first woman elected to the House of Commons, representing the riding of Grey South East as an independent, keeping close links with the United Farmers of Ontario party. Macphail was an ardent feminist and an advocate of social change and devoted most of her life to public service at a time when women were not welcomed in the public arena. Defeated federally in 1940, she moved to Toronto to become a newspaper columnist and in 1943 was nominated as the CCF candidate in the provincial riding of York East and won, thus becoming one of the first two women elected to the provincial legislature. She worked for women, miners and prisoners, founded the Canadian branch of the Elizabeth Fry Society and was largely responsible for Ontario's first pay equity legislation in 1951.

"That seems to be the haunting fear of mankind - that the advancement of women will some time, some way, some place, interfere with some man's comfort."
Agnes Macphail

Fanny "Bobbie" Rosenfeld

Bobbie Rosenfeld was a natural athlete. Born in Russia in 1903, she came to Canada with her family as a child. Her athletic ability showed itself early, and she became the star of championship basketball, softball and hockey teams in Ontario into the 1920s. She also excelled at golf, winning the Toronto grass court tennis championship in 1924 and a year later, astonished spectators at the Ontario Ladies Track and Field Championship watched when Bobbie, the sole representative of the Patterson's Athletic Club placed in every event on the programme - four firsts and two seconds - in events as diverse as discus, long jump and hurdles. At the 1928 Olympics in Amsterdam, Rosenfeld won a silver medal in the 100-metre sprint and a gold medal as a member of the women's relay team. She was named Canadian woman athlete of the first half-century in 1950, and elected to the Canadian Sports Hall of Fame.

Phyllis Munday

Phyllis Munday began climbing Vancouver's North Shore Mountains before the First World War, at a time when women still had to wear skirts in public. She would start out wearing a skirt and then change into pants part way up the trail. Munday went on to become one the most successful mountain climbers in Canada. She was the first woman to climb Mount Robson, the highest peak in the Canadian Rockies in 1924. Phyllis gave her time to supporting the Alpine Club of Canada and the Girl Guides (in 1909 she was the first girl in Vancouver to join the Girl Guides) and received many honours, culminating in the Order of Canada in 1973.

The Famous Five

In August 1927, Emily Murphy and four Alberta women - Nellie McClung, Henrietta Muir Edwards, Louise McKinney and Irene Parlby, later known as the "Famous Five," - petitioned the Judicial Committee of the Privy Council of Great Britain, for clarification on women's eligibility for appointment to the Senate. On October 18, 1929, the Committee ruled Section 24 of the British North America Act should apply equally to women. With that decision women became eligible for nomination to the Senate. One year later, Cairine Reay Wilson was the first woman to take her place in the Senate of Canada

The Edmonton Commercial Grads: This world famous women's basketball team of the 1920s and 30s, were North American champions for nearly 20 years. They won 502 of 522 games, a record unrivalled by any team in any sport. They were also champions at the 1928 Olympics in Amsterdam, however because basketball was only a demonstration sport at that there was no gold medal.

GREEN DRAGON PRESS

Activities
1920 – 1929

WOMEN'S FASHIONS

Discuss how clothing and fashion changed since the previous decade and how the changes reflected the politics and society of the 1920s. Plan a 1920s fashion show with political as well as fashion commentary.

NEW OPPORTUNITIES

Make a list of opportunities open to women according to the documents. Discuss opportunities not represented that were open during the previous decade. Recreate a job interview scenario for a woman applying for one of the jobs mentioned. What might she wear? What kind of questions could be asked? What kind of experience does she have? Did she do war work?

CANADIAN WOMAN AND SPORTS

Create a 1920s radio station that broadcasts only on women and sports. Write and perform a broadcast, including an interview with a well-known woman athlete. Ask questions about obstacles she has encountered as an athlete.

THE FAMOUS FIVE

Research the history behind the sculpture recently unveiled on Parliament Hill. What obstacles did the Famous 5 Foundation encounter? What does this reveal about the progress of women in politics today? Role-play a 1920s afternoon, where the famous five are discussing their pursuit of the "persons case." They have just been informed that the Supreme Court has rejected their demands. Make specific reference to the decision.

Resources

Crowley, Terry. *Agnes Macphail and the Politics of Equality,*Toronto: J. Lorimer, 1992.
Hotchkiss, Ron. "The Matchless Six: Canadian Women at the Olympics, 1928." *The Beaver,* 1993, 23-42.
"The Image of Women in Mass Circulation Magazines in the 1920s" in Trofimenkoff, Susan Mann & Alison Prentice, *The Neglected Majority: Essays in Canadian History,* Vol I. 116-124, McClelland & Stewart, 1977.

The Persons Case www.famous5.org

Videos:
Playing for Keeps & *The Lady From Grey County:* National Film Board.

Women & Sports poster: Green Dragon Press,www3.sympatico.ca/equity.greendragonpress

GREEN DRAGON PRESS

1930 – 1939

Persons before the Law

Swearing in ceremony of Canada's first woman senator, Cairine Wilson, during Opening of Parliament, Ottawa, February 1, 1930. National Archives of Canada/Cairine R. Wilson Collection, PA 126100.

GREEN DRAGON PRESS

1930 - 1939 Introduction

*"**Experts say that the depression is by no means the whole cause, and that the trend started some three years ago, women beginning then to lose ground in the business world. Clever young women who left university a year or two ago, confident of conquering the world, are to be found staying home with mother because there is nothing else to do. If girls cannot find jobs, the economic advantages of marrying them off again become apparent.**" (Isabel Turnbull Dingman, "Can She Manage Alone?" in Chatelaine, April 1932.)*

In 1929, the struggles of Emily Murphy and the Famous Five led to the landmark legal precedent as women were finally declared "persons" before the law. This same year, a shocked and unprepared world witnessed and experienced the crash of the stock market, leading North America down the long road of the Great Depression. For a majority of Canadians, this event marked a significant shift in their lives. For women, the Depression appeared to represent more than economic hardship. The post-war generation symbolized by the emancipated flapper seemed to have been replaced by a more conservative and traditionally feminine image of women. Economics dictated that married women give up their employment to allow men on relief to work. In fact, according to Statistics Canada, in 1931 only 3.5 --percent of working for pay women were married. It would appear that the progress of first wave feminism had suffered a significant setback.

Conversely, only 6 months after the famous Persons Case, on February 5, 1930, Cairine Wilson became the first woman to serve in the Canadian senate. Evidently, the struggle for women's liberation would continue, despite the obstacles imposed by the Great Depression. Agnes Macphail, along with Martha Black, continued to make waves in Parliament as the only two female voices. Their efforts to make their voices heard within the political sphere led to, amongst other things, important prison reform. The lives of Canadian women would continue to be influenced by the difficulties of the Depression until the outbreak of World War II, when once again, economic need would radically transform the roles they played within Canadian society.

The triumph of the Privy Council decision that women were indeed persons before the law was short-lived in the face of the economic difficulties of the thirties. The harsh reality of life for most ordinary women was summed up in an account by a farm wife from a *Chatelaine* series entitled "The World's Worst Job". The anonymous author gives an account of one summer day, which starts at five and ends at eleven at night. The day includes caring for livestock, cooking four meals, and carrying two of them on a half hour walk to the men in the fields.

GREEN DRAGON PRESS

The North Bay *Nugget* featured the following recipes on October 11 1933, with the lines: "Is the man in your family a mighty hunter who sallies forth with a gun and...brings home game in the form of squirrel ... [a]nd you wonder how on earth you do cook the things?":

☞ BRUNSWICK ☜ SQUIRREL PIE

3 squirrels, 3 slices salt pork, 2 onions, 4 cups tomatoes, 2 cups corn, 1 cup lima beans, 3-4 potatoes, 2 tsp. sugar, 1 tbsp. salt, 2 qt. boiling water, 4 tbsp. butter, 2 tbsp. flour. Clean wash and disjoint squirrels. Stand in cold salt water for an hour. Drain. Finely chop salt pork. 1 layer pork, onions, potatoes. 1 layer corn, beans, squirrels. Cover with veggies and pork. Season with pepper and cayenne, pour over boiling water, stew for 3 hours. Add tomatoes, salt, and sugar and cook another hour. Work flour and butter into smooth paste, stir into stew, boil 5 minutes and serve.

☞ SQUIRREL PIE ☜

2-3 squirrels, 1 onion, 1 lemon, 3 slices salt pork, 2 tbsp. flour, 3 cups water, baking powder, biscuit dough. Skin and dress squirrel, wash and disjoint, cover in salt water 1 hour. Simmer with onion 30 minutes, sprinkle lemon juice, roll in four, and fry in pork fat. Arrange squirrels in baking dish, stir flour into fat squirrels were fried in, boil it and pour over dish, cover with biscuit dough and bake 45 minutes.[1]

GREEN DRAGON PRESS

'THE STRONG ONES WERE WOMEN': THE EXPERIENCE OF CANADIAN WOMEN IN THE GREAT DEPRESSION

By Lara Campbell

The Great Depression was a devastating Canadian and international economic crisis. Even conservative estimates place unemployment rates at approximately 30 percent by 1933, and nearly two million Canadians on relief by 1934.i Relief for the unemployed was left to the responsibility of municipalities and was designed around the principle of "less eligibility" - a rate of support intended to be as meagre and humiliating as possible in order to preserve the work ethic. Relief policy gave preference to married men, unemployed single women were left to the care of private charities, and married women were labeled dependents of men, who were expected to apply for their relief provisions. In many municipalities across Canada, relief recipients were expected to perform manual labour in return for relief. They were rarely paid in cash, and most often paid in the form of supplies or with vouchers for food and clothing. Long viewed as a masculine tragedy of unemployment, few historians have examined the effect of the Great Depression on Canadian women and the family. The dominant images of the Great Depression, such as relief camps and riding the rods, are mainly images of unemployed men. However, women played roles of public and private importance during the Depression years. Examining the experiences and activities of women in the economy, politics, and the family leads to a fuller understanding of the Depression era in Canada.

Women, Work and Unemployment: High male unemployment brought women's participation in the labour force under public scrutiny for two reasons. First, longstanding beliefs in the idea of a family wage (the idea that men should support dependent wives and children) remained a powerful ideology even in times of high unemployment. Second, women who worked outside of the home, especially married women were either seen as usurping the role of the male breadwinner or selfishly working for "pin money." Thousands of Canadians wrote to provincial and federal governments to demand that women give up their jobs for men. The Quebec legislature debated legislation to keep women out of the workforce, and the Ontario government attempted to purge all married women from government jobs, though some women responded by continuing to work under their maiden names.ii

Some women's jobs were protected in the thirties because women were clustered in sex-typed occupations (such as domestic service and nursing), which would not attract male workers, or were not hit as hard as traditional male jobs, such as construction.iii Also, most female wage earners were single women between the ages of eighteen and nineteen who usually dropped out of the labour force on marriage. Women were a reserve army of labour in low-paying industries with no chance for upward movement. Furthermore, men could threaten women's jobs in the thirties. For example,

GREEN DRAGON PRESS

employers violated minimum-wage laws throughout the Depression. Because the minimum wage law was a form of protective legislation applying only to women, employers found they could fire women and hire men at lower wages. Female employees at a Valleyfield Quebec textile mill even drew up a petition asking the provincial government to spare their jobs by allowing the company to pay less than the minimum wage.iv

Census statistics also underestimated the extent of women's unemployment in the 1930s. A single unemployed woman who lived with her family or a married woman who lost her job was labelled a homemaker or a "dependent," not unemployed. Even though women suffered from unemployment, the government paid little attention to the problem, indicating that female unemployment was not taken as seriously as male joblessness. Domestic service training was the single government initiative to reduce female unemployment. Since the cost of living actually dropped for middle and upper class Canadians, many families could afford to hire a maid, and domestic service was the only female profession that increased during the Depression.v But it was also a job of last resort, because of its low wages and long hours. Non-white women were pushed into the lowest paying domestic jobs because factory and clerical work discriminated in favour of white men and women. One scholar estimates that at least 80 percent of Black urban women worked in domestic service in the thirties.vi

Despite opposition to workingwomen and government disinterest in the problems of unemployed women, by the 1930s it was clear than women were in the workforce to stay. Women's participation in the workforce slowly increased during the inter-war years, from 17.7% of the gainfully employed population in 1921 to 22.9% in 1941.vii With the advent of the Second World War, married women would enter the workforce in greater numbers than ever before.

Politics and Protest

Women were active in both formal politics and in various protest movements throughout the Depression. However, female politicians were still a minority in the 1930s: few female politicians held public office at the federal level in this decade.viii Women had a more visible political role through their involvement in a wide variety of groups that protested against unemployment and inadequate relief. Women who became active in public life often used traditional female roles to protest the conditions of the Depression. Many women based their activism on motherly concern, and this maternalism could become a militant force of political protest and an effective way to organize women. Therefore, much of women's activism revolved around the problems of unemployed men or concerns related to women's roles as homemakers, and not on the problems of female inequality. Housewives groups, often organized by the Communist Party (CP) and the Cooperative Commonwealth Federation (CCF), gave women the opportunity to protest over the well being of their family and children.ix
Even in explicitly political groups, many members were housewives concerned with the practicalities of feeding their families on a limited budget. In 1932, an amalgam of Jewish female factory workers, union organizers and housewives boycotted overpriced kosher butchers, spending several days picketing outside offending stores.x In Vancouver, a coalition from the CCF, the CP, and women's groups such as the Local Council of Women (LCW) and the Women's Christian

GREEN DRAGON PRESS

Temperance Union (WCTU) overlooked political differences to create a Mother's Day Committee in support of the Relief Camp Workers' Strike in 1935. This coalition organized a Mothers Day Protest in Stanley Park, where the women and the strikers formed a giant heart to protest against the strikers' situation.xi The collective actions of a group of mothers was a powerful form of protest in a society where the role of mother was glorified. While most women were excluded from traditional politics, these protest groups indicate that women developed their own forms, methods, and symbols of protest.

The Family

In the context of the nuclear family, women were under pressure to maintain their traditional roles as wife and mother, perhaps partly because the marriage rate fell as couples could not afford to marry.xii Women were expected to be psychological and emotional managers by helping to keep unemployed men feeling manly and secure. The editor of Chatelaine advised women to show "an extra special amount of thoughtfulness and tenderness toward the men who are feeling that they have not fulfilled their dreams of making your home life all they hoped..."xiii
Faced with the responsibility of keeping their family together and their husbands happy, women "made-do" in a variety of resourceful ways. Women's domestic labour was crucial to family survival. Women in the drought-ridden West often lacked electricity or appliances, and used methods of barter and co-operation to produce home-made soap, butter and vinegar: one prairie mother made gopher pie for meals.xiv "I knew where every last cent of my money went, feeding a husband and three boys," remembered one woman. "My grocery bill for the

month, if it was over ten dollars I was just sick."xv Making-do, however, could not compensate for poverty. One woman wrote to Prime Minister Bennett:
I have been fighting against worry until I feel as I am going to break down completely...I am very economical I bake all my own bread and use the flour bags for making undies for my little girl. There isn't a thing wasted in my house, and I couldn't get my rent light gas and water cheaper no matter how I tried.xvi

For single mothers, the Depression proved to be a difficult experience. As unemployment increased, and some men left to find work or disappeared in shame, women were left to struggle on their own.xvii Only five provinces had Mothers' Allowance Legislation, and deserted wives were eligible in only British Columbia and Ontario.xviii To qualify for aid, a woman had to be a British subject and be judged of good character by a local board. In all provinces except for British Columbia, unmarried mothers were automatically disqualified. Deserted and widowed mothers faced a difficult time getting enough money to survive. A mother from Vancouver recalled: "My husband walked out, just left like so many did...because they just couldn't take the shame of not being able to support their family." She supplemented her $10.00 a month in relief by pretending to be a nurse at a hospital, where she could feed and bathe her children for free.xix

Immigrant women had an even harder time keeping their families together in the depression years. Unemployed Anglo-Canadian men and women often relied on racist rhetoric and blamed immigrants for stealing their jobs. One woman complained to Ontario Premier George Henry: "It is the foreigner and the Jew who are taking our trades and work from

GREEN DRAGON PRESS

us."xx In 1931, Howard Ferguson, the Premier of Ontario, announced that his government was cutting off relief payments to unemployed immigrant workers.xxi In the Western provinces, where unemployment was intensified by drought conditions, the Manitoba Legislature passed a 1930 resolution that blamed unemployment on immigrant agricultural workers.xxii Eastern European immigrant women faced higher than average rates of unemployment,xxiii and often performed hard manual labour in homes and on farms. Farm women did the work of both men and women. Claimed a Polish woman from the prairies: "I did what a man did and more...When my husband ploughed and the pieces of prairie wouldn't turn over I'd turn the clods over by hand so the grass wouldn't rot...I'd take the children with me, along with some food and water."xxiv

  Maintaining the respectability of their families was important to women, but poverty often made it impossible to meet the ideals of motherhood. How could they be good wives and mothers when their laundry was always grey from the prairie dust and their children were starving? Many mothers refused to send their children to school without proper clothes or shoes. One woman, frustrated by the hypocrisy of a system that glorified motherhood but made it financially difficult for families to survive, complained: "When depression comes, my country rushes to the rescue. But when the S.O.S goes out, do Canadians say "Mothers and babies first? Is my name exalted when it appears on the relief list? Hardly."xxv

Canadian women's depression-era experiences differed depending on their class, their race, and where they lived in the country. Some middle-class and upper class women, for example, saw their standard of living increase. However, working women and homemakers, urban and rural women, Canadian-born and immigrant women all attempted to survive the Depression by creatively managing their limited resources. While more research remains to be done on the ways that women coped as the Depression changed the world around them, their experiences are a rich testimony to the many ways women struggled and worked together.

GREEN DRAGON PRESS

iJames Struthers, No Fault of their Own: Unemployment and the Canadian Welfare State (Toronto: University of Toronto Press, 1983), 83; Michiel Horn, The Great Depression of the 1930s in Canada (Ottawa: CHA Booklet #39, 1984), 10.

iiMederic Martin, "Go Home Young Woman!" Chatelaine (September 1933), 10; AO, RG 3-8, Henry Papers, MS 1738, file: Civil Service Positions, memo of 18 June, 1931.

iiiSee Ruth Milkman, "Women's Work and Economic Crisis: Some Lessons of the Great Depression," Review of Radical Political Economics 8 1 (Spring 1976); For example, women made up 96 percent of housekeepers and 100 percent of nurses. See Leonard Marsh, Employment Research (Oxford University Press, 1935), 240-244.

ivThe law was unlikely to be enforced, since there were only seventy minimum-wage and factory inspectors for all of Canada Canada, Royal Commission on Price Spreads, 129; Alison Prentice et al, Canadian Women: A History (Toronto: Harcourt, Brace Jovanovich, 1988), 234-5.

vLeonard Marsh, Canadians In and Out of Work, (Oxford University Press, 1940), 97. From 1921-31 there was a 7% increase in the number of women in domestic service. (Prentice et al, Canadian Women, 235).

vi Dionne Brand, "'We weren't allowed to go into factory work until Hitler started the war': the 1920s to the 1940s," in Peggy Bristow et al, eds. 'We're Rooted Here and They Can't Pull Us Up': Essays in African Canadian Women's History (Toronto: University of Toronto Press, 1994), 175-77.

viiBeth Light and Ruth Roach Pierson, eds., No Easy Road: Women in Canada 1920s to 1960s (Toronto: New Hogtown Press, 1990), 252.

viii Some of the women active in formal politics in this period were: MP Agnes Macphail, who first represented the United Farmers of Ontario and later the the Co-operative Commonwealth Federation (CCF), and Martha Black, who was elected in 1935 to replace her deceased husband in his Yukon riding. Cairine Wilson was appointed senator in 1930, and Iva Fallis was appointed in 1935. Women fared slightly better in provincial and municipal politics. Frances Hendersen was Deputy Mayor of Hamilton from 1932-45, and Helena Gutteridge was elected "alderman" in Vancouver in 1937. She, like many other female politicians at the time, believed that women were well-suited to political life because they "have a more sympathetic understanding of social problems." See Irene Howard, The Struggle for Social Justice in British Columbia: Helena Gutteridge, the Unknown Reformer (Vancouver: UBC Press, 1992), 187.

ixSee Joan Sangster, Dreams of Equality: Women on the Canadian Left, 1920-1950 (Toronto: McClelland and Stewart, 1989); Annelise Orleck, "We Are That Mythical Thing Called the Public: Militant Housewives During the Great Depression," Feminist Studies 1 (Spring 1993), 147-172.

xAlison Prentice et al, eds, Canadian Women: A History (Toronto: Harcourt, Brace Jovanovitch, 1988), 238.

xiSangster, Dreams of Equality, 141; Irene Howard, "The Mothers' Council of Vancouver: Holding the Fort for the Unemployed, 1935-38," BC Studies 69-70 (Spring-Summer 1986).

xiiVeronica Strong-Boag, The New Day Recalled: Lives of Girls and Women in English Canada, 1919-1939 (Toronto: Copp Clark Pitman, 1988), 83.

xiii Byrne Hope Sanders, "The Editor's Own Page," Chatelaine (February 1932), 4.

xivAnnie E. Hollis, "Our Western Heroines," Chatelaine (October 1931), 20; Barry Broadfoot, Ten Lost Years, 1929-1939: Memories of Canadians Who Survived the Depression (Toronto: Doubleday Canada Ltd., 1973), 84.

xvIbid., 274.

xviMichael Bliss and L.M Grayson, eds, The Wretched of Canada: Letters to R.B. Bennett, 1930-35 (Toronto: University of Toronto Press, 1971), 145.

xviiBy 1931, 285 541 families were officially female-headed, though this number would have excluded women and children who lived with a parent or relative. Census, The Family, 100.

xviiiAlberta, British Columbia, Ontario, Manitoba and Saskatchewan all had Mothers' Allowance Legislation by the 1930s. See Margaret Little, "The Blurring of Boundaries: Private and Public Welfare for Single Mothers in Ontario," Studies in Political Economy 47 (Summer 1995), 89-109.

xixIbid., 286-287.

xxArchives of Ontario, RG 3-8, George Henry Papers, MS 1750, file: Mothers' Allowance Commission, Miss A.M. to Henry, 26 August 1932.

xxiDonald Avery, Reluctant Host: Canada's Response to Immigrant Workers, 1896-1994. (Toronto: McClelland and Stewart, 1995)

xxiiIbid., 109.

xxiiiIbid., 111.

xxivIbid., 85.

xxv"A Canadian Mother," Chatelaine (October 1933), 13.

GREEN DRAGON PRESS

Thousands of men, women, and even children wrote to the Prime Minister, R.B. Bennett, telling him of their desperate condition. The Prime Minister was a wealthy man; his annual income was around $150,000 per annum during those years. He answered many of the letters, sometimes enclosing a few dollars. Bennett's private secretary sent five dollars to Christina Arnold of Raymore Saskatchewan, "which may be of some service to you in securing yourself a coat."

> *Raymore Sask*
> *Oct 11th/32*
>
> *Dear Sir, — I am a girl thirteen years old and I have to go to school every day its very cold now already and I haven't got a coat to put on. My parents can't afford to buy me anything for this winter. I have to walk to school four and a half miles every morning and night and I'm awfully cold every day. Would you be so kind to sent me enough money to so that I would get one.*
>
> *My name is*
>
> *Christina Arnold*
> *Raymore Sask*

Jean Lee recalled the struggles of her immigrant family during the Depression:

> *"I remember I was working even before I started school. I used to go down to the restaurant when I was very young and stand on a box to do the dishes. Later I waited on tables. I remember when we went to high school, I used to work until two in the morning, sometimes three, go to bed and then get up at eight for school.*
>
> *We had it rough, but it didn't do us any harm. I wasn't angry with my parents, We understood the situation, and we knew what had to be done. It's just a sense of responsibility. You had to help out when things were tough. We grew up during the Depression days. Almost everyone was on welfare.*
>
> *The unemployed people would go to city hall and get a ticket worth 11c for breakfast, and 16c for dinner. They were allowed two meals a day. They'd pay us with these tickets and we'd give them eggs, toast and coffee. For dinner they'd get a bowl of soup, beef stew, bread, butter and coffee. The next day we'd take all the tickets to city hall and cash them in for money to buy food for the following day."*
> *Jin Guo: Voices of Chinese Canadian Women, 149.*

GREEN DRAGON PRESS

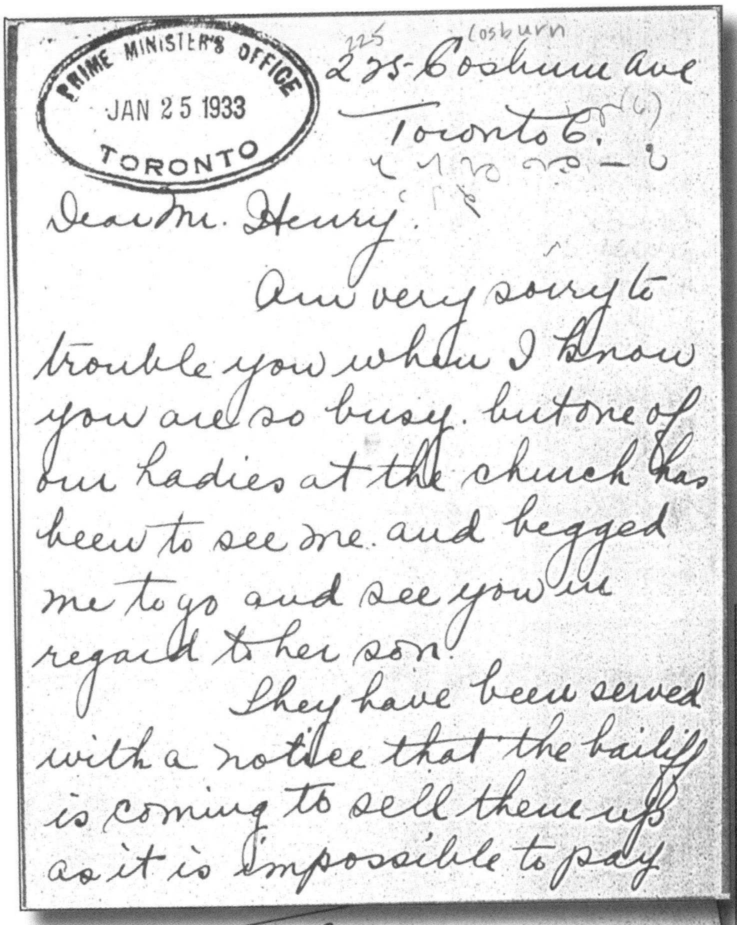

PRIME MINISTER'S OFFICE
JAN 25 1933
TORONTO

225 Cosburn
225 Cosburn Ave
Toronto 6.

Dear Mr. Henry.

Am very sorry to trouble you when I know you are so busy. but one of our ladies at the church has been to see me. and begged me to go and see you in regard to her son.

They have been served with a notice that the bailiff is coming to sell them up as it is impossible to pay

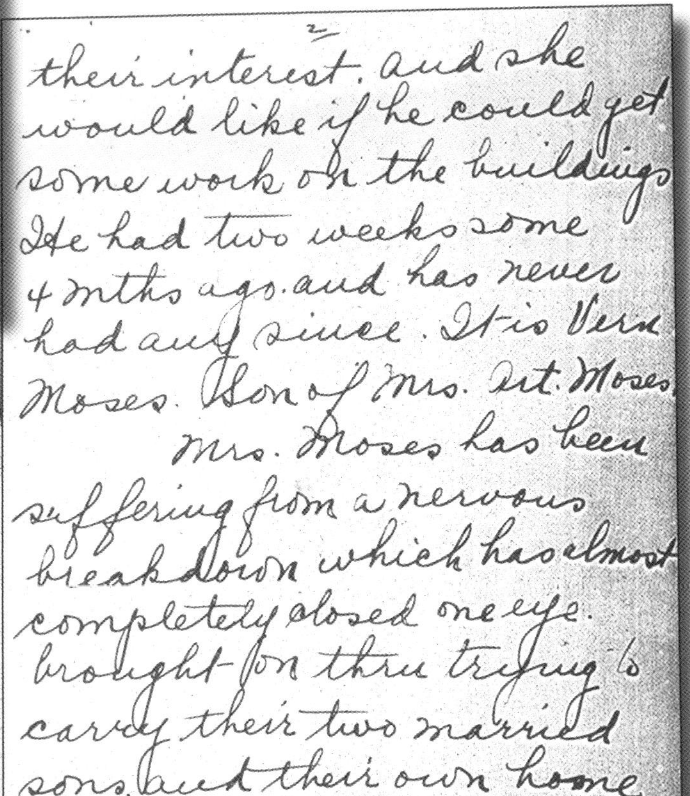

their interest. and she would like if he could get some work on the buildings. He had two weeks some 4 mths ago. and has never had any since. It is Vera Moses. Son of Mrs. Rt. Moses.

Mrs. Moses has been suffering from a nervous break down which has almost completely closed one eye. brought on thru trying to carry their two married sons, and their own home as well. thru these trying

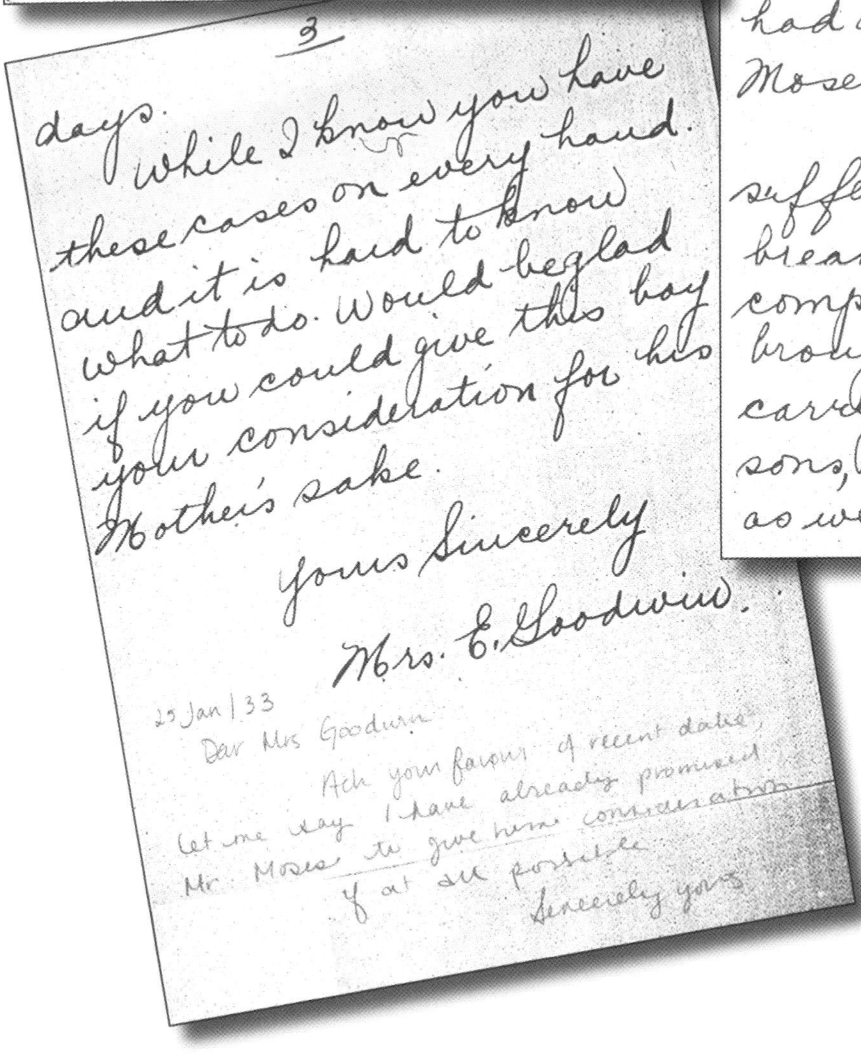

days. While I know you have these cases on every hand. and it is hard to know what to do. Would be glad if you could give this boy your consideration for his Mother's sake.

Yours Sincerely

Mrs. E. Goodwin.

25 Jan / 33
Dear Mrs Goodwin
Ach your favour of recent date,
Let me say I have already promised
Mr Moses to give him consideration
if at all possible
Sincerely yours

The premier of Ontario, George S. Henry also received his share of letters requesting assistance for themselves or others.

Archives of Ontario, RG 3-8, MS 1759, Office of the Premier, G.S. Henry.

GREEN DRAGON PRESS

TABLE 6
Budget for a man, woman and three children – 1926[2]
(one thirteen-year-old girl, two boys nine and eleven)

Commodity	Weekly Budget	Unit Price	Total
Milk and Cheese	14 Pints of milk	$0.14	$1.96
	1/2 pound of cheese	.25	.12 1/2
Eggs & Meat	3 pounds of rumpsteak	.20	.60
	3 pounds of salt beef	.22	.66
	2 pounds of haddock	.12 1/2	.25
	1 pound of liver	.30	.30
	1 dozen eggs	.45	.45
Vegetables	4 pounds of carrots	.03	.12
	2 pounds of rape cabbage	.03	.06
	2 pounds of onions	.05	.10
	12 pounds of potatoes	.02 1/2	.30
	2 tins of tomatoes	.10	.20
Fruits	6 oranges	.30	.15
	18 apples	.30	.30
	1 pound of plums	.12 1/2	.12 1/2
	1 pound of figs	.12 1/2	.12 1/2
	1/4 pound of grapes or gooseberries	.16	.04
Cereals	14 pounds of bread	.12	1.68
	2 pounds of flour	.07	.14
	1 pound of macaroni	.08	.08
	1 pound of rice	.09	.09
	1/2 pound of corn meal	.06	.03
	3 1/2 pounds of oatmeal	.06	.21
	1/4 pound of sago	.10	.02 1/2
	1/4 pound of tapioca	.10	.02 1/2
	1/4 pound of barley	.10	.02 1/2
	1/2 pound of split peas	.10	.05
	1/4 pound of beans	.09	.02 1/2
Desserts	1 pound of jelly	.12 1/2	.12 1/2
	1/2 pound of corn syrup	.09	.0
Fats	1 1/2 pounds of butter	.46	.69
	1 pound of fat	.21	.21
	1/2 pound of suet	.18	.09
	1 jar of peanut butter	.25	.25
	1/4 package of starch	.12	.03
Miscellaneous	1/2 pound of cocoa	.16	.08
	1/4 pound of tea	.60	.15
	1/4 package of baking powder	.32	.04
	1/4 tin of pepper	.09	.02 1/4
	1/4 sack of salt	.10	.02 1/4
	4 pounds of sugar	.07	.14

Budget for a man, woman and three children – 1926. *Quebec Women: a History*, 207.

GREEN DRAGON PRESS

In the 1930s, desperate times called for creative solutions in order to sustain a household. Women, traditionally the center of the domestic sphere, were often those who had to scrimp, save, delegate and improvise to make sure their families survived economic hardship. The following is a collection of anecdotes and memories of women who lived through the 1930s.
Compiled and published in the *Toronto Star*, by Bill Taylor, "We Wore Dad's Underwear."

Joan Taggart, of Toronto, grew up on a small, remote farm.:

"...snow suits [were] made from parts of Dad's old wool underwear dyed red. Dad hunted deer and the occasional grouse and this kept us in meat. Twice a year, basic supplied like flour, sugar, coffee, tea and so on were ordered in bulk and shipped in. No luxuries like toilet paper. Newspaper and old catalogues worked well in outdoor facilities! Medicine was a doctor's book and home remedies. The nearest doctor and dentist were 100 miles away and only gone to in extreme emergencies, when the CNR train could be flagged down for transportation. Trains were the lifeline of the community."

A woman from Shelburne did not want her name revealed, as she's afraid her siblings might still be embarrassed by the memories. Her family – three adults and six kids – lived in an eight-room house:

"We kept a cow...All the food was bought by the bag, such as flour, apples, turnips, sugar, potatoes. All that could be was canned from the garden during the growing season. Everyone went out to pick wild raspberries and strawberries, plus rhubarb and wild apples, which were made into jams or jellies. Two sets of clothes were given to each child when school started in the fall: blouses, skirts or jumpers, stockings, underwear (this had to be rinsed out every night). You took good care of everything you had because it was passed down to the next one in your family or traded with cousins or even neighbours. Most of the clothes we wore were made from adults' clothes torn apart and turned to the other side and remade. Entertainment was self-made – board games of all sorts were played. Most kids belonged to a church group...or Scouts. Everyone helped each other. My mother was often called out to assist at the birth of a neighbour's child. Sometimes the children's assistance was given to friends of the family, to go over and feed someone who was sick, take a little one out for a walk if the mother was busy, run uptown for supplies etc. We made our own shampoo by shaving off a bar of soap and heating it with vinegar."

GREEN DRAGON PRESS

Helen Whyte, of L'amable, near Bancroft, and her husband raised five children in rural Ontario during the Depression:

> "[The Depression was] a time when you always bought flour in 100-pound bags so you would have the flour sack for your pillow slips. We grew or made almost everything...There was never any waste! In the fall, we would have a special treat, partridge. One little bird, if that was all we got, could feed us all, supplemented with ample helpings of dumplings in the pot. On really cold nights, my husband would stay up to feed the fire. The winter meant porridge...and frozen clothes."

Lillian Marek of Penetanguishene, remembers saving:

> "[We saved] all the newspapers and rags we could get our hands on and when the rag man came around with his horse and wagon we would sometimes get 10 cents for them. That meant hamburger stew for supper. Poor as we were, Mom always fed any hobos who came to our door... We ate a lot of soup. My mother asked me to stop at the butchers on the way home from school to ask for bones for the dog. We didn't have a dog, but we had some good soup! The year 1937, being just a kid of 14, I had to drop out of school as a friend of ours offered me a job at a meat-packing house. I still remember the smell. My wages were 25 cents an hour; up at 5:30...to start at 7 a.m. Saturday was payday and I was so proud to be helping out the family. My little brown pay envelope went straight to my mom unopened...Looking back, it was a difficult life, but we were coping with it and at times were happy and content."

GREEN DRAGON PRESS

Images of Women

Margaret Lawrence, a well-known Canadian writer of the period, comes somewhat under attack in this article for her "time-worn, too familiar, and too regressive" views on women. Gwethalyn Graham writes a controversial critique of Miss Lawrence's School of Femininity in the context of the 1930s, an era where feminism seemed to have lost its momentum. Graham challenges Lawrence on her views of women, marriage, and careers, citing Canada, Germany, Italy and even the Soviet Union as examples of the status of women. It is evident in this article how larger historical movements impact women in their respective countries.

Women, Are They Human?

Gwethalyn Graham

On the evidence of the past six years of depression in Canada, and to a certain extent in the United States, it would appear that the position of women has begun to slip back and that women in general during that time have lost a good many of the advantages which took more than a hundred years to obtain. Partly because of the urgency of other issues considered more vital, partly because what has been happening to the women of Germany and Italy is so much more obvious that similar conditions in our own country seem negligible by comparison, the retrogressive movement has got under way here without…much notice or comment. Nevertheless there is a basic idea in common between Hitler…and the Board of Governors of a Canadian university who find it necessary to dismiss married women instructors because they are married. That idea is the traditional view of women as people of a purely secondary existence…wives, mothers, sisters, sweethearts…rather than as individuals, to be considered as such, independent of any relationships they may have… an idea which was accepted down through the ages until very recently and which now, in the autumn of 1936, find another exponent in Margaret Lawrence.

The Feminist Movement began in the first quarter of the 19th century with the publication of Mary Wolstonecraft's "Vindication of the Rights of Women", was fostered by the industrial revolution, and was precipitated by the Great War. During the twenties the upward and forward swing continued. In Italy it became gradually submerged in the Fascist point of view, the process being barely discernible because Italian women, having gained very little, had almost nothing to lose. In Germany it was brought to an abrupt halt with the election of Hitler in 1933, the contrast between pre-Fascist and Fascist conditions being blatantly apparent because, until then, German women had been the freest in Western Europe. In the United States and Canada the movement slowed down under an economic pressure which was unaccompanied by very much theorizing but was none the less effective. It is probable that Canadian women are in worse circumstances than American women, some phases of the movement having progressed further in the United States than in Canada…The whole question of what has unfortunately, come to be known as "Women's Rights" appears to have been shelved for the time being, although it is probable that Miss Lawrence's book will start fresh discussion….

GREEN DRAGON PRESS

Since the problem as it faces us at the moment, resolves itself into the immediate question of whether or not women, if married shall be considered as individuals or as dependent human beings, it is necessary to decide first of all if their actions are, as Miss Lawrence and a great many other people believe, primarily biological in their motivation. She envisages the normal woman as a "still, deep sexual being...a biological force under a compelling instinct to find a safe place to lay her babes, and before that she is in subconscious search for a man who will give her the babies and help her to find a place to lay them." In consequence, "When a young woman takes to writing"...or advertising copy, sculpture, engineering or designing...
" it is because something has hurt her biologically and she tries to escape the fate of womanhood." Of Jane Austin, Miss Lawrence remarks that she was "disappointed" as "every woman who does not get her man is disappointed"...

The stumbling block of marriage versus career has cropped up time and time again during the past fifty years, and continues to crop up after a temporary lull during the twenties when the cry of "Employ the men!" could not be raised upon economic grounds...Arguments based on the undeniable fact that women do give up their careers when they marry...take on a somewhat different light if one believes that the average man would probably give up working too, if he could afford it. It is doubtful if bricklaying is essential to the happiness of a bricklayer...

• 1947 - Married women released from jobs in the civil service and the Canadian Broadcasting Corporation, on the grounds that their wartime employment was only temporary.

GREEN DRAGON PRESS

Continuing the Fight for Equality

Idola Saint-Jean was the president of the Canadian Alliance for the Vote for the Women of Quebec. In 1931, on the eve of the Quebec Legislative Assembly's vote to extend the suffrage to women, Ms. Saint-Jean gave an impassioned radio address, urging Quebec's legislators to ensure women's equal rights. Despite her efforts, the Assembly voted 47 to 21 against women's suffrage. Women would not obtain the vote in Quebec until 1940.

Ladies, Gentlemen,

Tomorrow the Legislature will for the fifth time receive a bill demanding suffrage for the women of this province. A just and legitimate demand which, if it is finally realized, will put the women of Quebec on an equal footing with their sisters in the other eight provinces of Canada.

The women of Quebec were the first on the scene and as one looks back to the early pages of our history, we find them working with ardour at the admirable work of colonization.

...Let our legislators, when they are called tomorrow to vote yes or no on whether we will be admitted to full participation in our political life, remember that, in 1705, the first cloth manufactory in Canada was founded by a woman, Madam de Repentigny; let them recall the work of Marie Rollet, the great mistress of our Canadian farmers, who brought to our country the first plough. Then there was Jeanne Mance who set herself up as the municipal treasurer of Ville-Marie and found the necessary money to bring in a regiment charged with the defence of the colonists against the devastating attacks of the Iroquois. The founders of the first hospitals, the founders of the first schools, were they not, these women, whom we have the honour of calling our ancestors, the equivalent of Ministers of Commerce, Ministers of Social Welfare, Ministers of Education, and, I dare say, Ministers of Finance, filling these offices, in such a way, thanks to their organizational and economizing skills, as to even give pointers to a large number of men?

No man, witness to what our pioneers accomplished at the dawn of our history, would have refused them access to Parliament, if there had been one, at the time.

GREEN DRAGON PRESS

Moreover, this right that we are claiming, did we not possess it until 1834? And did we not exercise it with conscience and dignity...

We women have not lost our abilities; it seems to me, ladies and gentlemen, one finds us today in all the areas of charity and work. Economic conditions throw us into industry, into commerce, into education, in a word into all spheres of activity. As we have to work to live, then, why are we condemned to occupy only the subordinate positions? Why not allow us access to the professions and also the parliaments which make the laws that affect the woman as much as the man? Why, I ask you, Gentlemen, should we not bring to bear our qualities as teachers when a law concerning our schools is being discussed? Why should mothers not have the right to vote when the House studies a law concerning the welfare of the child, of the family, etc.? Are those not the problems that a woman will always understand better than a man?

In all sincerity, Gentlemen, tell us, are there questions that your mothers, your wives, your daughters could not understand, even if they had a very rudimentary education? And tell us, divested of your egotism, that brings you less happiness than you seem to think – tell us if you would be satisfied if, one day, a woman declared herself your arbitrary ruler, took upon herself, as you did sanctimoniously centuries ago, to dictate totally your way of life, making herself the only judge of your destiny. You would protest with good reason against such a state of affairs wouldn't you?..Let us elect our legislators. We are responsible human beings when treated as such. If a woman is guilty of an offense, your laws punish her, it is not her husband who mounts the scaffold, it is she who atones for her sin; therefore does it not seem to you to be unjust in the extreme that under statute law a good mother, a good wife does not have the right to conclude a transaction without having previously obtained her husband's signature whether it be good or bad?...Are those the laws of a country that calls itself Christian?...

Instead of treating us as dangerous rivals, let us become your companions in all spheres of activity. Be proud of our aptitudes and let us apply our talents to the service of our province. Born in another province, women can aspire to higher positions, but Quebec holds hers in tutelage and does not let them give their productivity to society.

Think about all these women, Gentlemen, and let your vote tomorrow be liberating...

[Excerpts from radio broadcast by Idola Saint-Jean, 1931]
Idola St. Jean. National Archives of Canada C68508.

GREEN DRAGON PRESS

Women and Work

At the end of World War I, women had been strongly encouraged to give up their jobs to returning service men. Now, as the Depression took its toll, women, particularly married women, felt the pressure to give up their jobs. It was even suggested by some that married women be fired to provide work for unemployed men. In 1936, the National Employment Commission received a letter recommending just such as course citing "the greatest good for the greatest number."
The Commissioner's reply was rather noncommittal, pointing out the practical difficulties involved in "taking employment from one group of persons and giving it to another." Nor did she respond to the suggestion that women's rights should only be honoured during "the good times."

Mrs. L. W. Sutherland, Ottawa

Dear Madam

I have read in the paper with a great deal of interest your speech on jobless men, and as you invite ideas, I will try in my humble way to supply mine. First I would have every married woman who applies for a job or is already working fill out a card stating where her husband works and how much he earns, if he has steady work, and a living wage, said living wage to be set by Government, if husband has hospitals bills to pay or such like.

Well if husband earns a living wage the wife should be discharged to make way for the young single girls who also want to get married and raise a family, also those who have school and want to help keep their parents who are sometimes out of work this way I am sure we could save a lot of families from being on relief, I venture to say that in Galt alone if all the married women were fired whose husbands have good jobs, we would not have a single unemployed person out of work, you don't have to take my word for it take a census of the married women working and find out for yourself.

Now it took a Hitler in Germany and also a Duce in Italy to put the married women out of industry and make way for the men and the young people who leave school, why not some one here in Canada who has courage enough to tackle this question, it does not need to work a hardship, if the woman's husband is sick all right let her work, if he cant find work let her work till he does, but make him look, if he does not earn a living wage find out why he don't, this is important, as some employers say his wife works he makes enough, if the woman is a widow she would be classed as single, this would all be on a card she would have to fill out sent to all factories and office and stores. Now I can hear the cry always raised about womens rights, that is fine they have a lot of rights in good times, when there is lots of employment, but what right have they who have husbands to provide good wages for them, to deprive the young workers male and female of the chance to advance, and also the young girls leaving school of the chance of going to work and helping their parents, in a local office a girl got married to a young man who has a real job in the city everyone thought she would quit her job several girls applied for job, but did she no, she did not but they did buy a new car a couple of months later, this is only one of the many cases I could name for you.

Now Mrs. Sutherland I hope I have not bored you with my letter I know you are doing a good job and a big job but someone will have to take up this question and fight the womens clubs, and womens rights and so forth, but the greatest good for the greatest number should be our stand and put it squarely up to the people...

C. Gardiner, Eq., 16 Todd Street, Galt, Ontario.

Records of the Department of Labour, RG 27, Vol. 3349, File 28, National Archives of Canada.

GREEN DRAGON PRESS

Notable Women

Elizabeth Bagshaw

Dr. Elizabeth Bagshaw was born near Cannington Ontario on October 18, 1881. One of the first women doctors in Canada (MB, University of Toronto, 1905), she had a successful 60 year practice but is best known as the founder of Canada's first birth control clinic in Hamilton, Ontario. She decided to flout the law against offering birth control information because of the suffering of the poor during the depression.

"There was no welfare and no unemployment payments, and these people were just about half-starved because there was no work...they couldn't afford to have children if they couldn't afford to eat. So the families came to the clinic and we gave them information."

Elizabeth graduated from the University of Toronto in 1905.

The clinic opened in 1930. There was no advertising except word of mouth and the clinic existed underground for 35 years. Dr. Bagshaw was its medical director for many of those years. She received many honours during her long life, including an honorary doctorate from McMaster University.

She also broke with tradition when as a single woman, she adopted a son. At that time this was unheard of. She arranged the adoption through a lawyer rather than the Children's Aid, reasoning that they would refuse her application. Dr. Bagshaw retired from practice in 1976 at the age of 95 and died in Hamilton on January 5, 1982.

Portia White

Portia White was born in 1911 in Truro, Nova Scotia, the third of thirteen children. After her father's service in WW I, the family moved to Halifax, Nova Scotia where he became the pastor of Cornwallis Street Baptist Church. By the age of 6, Portia was singing in the church choir. After taking a teacher training course at Dalhousie University, Portia taught during the Depression years in a rural Black settlement in Halifax County earning $30. a month. Once a week, she walked ten miles into Halifax for voice lessons. In 1937, the Halifax Ladies Music Club arranged for Portia to attend the Halifax Conservatory of Music. In the spring of 1944 Portia had her Town Hall debut in New York City. She performed in concerts until 1952 when she settled in Toronto where she taught and continued her studies. She gave a Command Performance before Queen Elizabeth II in Charlottetown, Prince Edward Island in October of 1964. She died four years later in 1968 at the relatively young age of 57.

Courtesy Nightingale Publishing.

GREEN DRAGON PRESS

Lea Roback

Lea Roback was born in Montreal in 1904, the second of nine children of Jewish immigrants from Poland. Lea had an independent streak from childhood and never hesitated to challenge authority. In her 20s Ms. Roback travelled to New York and Europe, where she studied literature, history and art while working to support herself. She returned to Montreal in 1932, and later managed Montreal's first Marxist bookstore. She had joined the Communist Party while in Berlin in 1931 as a rejection of the growth of Nazism. She eventually became very disillusioned with communism and left the party in 1958. Ms. Roback earned her place in Quebec's history books during a strike by the mainly female workforce in Montreal's textile and garment industries. In 1937she spoke out against the industry's terrible working conditions and led a strike by 5,000 workers. This was one of the province's first union struggles for women. Roback continued her efforts to organize workers - handing out fliers at factory doors, staging teaching sessions and trying to convince families of the value of unions. She was also a feminist long before the term was coined. In 1936 she fought side by side with noted Quebec suffragette Thérèse Casgrain. Lea Roback continued to fight against injustice for the rest of her life, living on her own into her 90s in a small apartment in Montreal's multicultural Côte des Neiges district. She died on August 28, 2000 at the age of 96.

GREEN DRAGON PRESS

THE SENATE
CANADA

June 11, '38.

This is being written in the
Senate Chamber of the House
of Parliament in Ottawa.
About one hundred representatives
of the Business Women's Club
are waiting, along with about
two hundred others including
senators and their wives and
representatives of other womens
organizations, for Prime Minister
Mackenzie King to unveil a
tablet, which has been placed

On June 11, 1938 Florence Partridge attended the unveiling of a bronze tablet by Prime Minister Mackenzie King in the Senate Chamber in Ottawa to honour the five Alberta women who fought to have the word "persons" in the British North America Act interpreted to include women, thus making possible the appointment of women to the Senate. Mrs. Partridge wrote to her mother, giving her account of the event.

2.

in the Senate Lobby by the
Canadian Business and Professional
Women's Clubs. The tablet is to
the five Alberta women who
were subjects of the "Persons"
case. The decision of the Privy
Council in this case was that
the word "persons" in the B.N.A.
act should be interpreted to mean
women as well as men. This
decision made possible the
appointment of women to the
Senate, and the two women
senators who have since been
appointed are also to be here
to-night.   The programme
is to be broadcast, and the

GREEN DRAGON PRESS

3.

radio technician and the photographer are both fussing about with their equipment.

We are all to be received, following the unveiling, by the Prime Minister, Dr. Ellen Douglas of Winnipeg who is the president of the B&P.W. Clubs of Canada, Mrs. Nellie McClung, Senator Cairine Wilson and Senator Iva Fallis.

This paper is supplied through the kindness, but without the knowledge of the Senate. We are sitting at the senators' desks. The desk from which this came had no name on it but had been well stocked with paper. —

4

Later — The dignitaries have arrived and departed. — Mackenzie King looking a bit frightened, Dr. Douglas wearing an orchid which was presented to her in Guelph last Tuesday and which was lost for some time in the refrigerator at her hotel here - but was produced in time for her appearance to-night — Mrs. McClung looking rather ordinary in black lace with a red rose, Senator Wilson looking hard as nails in white satin with gardenias, and Senator Fallis looking agreeable in something dark. We have all shaken their hands, and had a small amount of food and drink admitted to our systems. — and next time you visit the Parliament Buildings, the guide will point out to you the bronze tablet which we have been sitting on the wall to-night.

(Thought you might like to read this too.)

Mother

GREEN DRAGON PRESS

Activities
1930 – 1939

HE STRONG ONES WERE WOMEN

Read the article by Lara Campbell, p73. How does the title apply to what the author has written? Cite specific evidence of the strength of women during the 30s. Give direct quotes. Using your textbook, look up the chapter(s) on the Great Depression. Compare what Ms. Campbell's article reveals about the lives of women in the 1930's, and what your textbook presents. Do you feel your textbook has given adequate and equal representation of women in the Depression? Why or why not? Be prepared to justify your point of view. Create a 20-minute radio program designed for women in the 1930's titled "Creative tips to survive the current economic crisis".

BUDGET

The average Canadian family who was lucky enough to qualify for relief received approximately $10.00 per month. Imagine that you are a mother with a husband and three children, ages 3, 6, and 9. Create a meal plan that could feed your family based on the prices found in Table 6, p80. Don't forget, you may not be able to pay for electricity – therefore meat and other perishable products cannot be kept for long periods of time. As a class, discuss the different plans. Were you able to adequately feed your family? Look up what the basic nutritional requirements are for children of the above age. What consequences could this crisis have for the health of your children?

IDOLA ST JEAN

After reading her speech, p85, establish the arguments that Idola St. Jean put forth in favour of women's suffrage in Quebec. Evaluate her arguments. Do you believe they are logical? Effective? If so, why do you believe that the Assembly voted against allowing women to vote?

Resources

Brand, Dionne. *No Burden to Carry: Narratives of Black Working Women in Ontario 1920s to 1950s,* Toronto: Women's Press, 1991.
Goodall, Lian. *Singing Through the Future: the story of Portia White,* Toronto: Napoleon Publishing, 2004.
Strong-Boag, Veronica. *The New Day Recalled: Lives of Girls and Women in English Canada, 1919-1939.*
Prentice, Alison et al. *Canadian Women: A History.* Toronto: Harcourt, Brace, 1988.
The Clio Collective. Trans. Roger Gannon & Rosalind Gill. *Quebec Women: A History.*
Toronto: The Women's Press. 1987.

GREEN DRAGON PRESS

1940 – 1949

Women answer the call to duty

City of Toronto Reference Library, Baldwin Room.

City of Toronto
Reference Library,
Baldwin Room.

GREEN DRAGON PRESS

1940-1949 Introduction

"It's a great life for a girl, great in every way you look at it. You can't leave the task of winning the war all to the men...join up today!"

Advertisement for the Canadian Women's Army Corps, 1940.

"Aircraft need housecleaning, too!"

From the RCAF Women's Division Recruiting Handbook.

September 10, 1939, effectively marked the end of the Great Depression as Canada entered the Second World War alongside the Allies. Unemployment quickly dissipated as Canada mobilized for the war effort. As men enrolled in military service, and were shipped overseas, the labour force once again experienced a shortage of workers to fill the needs of a war economy. The government, recognizing this need, appealed to the patriotism of Canadian women to aid in the preparation for total war. Women were mobilized for the workforce as men were mobilized for the European front. Women had actually been working in factories for many years. Between 1891 and 1921 women in Ontario represented more than 25 percent of the total manufacturing work force, although concentrated in certain sectors such as textile, food and bookbinding. Some women had worked in munitions plants during the First World War. To attract married women, incentives such as daycare and reduced taxes were introduced. Propaganda played a vital role, glamorizing the image of the working woman. One of the most famous images was that of the "Bren Gun Girl," the Canadian version of "Rosie the Riveter." The model in this attractive image of a woman with hair upswept in a handkerchief, and carefully applied lipstick putting the finishing touches on a machine gun, was Toronto's Veronica

Foster who worked on the Bren Gun production line at the James Inglis Ltd. Plant. Economic need and the propaganda resulted in an influx of women in unprecedented numbers in traditional male roles, such as aircraft workers and machinists. Prime Minister King stated in a broadcast on September 1, 1940: "...Canadians will remember the debt they owe labour." In the military sphere, women's divisions were created within the army, navy and air force, recruited with promises of adventure, and of course with the appealing message of serving their country in a time of need. Interestingly, only one out of ten women in a survey reported in the *Toronto Star*, 1944, claimed they were motivated primarily by patriotism. The majority stated their motivation as being the dream of an improved standard of living.

This liberated atmosphere would not last. Although a number of women remained in the workforce after the war, the majority returned home. In the post war years, government initiatives such as daycare disappeared. The predominant message in the media underwent a less than subtle change, as the image of the determined workingwoman was replaced by the happy homemaker and/or the traditional female employee. One advertisement declared that when factory ID badges became a "souvenir," a brand new typewriter for secretarial work could

GREEN DRAGON PRESS

conveniently replace it. Another emphasized the need for women to return home; a young girl looks up at her mother and asks, "when will you stay home again?" Most women returned home, or to traditionally female jobs such as secretarial work.

Post-war Canadian society would reflect this shift in values. Once again economics had a decisive impact on the role of women. The successful transition from a war economy depended on selling the post-war dream of domestic bliss: the nuclear family who lived a luxurious life in the suburbs. The post-war lifestyle and its trials and tribulations are reflected in a September 1948 article in *Chatelaine* that examines the role of the soap opera in the life of the housewife. As one woman commented, the soap opera is "the sound of a human voice in a lonely house." The pressure on women in this society is more than evident in the title of a 1941 *Chatelaine* article: "A Note to Brides - Don't Delay Parenthood." The life of many Canadian women in the late 1940s foreshadowed the decade to come. The struggle to find meaning and satisfaction in a life filled with pressures to create a perfect home and raise the perfect family would prove to be a difficult one.

MADELEINE de VERCHÈRES - 1678-1747

YESTERDAY

BORN at Sorel, in the Province of Quebec, 1678, Madeleine de Verchères is one of Canada's National heroines. On October 22nd, 1692, at the age of fourteen and a half years, she, with the help of her two brothers, aged twelve and ten years, successfully defended FORT DE VERCHÈRES against attack by 45 Iroquois Indians. Madeleine de Verchères symbolizes the feminine heroism of CANADA. Died at Ste Anne de la Parade, Quebec.

TO-DAY

Artist: Adam Sherriff Scott
Title: Madeleine de Verchères 1678-1747, Yesterday, Today.
Accession Number: 19700036-002
Beaverbrook Collection of War Art
©Canadian War Museum (CWM)

GREEN DRAGON PRESS

TRADES OF THE WOMEN'S DIVISION

Information about the many trades open to Canadian women in the R.C.A.F. Women's Division will be gladly given, without obligation, at any of the Recruiting Centres listed on the back of this booklet. Below are listed some of these trades. If you do not think your particular ability would fit into any of them, enquire from the Recruiting Officer. She will be able to tell you where you can best serve.

Administrative	Hospital Assistant
Bandswoman	Instrument Maker
Clerk (Accounting)	Laboratory Assistant
Clerk (General)	Laundrywoman
Clerk (General) (Medical)	Meteorological Observer
Clerk (Operations Room)	Operator (Telephone)
Clerk (Stenographer)	Pharmacist
Clerk (Stenographer) (Medical)	Photographer
Cook	Postal Clerk
Dental Assistant	Radiographer
Dispenser	Standard (General Duties)
Driver (Transport)	Tailoress
Equipment Assistant	Teleprinter Operator
Fabric Worker	Wireless Operator (Ground)

QUALIFICATIONS

Canadian women over 18 but not yet 41 are eligible for enlistment if they are:

Physically fit.
Have High School entrance or better.
5 feet or over in height.
Able to pass appropriate trade test.

The following documents should be produced:

Evidence of birth.
Proof of education.
National Registration Certificate.

Do not let the absence of documents prevent you from applying, however. The Recruiting Officer will be glad to help you obtain them.

RCAF Handbook - Women's Division 1939-45. City of Toronto Reference Library - Baldwin Room.

GREEN DRAGON PRESS

"The hand that rocks the cradle can also do a mean job on a tracer bullet - if it's kept happy. If it's kept soft and smooth and feminine. If the nails are clean, bright and well-groomed; the skin white and supple through proper care. Give your nails the victory cut..."

> -Nail polish advertisement, 1943.

Advertising, posters and pamphlets - all were used to encourage women to join the armed forces or work in factories. Such wartime propaganda was also used to warn against saboteurs and spies and hoarding, as well as to urge the purchase of Victory Bonds and the collection of rubber, fat, and tinfoil. School children took part in a War Savings Certificate program. Stamps were purchased for .25 each and stuck into special passbooks. Almost all advertisements, whether for clothing, groceries, or indeed any item for sale, combined praise for the particular produce with exhortations to work for the war effort. For example, The William Paterson candy company and George Weston Bakery advertised on ration card holders, combining the call to "Work Harder for Canada" with the statement that "Good Candy is Good Food: Eat Some Every Day!"

GREEN DRAGON PRESS

"It was flannelette Grandma was after, twelve yards for three nightshirts. But when the clerk mentioned flannelette was getting scarce, she bought the whole bolt! Grandma didn't mean to be a saboteur. But she is...she's a hoarder.

You know, of course, that many products are getting scarce. That's why it's so terribly important to buy wisely. In the case of all washables, for instance - shirts, shorts, dresses, overalls, pyjamas - it's important to get them Sanforized if you can to avoid waste from shrinkage. And for heaven's sake don't buy any more than you need. It's one thing you can do to help win."

The Whispering Campaign

"Spreading of harmful and irresponsible rumours is undoubtedly one of the factors most damaging in Canada's war effort. There are rumours of all kinds and descriptions and unfortunately many people seem to take an unthinking, inane and even mischievous delight in passing them on. Naturally the farther such stories go, the more fanciful and exaggerated they become. We may not believe them ourselves, but inevitably they stick persistently in the minds of some, exerting an insidiously disruptive effect."

"Most inexcusable of the current crop of rumours are certain reports concerning women serving in the Army Corps and in the Women's Division in this time of urgent need.

People who deliberately slander these fine forces are 'not worthy to polish the shoes of Canada's women in uniform."

W. Hugh Conrad, *Athene, Goddess of War: The Canadian Women's Army Corps, Their Story* (Ottawa: Consumer and Corporate Affairs, 1983), 112.

GREEN DRAGON PRESS

But not every one supported the idea of women in the military. One young woman wrote to the Hollywood actress Bette Davis asking for advice when her boyfriend opposed her desire to enlist in the air force. Miss Davis did not mince words.

☞ YOUR PROBLEMS ANSWERED BY ☜ BETTE DAVIS

Dear Miss Davis:

I am a girl of seventeen and I have a boy friend overseas whom I love very much. As I am Canadian, I wish to join the Air Force -I am eligible but he won't hear of it. He says he is fighting so we girls won't have to. He also doesn't think it is a girl's place to join up and be put in uniform.

He says that if I do join up, he will have nothing to do with me. Now, Miss Davis, I would like to know what you would do in my place: Join up and fight for the love of my country, or stay at home and wait for him to return, as he wishes.

Carol D.

Dear Miss D:

If joining the Air Force is something that you sincerely want to do, if you honestly feel that it will contribute toward winning the war more quickly, you must do it. You have to live with yourself; you must behave in accordance with your convictions.

As for your beau, he must realise how much we need every person to do what he can. The time has passed when women must simply sit at home and wait for a soldier's return, without doing anything constructive. What would other allied nations have done if their women hadn't contributed to the war effort as well as the men?

It seems to me that you must do what you feel is right in this situation and in the long run I'm sure your beau will understand.

Bette Davis

GREEN DRAGON PRESS

"Women between the ages of 18 and 35 and in good health are wanted to work in eastern war plants. 'Keep 'em firing' is the motto used. The kind of girl we want is the girl with a good head on her shoulders. We take girls absolutely unskilled in war industries and train them right at the plant. A Saskatchewan girl - whether she's a farmer's daughter, domestic servant, waitress, clerk, stenographer, college graduate or debutante - if she is willing to learn - has the qualities of a good war worker. Wages are 0.35 an hour for a 48-hour week. Time and a half for all overtime. At the end of 4 to 6 weeks, the rate of pay will be increased according to the individual's ability."
The *Leader-Post*, Regina, December 5, 1942.

A woman's lipstick is an instrument of personal morale that helps her to conceal heartbreak or sorrow; gives her self-confidence when it's badly needed; heightens her loveliness when she wants to look her loveliest.
No lipstick will win the war. But it symbolizes one of the reasons why we are fighting...the precious right of women to be feminine and lovely - under any circumstances.

Lipstick advertisement, October 1942.

[My husband] had the idea that when we got married I shouldn't work. We had one room and the use of the kitchen, and I was going stir crazy. Nothing to do all day. You'd go out and window shop, but then you'd spend money. So finally - that was the first time I'd bucked him - I went out and got a job, a job in a war plant. I worked on what they call the high explosives side, where you got paid a little extra because you were working with dangerous powders. We made detonators for torpedoes, and it wasn't a bad job. I learned every job on the line because it was awful boring just to stay in one. Some of the women stayed in one job all the time they were there, but I made the rounds - learned them all - and I liked every shift excepting the night shift.

Grace Fowler in: *No Burden To Carry: Narratives of Black Working Women in Ontario 1920s to 1950s*, 124.

GREEN DRAGON PRESS

Grace Fowler enjoyed her work in the munitions factory, however she met with discrimination: "When I worked in that war plant - especially on the night shift, when all the machinery breaks down - we used to get into some real good discussions.

So that stopped that conversation!" Grace Fowler in: *No Burden To Carry: Narratives of Black Working Women in Ontario 1920s to 1950s*, 124.

Kathleen Carter and Geraldine Carter, Munitions workers, December 2, 1944. Toronto Telegram Photograph Collection, York University Archives and Special Collections, ASC1338.

The experiences of Diana Rickey and her sisters were typical of many women who worked in munitions plants. Diana married Alfred Rickey who was serving with the Strathcona Horse regiment and in 1941 he was transferred to southern Ontario. Diana moved to Toronto to work when her husband was sent to North Africa. As Canada's participation in the war effort increased so did the involvement of women in the machines that sewed parachutes. Soon another sister, Mary, joined them and all three worked for the war effort, Pearl and Mary worked on the Inglis assembly line making Bren guns. All three sisters lived together in a one-bedroom suite on the top floor of a house. They worked shift work, ate meals at the subsidized cafeterias at work and entertained themselves at dance halls and movie theatres. They continued their participation in the war effort in 1942 by wiring panels for destroyers, corvettes and frigates, soldering, drilling and making gunpowder. After the war, most women lost their factory jobs but many looked for work elsewhere. Mary got an office job where she met her husband. Pearl worked for Canada Packers and Diana reunited with her husband.

This one night we talked about nursing, and I was saying how they wouldn't let Black girls go into nursing at that time - and this supervisor was trying to explain to me why they didn't and was trying to be delicate about it. She was saying, "Well, you know your people have a different odour and somebody sick, they don't want somebody [like that] around them."

Grace fought back, asking the woman "How many Black people are working in this shop right now?" And she said, "Well, you're the only one." I said, "I work alongside of some of these women. If I smelled as bad as them, I'd shoot myself, so don't talk to me about bad smell because you've got it here, and you don't have a Black person in it."

GREEN DRAGON PRESS

Excerpts from a Vancouver war worker's diary, 1942:

Jan. 7 - The blackout shutters were put on the school windows today...Marks in my exam were 64. Just average. Did the best in manual work.

Jan. 8-They're really rushing us at the school. Today we were divided into two classes. I'm in the advanced and we had fun taking an old plane apart. Some of us will be starting at Boeing's plant soon.

Jan .17 - Finally worked today. Filed hinges. At 9:30 we were taken all through the plant in single file right through to the offices to the "ladies", where we all took turns. There are no washrooms as yet.

Jan. 20 - I'm working the band-saw. At 10:30 we were all given ice cream to protect our tummies against all the sprays etc. I'm on night shift.

Jan. 23 - No wonder we don't turn out planes very fast. The boys sure don't strain themselves. It will be a good thing when the girls take over. They are more conscientious.

Feb. 2 - Riveted for the first time today.

Feb. 6 - This morning a girl in the machine shop had a big glob of hair pulled out when she got caught in the drill press. Now we have to cover our hair completely or else wear dust hats. Got first pay cheque, $48.53 for two weeks with deductions. We make 40 cents an hour.

Feb 23. - After work went to town to buy a suitcase to carry my overalls in. It has no lock due to the shortage of metals.

Mar. 1 - Andy [the foreman] called me over today and told me I was to be in charge of the girls and the one boy on the job. There have been too many mistakes on the parts. It's a compliment. The Japanese are being evacuated from the coast.

Mar. 3 - Had most of the shop hammering on the D-brackets. Most of us felt light-headed. We think it's from the fumes from the paint shop. We were told to drink milk.

Mar. 18 - Today I became butcher and took Joyce's fingernail off on the rivet squeezer. I felt awful and I guess she felt worse.

Apr. 27 - Today we're voting "Yes" or "No" for conscription. The answer will be "Yes".

Apr. 30 - Deburred Lucite for eight hours steady. Had a nosebleed, then my nose ran like a sieve. Every time I work on Lucite this happens. I must be allergic to it. If I feel like this tomorrow I'll have to stay home.

May 30 - Drove home on the bus and the driver said he didn't recognize me in my street clothes. He's so used to my overalls. We wear them so we don't have to change at work.

June 14 - Rained torrents but 969 turned up at the picnic and we had a wonderful time, dancing, drinking and running around in the rain, eating wet sandwiches, drinking sugarless coffee.

June 24 - Am now riding to work on my bike. Five miles. Buses don't stop in West Van any more.

July 11 - Congratulations Viv! Today Mr. Griffin told me I was to act as instructor and check all riveting done by the girls, also train the new ones. He says it's an honour as I'm the first girl to hold the position in the Boeing Plants. I also get a five cent raise.

Sept. 24 - Pay day. $55.60. Not bad. We went to town to cash our cheques and there were literally thousands of girls in overalls doing the same thing.

GREEN DRAGON PRESS

But not all Canadian women had the option of choosing to join the forces or work in factories. Japanese Canadian women, even those who were second-generation citizens, endured shameful treatment. Following the Japanese bombing of Pearl Harbour, the Canadian government ordered 21,000 people of Japanese ancestry, more than 80% of them Canadian citizens to leave their homes in British Columbia. They were taken to camps and lonely towns in the BC interior or to farms in Alberta and Manitoba. More than 4,000 of them moved to Ontario and Quebec. Their property, including houses, farms and fishing boats were either confiscated or sold cheaply. Muriel Kitagawa, a young mother, wrote to her brother.

March 2, 1942.

Dear Wes:

What a heavenly relief to get your letter. I was just about getting frantic with worry over you. That's why I hope you'll forgive me for writing to Kim Carson. Eddie [Muriel's husband] and I thought that was the only way to find out what really was happening to you. Oh Wes, the things that have been happening out here are beyond words, and though at times I thank goodness you're out of it, at other times I think we really need people like you around to keep us from getting too wrought up for our own good.

Eiko and Fumi [Muriel's friends] were here yesterday, crying, nearly hysterical with hurt and outrage and impotence. All student nurses have been fired from the General [Hospital.]

They took our beautiful radio...what does it matter that someone bought it off us for a song...it's the same thing because we had to do that or suffer the ignominy of having it taken forcibly from us by the RCMP. Not a single being of Japanese race in the protected area will escape. Our cameras, even [young brother] Nobi's toy one, all are confiscated. They can search our homes without warrant.

This is My Own: Letters to Wes and Other Writings, 77, 78.

GREEN DRAGON PRESS

Aftermath: Exchanging Overalls for Aprons.

During World War II women had entered the paid labour force in droves as part of the victory effort. But when the men came back women were urged to return to their kitchens. Through that period, labour unions and social activists lobbied strenuously for the "male breadwinner's wage..." to allow one workingman to support his family while his wife cared for the children and home. But not all workingwomen could afford to go back to the home. In fact, the number of women in the paid work force continued to grow after the war. For example, in Quebec, between 1941 and 1951, the number of workingwomen increased by almost a third. In Quebec, the church, nationalists and intellectuals were hostile to workingwomen, but their hostility did not keep all women at home. Historian Francine Barry notes that in 1941, 8 per cent of workingwomen were married; in 1951, the rate was more than 17 per cent. The increase was most noticeable in the manufacturing sector, not surprisingly, as the working class is the most vulnerable to price increases. And a working-class family could not survive without two breadwinners. (*Quebec Women: A History*, 294)

Homecoming was often a mixed blessing for veterans and their families. They had to make tremendous adjustments. Many of those who served overseas had undergone shattering experiences, and those who waited and worked for those who fought, endured loneliness and fear. Many women had gained experience and confidence and were not willing to return to positions of dependence.

A former CWAC member wrote:
"It was quite a shock when you left the service. When it was all over. It was an unforgettable experience and I certainly have no regrets. It changed everyone. You'd been protected in the service. Everything was part of a routine and there was a lot of adjusting to do afterwards, for women as well as for men. I don't think some of the men ever adjusted, for that matter. There were a lot of divorces after the war because of it. Everything had changed!"

On the other hand, many veterans, both female and male, had spent years being told what to do and had to become accustomed to freedom of choice.

A former WRCNS member wrote:

"I had a good job waiting for me when I got out, but some of my friends were scared to death of getting back into civilian life. Being in the service meant that everything was decided for you. You knew what you were going to wear and where you were going to eat and the whole routine was laid out. So a lot of people were feeling really lost when they got out, because they weren't used to thinking for themselves."
Greatcoats and Glamour Boots, Canadian Women at War (1939-1945) 199.

GREEN DRAGON PRESS

BACK HOME
FOR KEEPS

CANADA

Chatelaine Magazine
May, 1945.

Victory

with heartfelt
gratitude.....
we join in the
rejoicing and
thanksgiving
for this day of
victory.

Famous Players
Canadian
Corporation

Evening Telegram, n.d.

GREEN DRAGON PRESS

Early in the war L.S.B. Shapiro, writing in *Saturday Night* expressed the not so hidden concern that there would be increasing challenges to the concept of "it's a man's world:"

"...After countless centuries of existence as the underrated sex, women are proving that they can do a man's job. But are they taking advantage of this opportunity?... They are not. They are being women - first and foremost - useful women, to be sure, but fundamentally feminine. I foresee no difficulty after the war in renewing the tradition that this is a man's world."
"...They have not allowed their utilitarian function, which is absolutely invaluable to the war effort, to interfere with their primary inclination for being coy, charming, very feminine individuals whose chief aim in life (at least one of them) is to make themselves attractive to men.."
"They're Still Women After All,"
Saturday Night, September 26, 1942.

Among the things that did not change, were gender stereotypes. For despite the contributions made by women during the war, post-war society did not reject stereotypical views of gender roles. In a 1947 advertisement, the gifts Mr. Bowman carries are "boy" toys. Appropriate girl toys at this time would have included dolls, baby carriages and dollhouses. Sports equipment was reserved for males.

"It's a girl?"

"You must be mistaken, nurse...it's Mrs. WILLIAM Bowman that I mean. We're going to have a boy - later on today."

"No mistake, Mr. Bowman - your surprise party's over! Go right in to see her - and that beautiful seven-pound daughter of yours!"

GREEN DRAGON PRESS

Some calls for women to return to their "proper sphere" were unsubtle and deeply demeaning to both men and women, in that they assumed men could not cope with capable women. The author of this (possibly tongue-in-cheek) magazine article gives women the choice - a monkey wrench or matrimony.

Liberation Deferred

Look Ladies: it's reconversion time. Tanks and tail guns have vacated the priority list in favour of new refrigerators and nail scissors. We've written two V-Days into the record, and re-establishment, rather than re-armament, is the order.

So how about coming out from behind those welders' masks and swapping your overalls for aprons? The men folk are returning from overseas; they will take a very dim view of the situation if they find that you have permanently muscled in on their toiling territory...

He's sick of whipcord. He wants a clinging vine.

It will be quite a shock to him to discover that instead of staying home and crocheting borders for the hand towels, his better half is driving a streetcar...

In England it was commonplace to see a gal step up to a packing case almost as big as herself, fluff out her back curls, and casually toss the load onto a lorry. Another gal would be standing by, ready to drive the load away.

The spectacle was successively astonishing, amusing, and boring. In due course a woman porter became just a porter. She literally worked herself sexless...

Refrain from any act which would even suggest your ability to lift anything heavier than a dry mop. Make like a lady, not like a lady wrestler...

Let a repatriated fighter pilot illustrate our position in the matter.

"I got the car out the other evening and went out for a spin in the country. The machine hadn't been used for over three years, so I wasn't really surprised when it conked. I pulled off the road and lifted the hood.

"Well, I was standing there, giving the job the once over, when another car stopped beside me, and out stepped a babe in something green. "Having some trouble?" she asks, giving me a nice smile. "Maybe I can help."

"The next thing I know, I'm elbowed right out of the play. This doll fiddled around with a couple of wires, then stepped away and turned the smile back on. "That should do it." And before I could even ask her name, much less her phone number, she was away. What makes it really bad, my bus has been running like a rocket ever since."

"So," the pilot concluded. "I've decided to find me a girl who doesn't know a basket from a grease gun. I'm going to give her a vehicle maintenance test. If she flunks, I'll lay my heart in her lap. But if she passes - so will I."

Which will it be, ladies? Matrimony or a monkey wrench?"

Mayfair, December 1945, 40-41.

GREEN DRAGON PRESS

Making a home in a new land

During and immediately after the end of the war, close to 45,000 British and European women left their homes and families to start a new life in post-war Canada as "war brides." Because they were wartime dependents, the Canadian government took responsibility for bringing them to Canada. Their husbands had served as part of the Canadian war effort and they had met their husbands at camp dances, and in hospitals.

The arrival of these women and their children marked the single largest wave of immigration since the Great Depression. These women came mostly from England but also from other parts of the United Kingdom and continental Europe. The war brides had much in common; they were young and many were either pregnant or already had one or more children. Over 22,000 babies or young children arrived with their mothers during this time. Most of them entered Canada at Pier 21 in Halifax, often to cheers from waiting Canadians. Because most of them were British subjects, there were few immigration difficulties. Many of the women, especially those from England expected to find living conditions similar to those they had known and were surprised at the differences they experienced. Many felt a strong need to unite through various associations in order to gather together and share their past and their new experiences.

Dutch War Brides National Archives of Canada CN 45293-3 (CNR)

GREEN DRAGON PRESS

Myrtle Wong was born in Bendigo, Australia in 1922. She immigrated to Canada from Australia in 1946 as a war bride. Myrtle described her experiences of racism, some kindness and her decision to "fit in."

"I came to Canada from Australia in 1946. I lived in the home of a Canadian who had looked after my husband from the time he was nineteen years old. This man was a highly respected Queen's Council lawyer. On the days when the maid was not in, I helped with the laundry and cooking. I was not glad to be here at first because I missed my family and I had to face a lot of racism from people who mistook me for a Japanese. When I arrived in London, Ontario, nobody knew me. I wasn't very well accepted. I'd walk into a store and people would slam the door in my face, thinking I was Japanese. In Australia my whole family was well known and respected, but here I was just like an ant. So that was an adjustment. It was like I fell off the ladder.

But there was one very kind family nearby who made me feel welcome and helped me bridge the gap. If I had to go anywhere they would accompany me so I wouldn't get lost. They got me accustomed to the Canadian way of doing things: the right clothing, food, transportation, holidays. The mother of this family treated me like a daughter. This family really made it easy for me. I was already fluent in English, so I adapted very quickly...you know the saying, "When in Rome, do as the Romans do"? That's exactly what I did.

Jin Guo: Voices of Chinese Canadian Women, 103-4.

Doris M. Richards, a widowed war bride, had to be even more courageous than most, for she did not have a happy reunion with her husband to look forward to:

"As the train from Halifax conveyed us to different villages and towns across Canada, we were witness to numerous joyful scenes as men and women were reunited and children acquainted with their daddies. Viewing this increased my personal sorrow and secret dread of meeting strangers in a strange land, speaking a strange language. When the time came at the station in Trois-Rivières, Quebec, it was necessary for Red Cross officials to introduce us to our newly acquired family of in-laws. Emotion was high on both sides and tears flowed freely. But to this day I have never forgotten the incredible loving feeling that immediately surrounded us.

Despite the differences in background, culture, and tongue, I felt I had arrived "home." Cousins, aunts, uncles, brothers, and sisters, of all ages, welcomed us wholeheartedly and took us home to meet my ailing mother-in-law. It had been her wish to see and hold her English baby granddaughter, the legacy of her son who was destined never to return."

Promise You'll Take Care of My Daughter: The Remarkable War Brides of World War II, 109.

GREEN DRAGON PRESS

Notable Women

Joy Kogawa

Joy Kogawa was born Joy Nakayama in Vancouver, BC, in 1935. She and her family were moved to an internment camp in Slocan, BC in 1942, and all of their property was taken away. She studied education at the University of Alberta, then music at the University of Toronto. She taught for a while, then began writing for the Prime Minister's Office in the 70s. Her experience in the camp at Slocan affected her deeply, but her reaction for the first part of her adult life was to deny her Japanese-ness by not having Japanese friends, not speaking the language and by trying to blend into white Canada. Then, she came across the material of Muriel Kitagawa in the Public Archives, and it was this outspoken woman's work that jolted Kogawa into facing the reality of what happened to her and other Japanese Canadians. Also, she says, the pen has a power and direction of its own, and it seemed to want to write about that time. www.coolwomen.org

Photo: courtesy G. Kogawa.

Viola Desmond

On Friday, November 8, 1946 Viola Desmond, a Black Halifax businesswoman, was thrown out of the Roseland Theatre, in New Glasgow, Nova Scotia. This unjust action was symbolic of the racist policies and laws that still existed during this period in Canadian history. Ms. Desmond sat in the white section of the movie house, and refused to move when ordered to do so. As a result, she was jailed overnight and convicted the next day of defrauding the Province of Nova Scotia of one-cent tax. Though no signs were posted, there was in Nova Scotia and other parts of Canada at the time de facto segregation in some public places like bars and movie theatres. At the Roseland, tickets to the white section carried a one-cent extra tax. Ms. Desmond had requested a ticket to the house but was refused and was sold instead a ticket to the balcony. Readers of *The Clarion*, a local paper, edited by social activist Carrie Best, donated money to fund her legal defence. The Supreme Court of Nova Scotia rejected her appeal.

Thérèse Casgrain

Thérèse Casgrain entered the public sphere during the federal election of 1921 when she conducted a highly successful campaign for her husband who was ill. She became president of the Provincial Franchise Committee (later, the League for Women's Rights) in 1928 - a position she held for 14 years. One of the main obstacles to winning suffrage in Quebec was the lack of support from rural French women. She was able to reach many of them through her radio program. " Femina," which was broadcast on French and English networks, and by speaking at conventions.

Following the war and the final achievement of the vote in 1940 she continued faithfully to press for child protection laws, prison reform, government appointments for women and amendments to the civil code. She became vice-president of the National Federation of Liberal Women and in 1948 resigned to join the CCF Party. She soon became vice-chairperson of the national CCF executive and in 1951 was chosen Quebec Social Democratic Party leader, a post she held until 1957 - the first woman party leader anywhere in Canada. When the NDP succeeded the CCF in 1961, Casgrain continued her active support, as national vice-chairperson. "I can't imagine a woman who has the best interest of her children at heart not taking an interest in politics," she said. www.herstorycalendar.ca

GREEN DRAGON PRESS

Activities
1940 – 1949

WAR TIME EXPERIENCES

Research the propaganda and images that made the wartime personalities of the American "Rosie the Riveter", and the Canadian "Bren Gun Girl". What do these two famous characters have in common? i.e. did they serve the same purpose? Was their message fairly similar? Give specific examples.

In the form of an analytical essay, compare and contrast the experience of Canadian women in World War One, and World War Two. Use the documents in this book to aid your research. Focus on the following: propaganda and images of women at work. Using the Vancouver war worker's diary write and perform a skit entitled "a day in the life of a woman war worker".

BETTE DAVIS SOLVES YOUR PROBLEMS

Provide your class with only the question sent to Ms. Davis, p100. Ask the students to write their own responses. Compare and contrast with the advice offered by Bette Davis. Ask the students to imagine other scenarios that would arise, posing moral, ethical, emotional or simply societal dilemmas for young women during the war. Examples might include harassment by a supervisor at a factory, or the agony of not knowing if your father/husband/brother/boyfriend would ever return.

ADVERTISING

Create a 2-3 minute commercial for a product of your choice that sells not only the product, but also a "war time moral message."

Resources

Gossage, Carolyn. *Greatcoats and Glamour Boots: Canadian Women at War (1939-1945),* Toronto: Dundurn Press, 1991.
Jin Guo: *Voices of Chinese Canadian Women,* Toronto: Women's Committee, Chinese Canadian National Council, 1992.
Kitagawa, Muriel. *This is My Own: Letters to Wes and Other Writings,* Vancouver: Talonbooks, 1985.
Joy Kogawa. *Obasan,* Toronto: Penguin Books, 1983.
Lambton, Gunda. *Sun in Winter: A Toronto Wartime Journal, 1942-45.* McGill-Queen's University Press, 2003.
Lennon, Mary Jane & Syd Charendoff. *On the Homefront,* Erin: Boston Mills Press, 1981.
Wicks, Ben. *Promise You'll Take Care of My Daughter: The Remarkable War Brides of World War II,* Toronto: Stoddart Co. Ltd., 1992.

Video: *Rosie the Riveter:* National Film Board.

GREEN DRAGON PRESS

1950 – 1959

The joys of suburbia illusion and reality

Photo courtesy Mary Morden

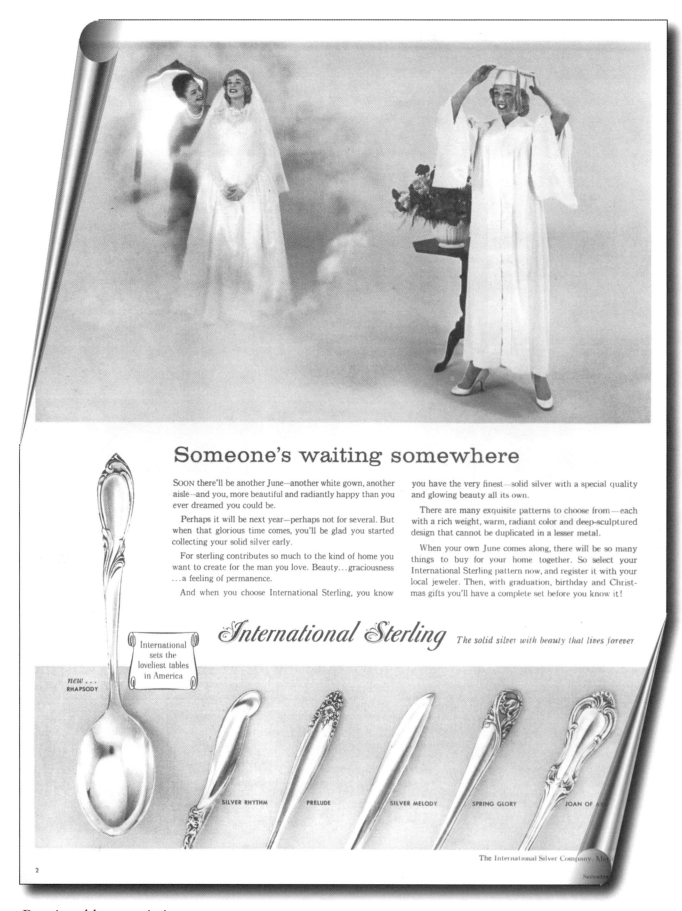

Someone's waiting somewhere

SOON there'll be another June—another white gown, another aisle—and you, more beautiful and radiantly happy than you ever dreamed you could be.

Perhaps it will be next year—perhaps not for several. But when that glorious time comes, you'll be glad you started collecting your solid silver early.

For sterling contributes so much to the kind of home you want to create for the man you love. Beauty...graciousness ...a feeling of permanence.

And when you choose International Sterling, you know you have the very finest—solid silver with a special quality and glowing beauty all its own.

There are many exquisite patterns to choose from—each with a rich weight, warm, radiant color and deep-sculptured design that cannot be duplicated in a lesser metal.

When your own June comes along, there will be so many things to buy for your home together. So select your International Sterling pattern now, and register it with your local jeweler. Then, with graduation, birthday and Christmas gifts you'll have a complete set before you know it!

International Sterling The solid silver with beauty that lives forever

International sets the loveliest tables in America

new ... RHAPSODY

SILVER RHYTHM   PRELUDE   SILVER MELODY   SPRING GLORY   JOAN OF ARC

The International Silver Company, Me...

2

Reprinted by permission.

During the 1950s, women were encouraged to finish school and prepare for marriage. Linking the two suggested that education served the purpose to prepare better wives and mothers. This ad reinforces the message - the women share common characteristics: a happy smile, wearing white, and a sense of accomplishment.

GREEN DRAGON PRESS

1950-1959 Introduction

"The decade of the fifties can be skipped over lightly. Nothing much happened except that we all donned housedresses and aprons and devoted our lives to keeping our homes squeaky clean and raising perfect children. We did find our place in this era, but it offered nothing over which one could wax sentimental in future years. I actually remember sitting having coffee and listening to one of my neighbours describe in detail how she organized her kitchen drawers."

"A Generation Caught between Two Tides,"
by Audrey Jenkinson, The Globe & Mail, December 14, 1992.

Economics have often, if not always, dictated the role of women in society. During World War II, a shortage in the work force created a need for women's labour. A full employment economy and a shortage of consumer goods meant that at the end of the war the general public had disposable income and the urge to spend it. A new era of mass consumption fuelled by advertising, sophisticated market research and new forms of credit, like charge cards accompanied a rush to the rapidly expanding suburbs, the construction supported in part by low-cost mortgages for veterans. Post-war prosperity seemed like a miracle and it appeared, on the surface at least, that the economic boom also increased equality and opportunity by spreading more wealth among more people. For the most part though, women, people of colour and working-class whites benefited far less from government offerings of university tuition for veterans and mortgage funding. In *A Consumers' Republic*, Alfred A. Knopf, 2003, Lizabeth Cohen, professor of American Studies at Harvard University, writes that the American suburban metropolis was rigidly segregated by class and race, developers using their power to redefine public space, from shopping centres to ocean beaches, in an effort to keep profits up - and undesirables out - a situation mirrored in Canada.

The Levittown of the U.S. was being duplicated here as new suburban communities, sprang up across the country.

Along with the economic boom of the 1950's came the call for women to return to their traditional role as mother and homemaker. Just as at the end of World War I, day care centres closed, returning veterans claimed their jobs, the civil service renewed its rule barring married women, and the pressure was on for life to "return to normal." Gender roles were reinforced for both men and women, as men replaced their army uniforms with their grey suits, suitable for climbing the corporate ladder. A wife was expected to play her role within this scenario, aided by the many new and wonderful household appliances now available to her. Certainly, the glorification of traditional family values and of suburban lifestyle is evident in the documents from this time period. *McCall's* was deemed the magazine of togetherness. Magazines targeted at young women reinforced this priority in the form of Valentine's Day specials on hope chests and silverware for that special day "when the white graduation gown is replaced by another white gown as you walk down another aisle." In 1959, Barbie appeared on the scene, becoming an icon of the impossibly perfect female form, representative of less than 1% of the female population.

GREEN DRAGON PRESS

In fact, despite this permeating image of the happy mother and housewife, many women felt isolated and frustrated by the limitations and expectations imposed during this time period and many women, having grown used to earning their own money and making family decisions were unwilling to return to the new "normal." Canadian women continued to enter into the workforce, challenging limits and overcoming obstacles despite the oppressive atmosphere of 1950's culture. Women such as Doris Anderson, editor of *Chatelaine*, represented the continued struggle for equality. Charlotte Whitton became the first female mayor in 1951. In fact, a new generation of women was growing up in this environment, and in the following decades, would actively take part in a second wave of feminism.

As in the past, the idealized role was not open to all women. The suburban housewife with smiling children and shiny appliances was a construct that required a certain level of income. Although some opportunities had opened for women of colour during the war, this was not as a result of an effort to deal with racial segregation, but rather because of the labour shortage. Jobs traditionally reserved for white women became open as they left for higher paying employment in war industries. Hospitals, laundries, and dry cleaners were desperate for staff. Some Black women were finally able to train as teachers and some found work in factories. One factory worker, Marjorie Lewsey reflected with great irony: "We weren't allowed into the factory until Hitler started the war." *We're Rooted Here and They Can't Pull Us Up*, Dionne Brand et al, 179. One occupation that had always been open to Black women - domestic work - took on a new importance with the economic upswing, as middle-class families had extra income to employ others to help look after their homes. This was aided by a Canadian government sponsored domestic immigration scheme that successfully brought female domestics from the Caribbean into Canada. A "brain drain" out of the Caribbean, many of these women were educated and highly trained, but were often disappointed in the domestic jobs they received after arriving in Canada. Despite the issues, labour schemes remained a popular solution to the post-war economic challenges.

GREEN DRAGON PRESS

The Suburbs and the Consumer Society

After the War, one of the biggest national problems was a shortage of housing. The Depression and the War had stunted housing development. Returning veterans were demanding a solution from the government. The National Housing Act created vast subdivisions, the suburbs, which redefined the nature of Canadian society. Public transportation was often poor, and most of the suburbs had been designed for people with cars. For both these reasons, the housewife often doubled as a chauffeur for the rest of the family and could easily find herself behind the wheel of a car for 20 hours a week.

Life in a Suburban Toronto Community

"...At about the time when the male is ready to launch his career, he seeks a life partner, a woman who will assume the traditional responsibilities of helpmate, confidante, companion, and mother of his children. He marries a girl who occupies about the same position in the class structure as himself. She is about as well educated as he is... Upon marriage, the woman takes charge of the home. When children come, they are her main responsibility. It was exceedingly difficult to find women in Crestwood Heights who had continued their vocations past motherhood. After marriage, the claims of the husband and, later, of the children on the woman's time and energy are so dominant that she must abandon her aspirations towards a career...The role of wife and mother in these circumstances lacks many of the satisfactions commonly associated with it in a more stable rural type of society, even though the biological and emotional fulfilments it provides are still powerful. Many a mother in Crestwood Heights stated somewhat ruefully that motherhood had "cut short" her career. She was unlikely to think of motherhood itself as a career...If questioned directly, she would aver that motherhood was a career, but she would omit mention of housekeeping, unless closely questioned as to her attitude towards it. Then, although she might not dismiss housekeeping as plain drudgery and lament the lack of domestic help, she would nevertheless qualify her acceptance of housekeeping by linking it to other ends: child-rearing, making her husband happy, or her interest in entertaining..."

John R. Seeley, R. Alexander Sim, and Elizabeth W. Loosley; *Crestwood Heights: A Study of the Culture of Suburban Life*, (New York: Basic Books, 1956), 139-140.

Images of Women

During the 1950s, there was enormous pressure on women to be successful housekeepers. Keeping a home "clean, organized, and orderly" were important aspirations for most wives and mothers. Women's magazines capitalized on this concern and featured numerous articles that addressed ways in which to perform wifely duties. The article which appeared in Good *Housekeeping Monthly*, 1955, is typical of the time, giving specific advice for women to be good wives and homemakers.

• Men may cook or weave or dress dolls or hunt humming birds but if such activities are appropriate occupations of men, then the whole society, men and women alike, votes them as important. When the same activities are performed by women, they are regarded as less important.

Anthropologist Margaret Mead - 1950.

HOW TO STAY MARRIED

BY JOHN K. THOMAS, M.A.
Director of the Personnel Laboratory, Psychological Consultants, Toronto. Mr. Thomas, happily married and the father of three, conducts Canadian Home Journal's marriage-clinic column each month.

The belittling wife: a message for Mrs. Dagwood

THE MAN from Montreal was desperately unhappy; he came to see me because he was having difficulty with his marriage.

Outwardly there were no signs of disaster. He described his wife as a good mother to his three children, a good housewife, and in no sense a social climber. He had worked very hard to build up his own business, and during twenty years had been most successful. His wife was now better off financially than she had ever been, and neither of them had any romantic interests elsewhere. Yet in spite of all this, he was genuinely sick at heart because he no longer felt like a man; in fact, he had attempted suicide.

He complained that his wife humiliated him.

Perhaps since we take the comic-strip character, Dagwood, for granted, we are not too upset over the pathetic little man who is bawled out by his boss, outsmarted by his wife and never given a moment's peace. We may regard this as funny because it is frustration recollected in tranquillity—but the man who endures it has little dignity. Dagwood's only answer to a matriarchal world is the refuge of sleep, of escape into fantasy, but here again it is quite probable that the dogs will have usurped his sofa.

My friend was no Dagwood. A tall, good-looking man, still youthful in appearance, the humiliation he complained of was an unending succession of small incidents.

For instance, when he started to tell a story his wife would explain to the audience that he never was very good at stories. If a friend told one, however, no matter how bad or off-color, she would laugh uproariously. If he told a bawdy story she would reproach him publicly for his bad taste. If he attempted to speak at a Home and School meeting, she nudged him to sit down and not embarrass her. If he told the children to go to bed at an agreed-upon hour, she countermanded his orders and gave them an extension. When he wanted to go out, she felt tired. When he was tired, she reproached him for their dull social life.

Their love life was of course on the same pattern: she was too tired, too disinterested, and they had violent arguments on this score. When he wanted to talk of love and the pleasures of the shared life, she would talk of taxes, and remember that she had forgotten to put out the milk bottles.

We have come a long way from the domineering father and the tyrannical husband. The economic freedom that women now enjoy has given them an independence that is revolutionary. "Himself" no longer rules on all matters and "his" final word is not the law of the house. In a democratic country, this is to the good, and gives women an increased dignity. But at the opposite end of the scale from "Himself" is Dagwood.

Dagwood enjoys popularity as a comic strip because, in a wry way, it registers with many people as being fairly close to the facts as they know them. Thoreau referred to the days of most men as being lives of quiet desperation. And here we have the male of the species reduced, diminished, robbed of his virility and dignity. His office is a place of frustration and when he gets home and cannot doze on the couch any longer, he creeps off—to find his only satisfaction in a Dagwood sandwich.

AS A BOY grows up he tries to identify himself with the masculine role in our culture. His play, his reading, and the movies are constantly supplying him with a series of roles which he tries on for size. He may be a fireman, or Nelson, or Scott of the Antarctic. He's a tough cowboy, a G-man, or a Private Eye: He dreams of carrying the ball over the line in the last moments of play or fighting to the end in a rearguard action. Later on he takes over the role of the Prince in Cinderella. He has held in front of him as models bold, gallant, virile men who are aggressive, decisive, and able to handle the role of a man. He also expects to have to go out and earn a living and be successful.

In our culture mothers raise their children to follow this line of activity. And by their loving encouragement, they suggest to the boy the sort of man they hope he will be.

Then he gets married. He has learned by this time that he is no Nelson or Ulysses, and has had some experience of the difficulty of earning a living. In a fiercely competitive world, he can rarely earn the living he dreams of, or provide a standard of living commensurate with his ambitions. His world is one of uncertainty and insecurity. He may be fired tomorrow, or the firm may fail. Everyone he works with is under tension—and his bosses too are men usually living under great stress. He has to deliver the goods, or get out.

But he wants to be respected by his fellows and to feel that he is loved. Even though his job does not carry a long title, he wants some status in his own community—respect for his skill and commendation for a job well done.

In other words he wants to feel like a man.

Now if his home life is one that constantly diminishes him, if the way he is treated has little relation to the way he sees himself, he is bound to be unhappy.

If he is made to feel inadequate as a man, he will in all probability function badly. This is particularly true if his mother was a warm, supporting sort of person, and his wife is a frigid shrew. She, of course, may have many reasons for being like that, but it does not alter the fact that she is defeating her husband.

WHAT to do? If possible, she should try to put herself in her husband's place and try to understand his own picture of himself. And also try to realize the stresses he is subject to in the course of a day. Then she can help him.

I don't mean that she should reassure him in a rather abstracted way, as doting parents build up a precocious child. Nor that she should gushily keep telling him that he is wonderful all the time. Men can spot the phony act as easily as can a child.

I don't mean that she should flatter him—because flattery is a form of cynicism. It presumes that the person is rather a fool and that he can be persuaded to do things because he won't see through the pretense.

She should help him to see things as they are; but there is a time and a place for doing this. Women who nag are quite often telling the truth; but nagging is usually a presentation of the right facts at the wrong time.

She does not have to treat him as an invalid and think that he cannot pick himself up after a fall. But neither does she have to keep pushing him down! She knows that as a man, *he* will have to "suffer the slings and arrows of outrageous fortune" and learn how to master his difficulties.

She can:

1. Try to live on his income without constantly complaining. She can remember he is doing the best he can.

2. Agree on disciplinary problems in the home and avoid countermanding his wishes.

3. Talk over his problems with him and understand the working world he lives in.

4. Try to see eye to eye with him on the major issues of life—faith, friendships, loyalties.

5. Encourage him.

6. Love him.

Her reward will be a husband whose energy is not steadily drained by emotional crises, and their consequent wear and tear on the body. A man who is freed from the pinpricks of the Dagwood world can throw himself wholeheartedly into his work. And he will also be the man who can't wait to get home because he will feel happy there, sustained, constantly renewed and ready to meet all the tomorrows.

COPYRIGHT: KING FEATURES SYNDICATE 1955

©Reprinted with special permission of King Features Syndicate.

☞ A GOOD WIFE'S GUIDE ☜

- ✔ Have dinner ready. Plan ahead even the night before, to have a delicious meal ready, on time for his return. This is a way of letting him know you have been thinking about him and are concerned about his needs. Most men are hungry when they come home and the prospect of a good meal (especially his favourite dish) is part of the warm welcome needed.

- ✔ Prepare yourself. Take 15 minutes to rest so you'll be refreshed when he arrives. Touch up your make-up, put a ribbon in your hair and be fresh looking. He has just been with a lot of work weary people.

- ✔ Be a little gay and a little more interesting for him. His boring day may need a lift and one of your duties is to provide it.

- ✔ Clear away the clutter. Make one last trip through the main part of the house just before your husband arrives.

- ✔ Gather up schoolbooks, toys, paper, etc. and then run a duster over the tables.

- ✔ Over the cooler months of the year you should prepare and light a fire for him to unwind by. Your husband will feel he has reached a haven of rest and order, and it will give you a lift too. After all, catering to his comfort will provide you with immense personal satisfaction.

- ✔ Prepare the children. Take a few minutes to wash the children's hands and faces (if they are small), comb their hair and if necessary change their clothes. They are little treasures and he would like to see them playing the part. Minimize all noise. At the time of his arrival, eliminate all noise of the washer, dryer or vacuum.
Try to encourage the children to remain quiet.

- ✔ Be happy to see him.

- ✔ Greet him with a warm smile and show sincerity in your desire to please him.

- ✔ Listen to him. You may have a dozen important things to tell him, but the moment of his arrival is not the time. Let him talk first - remember, his topics of conversation are more important than yours.

- ✔ Make the evening his. Never complain if he comes home late or goes out to dinner, or other places of entertainment without you. Instead try to understand his world of strain and pressure and his very real need to be at home and relax.

- ✔ Your goal: Try to make sure your home is a place of peace, order and tranquility where your husband can renew himself in body and spirit.

- ✔ Don't greet him with complaints and problems.

- ✔ Don't complain if he's late home for dinner or even if he stays out all night. Count this as minor compared to what he might have gone through that day.

- ✔ Make him comfortable. Have him lean back in a comfortable chair or have him lie down in the bedroom. Have a cool or warm drink ready for him.

- ✔ Arrange his pillow and offer to take off his shoes. Speak in a low soothing and pleasant voice.

- ✔ Don't ask him questions about his actions or question his judgement or integrity. Remember he is the master of the house and as such will always exercise his will with fairness and truthfulness. You have no right to question him.

- ✔ A good wife always knows her place.

Good Housekeeping Monthly, May 13, 1955, cited in an article titled "Women of '90s: You've come a long way... by Dale Anne Freed, *Toronto Star*, March 8, 1994.

GREEN DRAGON PRESS

The Role of "wife" in the Media

Lucille Ball was undoubtedly an icon of the 1950s. Born in 1911, Lucille became famous following a successful movie career, when her television show, with her husband Desi Arnaz, "I Love Lucy" skyrocketed to fame. Her success came as a result of hard work, commitment and intelligence. Her TV persona, however, was of a silly, forgetful woman who, although living life as a housewife, was waiting for the day she might break into her own career in show business. How could someone so capable and successful convincingly portray someone so irrational and scheming? One can give credit to her enormous talent as a comedic actor, but what exactly was Lucy portraying on her "I Love Lucy" show? Was this an image of the traditional 1950s housewife or was there something more to her image? Did people laugh because they recognized their own lives in her comedy or did Lucy allow the women of the 1950s a chance to ridicule the status quo of the day, recognizing that women might find fulfillment outside the home. The opposing views of two commentators, Joyce Millman and Anita Gates, writing in the *New York Times*, October 14, 2001, are summarized below.

Joyce Millman sees in the character of Lucy Ricardo a complex woman, envious, stubborn, undisciplined and imperfect, and suggests that it was these qualities that made her show "I Love Lucy" so enduringly hilarious and so relevant. Lucy wanted it all, family, fame, a part in her husband Ricky's movie, and admittance to an exclusive ladies club, a Paris frock and a movie star's autograph. Nearly every plan Lucy undertook was rooted in the desire to create a life of her own. She usually did get what she wanted, often fighting her husband's attitude of male superiority. Her sense of injustice might have been understood by the thousands of women who had played a significant role in the war economy yet were encouraged in the post-war period to play a supportive role to the men in their homes and workplace. These women, however, didn't feel entirely comfortable openly challenging these roles. Lucy did it for them. Lucy was a woman aggressively pursuing her greatest ambitions. But because she did so in a clown like manner, her challenges seemed more acceptable. Lucy used her clowning to assert her confidence in herself. Her schemes were creative, logical and courageous and often had funny but successful outcomes. She may have been delusional about her talents and abilities, but she was always clever and tenacious. She was a radical and powerful figure who became an important television icon for women desperate to liberate themselves from the demanding, conservative attitudes of the day.

Anita Gates, on the other hand, writes that despite the fact that by 1951, 25% of American women were in the workforce, Lucy Ricardo did her part in making the stereotype subservient housewife not only real but also rather adorable. Lucy taught the 1950s women about life in New York, marriage and gender roles. But while Gates agrees that the show was extremely funny, she doesn't think Lucy offered much of a role model. Lucy did not succeed at anything, losing airline tickets, overdosing on seasickness pills, sending her passport ahead in her luggage, failing to maintain part-time jobs, and even demonstrating a lack of artistic talent whenever allowed a small part in a show. Lucy finally landed a movie studio contract but changed her mind in the end. Isn't that typical of a woman? Ricky regularly shouted at her inability to balance the household budget and her schemes that ended up costing him money. He actually spanks her in one episode. And although the real Lucille Ball pulled Desilu Productions out of a financial slump, and proved more financially successful than her husband, she portrayed herself as an idiot with money. Perhaps in an effort to produce a successful show, the producers decided to capitalize on the uncertain labour qualifications of women. Gates feels this negative role model affected the first wave baby boomer girls, encouraged the status quo, and reflected the stereotype of women as manipulative.

- 1950 Bobbie Rosenfeld is named Outstanding Canadian Athlete of the half-century. Over the years, she competed in seven track and field disciplines, won tennis titles and starred in basketball and baseball. She is one of only three Canadians to have two Olympic track and field medals.

GREEN DRAGON PRESS

Gender Roles

In the 1950s *Seventeen* magazine sold a very specific message to teenage girls. The pressures and expectations of middle-class North America are overwhelmingly present in the advertisements and articles: *Seventeen* magazine prepared young women for the prospect of marriage. One of the most dramatic examples, in addition to ads for silverware and engagement rings, were the numerous sales pitches for hope chests. "Some special occasion is surely coming up soon - your birthday, graduation, engagement perhaps..." The message is clear.

Classic Modern in blond oak—a charming design for any room in the house. Self-lifting tray; rubbed and polished finish. Model #3025. Lane Table, #247. Chest price, $59⁹⁵*

Smart girls ask for the gift that gathers more gifts...

Seventeen magazine, May, 1954, 25.
Reprinted with permission:
Lane Furniture Industries.

• 1951 - Employees strike at Eaton's department stores.

GREEN DRAGON PRESS

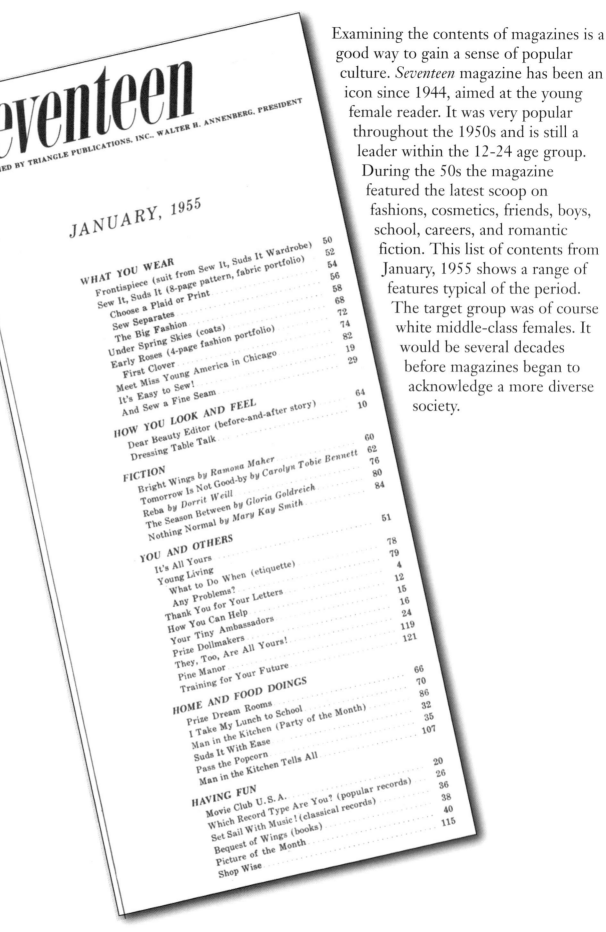

seventeen

PUBLISHED BY TRIANGLE PUBLICATIONS, INC., WALTER H. ANNENBERG, PRESIDENT

JANUARY, 1955

Examining the contents of magazines is a good way to gain a sense of popular culture. *Seventeen* magazine has been an icon since 1944, aimed at the young female reader. It was very popular throughout the 1950s and is still a leader within the 12-24 age group. During the 50s the magazine featured the latest scoop on fashions, cosmetics, friends, boys, school, careers, and romantic fiction. This list of contents from January, 1955 shows a range of features typical of the period. The target group was of course white middle-class females. It would be several decades before magazines began to acknowledge a more diverse society.

Seventeen, January 1955, 3. Reprinted by permission.

GREEN DRAGON PRESS

During the 1950s, a boy's future was also clearly defined. He was expected to marry and find a well-paying job to provide for his large family. This article (excerpt) provides insight into the mind of the adolescent boy in the 1950s.

The following excerpt from an article that appeared in the May 1954 issue of *Seventeen* is of particular interest because a young woman's future is being previewed by an adolescent boy through the looking glass of current statistics.

FROM A BOY'S POINT OF VIEW

BY PFC. PETER LEAVY

WABER

A Look at Tomorrow

Some facts on what your life may be like in your fast-approaching future

Seventeen magazine, May 1954, 20. Reprinted with permission.

The article outlines some of the key issues of the 1950s, including the impact of economics on the family, and the growth of suburbia.

Everybody dreams about the life He (or She) with whom he (or she) will someday share holy vows, wedding cake and blueprints for a little white house on a hill.

One day I began to wonder how the hazy, hopeful image of her future husband in many a girl's imagination stacks up against the hard reality she eventually meets at the end of the aisle. So just for fun I began to put together...an actual composite picture of the contemporary United States male, call him Andy, whom every young girl will someday call her own.

If you are a statistically typical girl and you marry a statistically typical guy, Old Prophet Peter can now tell you a lot about what your future holds in store...

You and Andy will be members of the youngest-marrying generation in American history...Andy will be twenty-two years old when he says you-know-what. You, believe it or not, will be only twenty... If this flabbergasts any grand-fatherly graybeard who slipped uninvited into my audience, it may appease him to know that you and Andy will be far better prepared for marriage than he was in his time. Both of you will have much longer and fuller educations than Granddad, and certainly his wife, could claim. As a result, your grasp of the exigencies of life will be clear-eyed, knowledgeable, firm...

What will husband Andy do for a living? Well, statistically, he won't have a "glamour" job in advertising, television, or radio; he won't be a farmer or a doctor or a lawyer. His paycheck will come from a manufacturing industry, a trade, or government work. These three occupations account for most of the country's breadwinners.

GREEN DRAGON PRESS

You, too, will earn your keep for a couple of years after you are married. But as soon as your family begins to expand you'll cover your typewriter and call it a day. From there on in, statistically anyhow, your sole occupation will be that of housewife and mother. Andy will be your only employer...

Before the arrival of your offspring, you as Andy's wife will be an out-and-out financial asset. This is another reason you can anticipate an early plunge into the blue seas of married bliss without economic trepidation. If years of post-service study or professional training loom on Andy's horizon, the odds are good that you, as a breadwinner, will help work Andy's way through college or it's equivalent.

And you will give your help with the best will in the world. The marriage picture in Andy's mind and yours is of a partnership, not a patriarchy. The rapid rise of joint checking accounts during the last twenty years is circumstantial evidence of how genuinely husbands and wives today are sharing their wealth as well as their lives...

How big a family will you and Andy have? The Census Bureau tell us the probabilities indicate that your handsome brood will well outnumber your parents' earlier-period little one. The "only child" seems to belong to history. In ten years the number of fourth children in families jumped 160% beyond the 1940 figure! Since 1950, four-children families have taken another leap...

In whatever part of the country you and Andy call home, you will rent, not own, your first dwelling. But you'll only be biding your time until your bank account indicates "buy". At that point you'll probably settle down in a ranch house in Suburbia, a commuting community about forty-five minutes by train from the fairly big city in which Andy will work...Big families and big incomes are apparently causing the young-marrieds of our generation to desert the cities as quickly as they can find a piece of out-of-town property and the means to pay for it.

This, then, is a statistical forecast of your future with Andy, the fellow you'll meet down front as the music stops. From my point of view, both of you deserve congratulations. It looks like a very solid match.

GREEN DRAGON PRESS

EILEEN DARBY/GRAPHIC HOUSE

Indianapolis high-school students who brain-stormed answers to problem of teen-age popularity could joke about it, but many answers were thoughtful and sober. Moderator-author Jhan Robbins sits third left

by JHAN and JUNE ROBBINS

A lively group of high-school students

proves that this is a problem

they are well equipped to solve for themselves

teen-agers tell
HOW TO BE POPULAR

How to make yourself popular is a problem for all ages, but it can be a particularly disturbing one for teen-agers. "A fifteen-year-old who feels that he hasn't any friends suffers day-to-day emotional agony most grownups mercifully have forgotten," a teacher we know once observed. Abundant advice on the subject for both young and old is available from psychologists, educators, sociologists and physicians. It is seldom followed. Less often does it work.

For the most part, as far as youngsters are concerned, adult viewpoints are too remote or too complicated.

Can teen-agers themselves think the problem through? Can those who are already popular help others? Many high-school boys and girls enjoy harmonious relations with their families. They have secured the trust and approval of their school and community, the ready welcome of good friends of both sexes. Do they know how they do it? McCALL'S decided to use "brain-storming"—a new technique for creative thinking—to find out. A group of students at the handsome new $3,000,000 North Central High School on the outskirts of Indianapolis, Indiana, agreed to help.

Attractive and lively-minded—eight boys and nine girls ranging in age from fifteen to seventeen—they all were good students and rated "very popular" by both teachers and classmates. There were athletes, class officers, nature hobbyists, science hobbyists (one amateur rocketeer: one bandaged hand), and were planning to be teachers, nurses, businessmen, engineers, actresses, pilots and politicians. They took eagerly to the idea of brain-storming.

Brain-storming is a system of producing a great many ideas in a hurry. Members of the group are encouraged to spout out whatever thoughts come into their heads—good or bad, new or old — on the subject under discussion. "In this session," the Indianapolis students were told, "we're going to think about popularity. What are the characteristics of popular boys and girls? Why are they well liked? What can a person your age do to widen friendships and become trusted and respected by others? What original ideas can you offer?"

The students were cautioned that nobody's idea was right or wrong and no criticism of ideas would be tolerated. Don't be afraid to come up with a zany suggestion — the more ideas, the better — combinations of two or more may be best of all.

College-educated adults, brain-storming in business and industry, have produced as many as 400 ideas in a single session. The average brain-storming produces 200. This delightful group of high-school youngsters suggested 715. They hurled them out, one right after another, at a furious clip, until they ran out of breath and the moderator and stenotyper pleaded exhaustion.

Of course, as in every brain-storming session, many were partly duplicated, some were off the track, some were too obvious, others too personal to be of general use. So we pruned the list down to 142 offering sound, if sometimes humorous, advice. We believe they will be of help to anyone of any age who needs to form new social habits in order to get along better with his family, his friends and the community he lives in.

1 Let the kids you are with know you like them.
2 Record your laugh on tape and play it back. If it sounds awful, change it.
3 Don't monopolize the conversation.
4 Don't have one set of manners for the people you want to make time with and another set for everybody else.
5 Even if you dress sloppily, look clean.
6 Don't become a twosome hermit. Even if you are going steady, continue to see your other friends.
7 If you were going steady but suddenly broke up, don't go around cutting down your former date.
8 Be friendly. Smile at people even if you don't have a reason to.
9 Give yourself a snappy new nickname like "Smoke," "Speed" or "Atom."
10 Think of ways to make others feel important.
11 Don't carry grudges. If you get mad, get over it quickly.
12 Admit your mistakes cheerfully by saying, "Boy, when I goof, it's a real beaut!"
13 Be willing to try longhair things like a museum, a concert or a ballet.
14 Don't tell long-drawn-out or involved jokes.
15 Don't be the person who's pointed out for having a big collection of dirty jokes.
16 Visit people in the hospital, but not so often that you become a pest.
17 Don't steal their fruit.
18 Keep your nose out of the upper atmosphere.
19 Don't chew gum on dates.

Continued on page 54

Teenage culture in the 1950s was of great interest and concern to adults, particularly parents. In the August 1958 issue of *McCall's*, the following article provided the "older generation" with advice for teenagers on improving their social life. The article is based on interviews with a panel of teenagers, therefore the list of "142 ways to be popular" is itself a wonderful insight into the values and concerns of middle-class North American adolescents. Advice targeting "girls", and "especially boys" offers added insight into sex-role stereotyping of 1950s.

How to be popular

Continued from page 52

20 Don't blow bubble gum.
21 Don't crack your knuckles.
22 Don't burn people down just for a laugh.
23 Listen politely to the other kids' ideas even if they sound real crazy.
24 Don't pet just because you're too dull to think of anything else to do.
25 Work on community projects—Cancer Fund, Red Cross or Y.M.C.A. Offer to help your minister.
26 Don't make a great show of your superiority even if you know you're superior.
27 Learn to duck a fight without losing your dignity.
28 Be a good loser.
29 Be a good winner.
30 Don't be a constant moocher.
31 Don't lend money too easily.
32 Don't be a night owl—it produces circles under your eyes and zeros on your exams.
33 Keep attending games even when your team is losing.
34 Don't boo the umpire or referee.
35 Don't always take snap courses.
36 Don't be a teacher-polisher.
37 Learn to play a musical instrument.
38 Don't think a car is the most important thing in the world.
39 Have friends from other schools.
40 Show appreciation for presents even if you had hoped for something else.
41 Don't spend too much on your girl friend's or boy friend's presents.
42 Don't be afraid to start a fad—someone has to.
43 Keep your fingernails trimmed.
44 Find out beforehand what your date is going to be wearing and dress accordingly.
45 Think up unusual parties like going to the county fair, or picknicking after swimming, or having a hobo party.
46 Don't drink.
47 Don't take foolish dares.
48 Shake hands with people when you are introduced to them. Not a "fish" handshake, but a nice firm one.
49 Never call older people by their first names unless they ask you to.
50 Don't tell the same joke or story over and over.
51 Act as if you are having a good time even if you're not.
52 Don't laugh at someone trying to learn to water ski.
53 Discuss other people's religions open-mindedly.
54 Don't exclude someone from your social group because of prejudice.
55 Let your friends know that in an emergency they can depend on you.
56 Don't take an apple to your teacher; take a pizza or a knockwurst.
57 Learn to write legibly.
58 Don't join school clubs just to get your picture in the yearbook.
59 Don't confide in everyone.
60 Make a list of your bad habits and try to overcome them.
61 Even if you're not as popular as you'd like, don't be a bookworm all the time.
62 Don't use big words unless you know what they mean.
63 Don't be a name dropper.
64 Always carry some food or candy with you—people will flock around you.

Especially for Girls

65 Learn all about sports and cars.
66 Know how to follow when you dance.
67 If he apologizes for his dancing, compliment him on his natural rhythm.
68 Don't break a date once you've made it—even if someone you like better asks you.
69 Don't pile on make-up an inch thick. Boys are scared of all that junk.
70 Have a wide circle of girl friends, not just one or two.
71 On a date don't yak all the time.
72 Don't suspect the boy of being up to no good if he runs out of gas—give him the benefit of the doubt unless it happens all the time.
73 If dancing with one boy, don't be looking around trying to find another.
74 Go home with the date you came with.
75 If you are fond of an egghead, ask him to help you with your homework.
76 If you are the "A" student, offer to help him with his homework.
77 Wait for the boy to get around to open the car door. If you expect good manners, you'll get them.
78 Ask your boy friend's mother if you can help her.
79 Offer your services as water boy to the football team.
80 Be the first one to wear the new hairdos.
81 Don't wear too tight clothing.
82 Don't comb your hair in class.
83 Develop a perfume that smells of ham and eggs to wear in the morning. The boys will love it.
84 Don't invite your boy friends over without permission when you are baby-sitting.
85 Don't brag about your date last night.
86 Don't go on crazy fad diets.
87 Start a charm class for shy boys and then date your best pupils.

Especially for Boys

88 Drive sensibly. The girl's parents will like it—and they can help you.
89 Avoid loud, boisterous language. Don't get in the habit of swearing or calling everybody a jerk.
90 Don't lead a girl on to think you like her best if you don't.
91 Learn how to dance well. It's not sissy to take lessons.
92 Stand up when your girl's parents come into the room.
93 Always have the girl home at the time she says.
94 Don't brag about girls you have gone with.
95 Don't gossip about girls you are going with now.
96 On a date don't be too stingy with your money—but don't be too extravagant either.
97 Don't take her Dutch treat all the time.
98 Tell her you like her dress.
99 Paint your car purple or bright red or yellow.
100 Get a sports jacket to match it.
101 Whistle at girls, but be different—whistle symphonies.
102 Make the best grades you possibly can—girls are impressed by men with brains.
103 Build a rocket and take your date with you. Who cares if it never gets off the ground?
104 Let the girls know you have a savings account.
105 Don't always ask what she wants to do—girls like fellows with initiative.
106 If your girl is on a diet, don't eat a chocolate sundae in front of her.
107 Get a tandem bike and ride your girl to school on it.
108 Spread the rumor you are a woman hater. It will work in reverse.
109 When riding in a friend's car offer to pay for the gas.
110 Don't roll down all the car windows so it will mess up the girl's hair.
111 Don't eat too much at your friends' houses.
112 If your girl friend wears braces on her teeth, get a set for yourself.
113 Learn to quote some poetry—girls are impressed by it.
114 Get a job this summer as a life guard at a girls' camp.

How To Be Popular With Your Parents

115 Don't leave the family car with an empty gas tank.
116 Improve your manners.
117 Confide in your parents. Let them know you trust them.
118 Let them know what you are doing.
119 Don't hog the phone.
120 Don't take advantage of charge accounts.
121 Try jokes out on parents.
122 Be proud of them—introduce them to your friends.
123 Don't make them sit up worrying about what time you will be home.
124 Keep your room clean.
125 Don't change clothes all the time unless you do the washing.
126 Offer to baby-sit with younger brothers and sisters.
127 Bring your parents into your sports and other activities.
128 Introduce them to your friends' parents.
129 Always remember their birthdays and anniversaries.
130 Be interested in the things your father does at his job.
131 Don't do homework in the middle of the kitchen.
132 Don't leave food all over the house.
133 Try to understand the kind of music your parents like.
134 Don't play them out of the house with one particular record.
135 If you have done something wrong, be ready to take your punishment. Don't lie your way out of it.
136 Don't make fun of the older generation.
137 Be tolerant if your parents don't understand some things. Take time to explain it.
138 Double-date with them once in a while.
139 Compliment your mother's meals.
140 Don't get embarrassed when your mother brings out your baby pictures.
141 When your father is within hearing, tell your friends what a fine golfer he is.
142 Indian wrestle your father and let him win.   THE END

Who Was on the Panel

Moderator: *Jhan Robbins*
Seniors: *Larry Coffey, Chuck Harrison, Marcia Maher, George Quigley, Mary Lou Stark, Marilyn Wilmore*
Juniors: *Nancy Colville, Judy Lybrook, Pat Merriman, Tim Steele, Chip Wilhoite, Joe Wood*
Sophomores: *Sue Ann Barlet, Jim Birr, Tamra Edgington, Janet Graves, Brad Waltman*

McCall's, August 1958.

GREEN DRAGON PRESS

The following excerpt from *Canadian Home Journal*, April 1955 offers a unique perspective in the form of a father's advice for his daughter and her future role as a wife and mother. Although it is still a given that the young woman will fulfill this role, how she will accomplish this appears to be questioned by her father who hopes she may have a more "enlightened" experience with a man who will regard her as an "equal partner."

Letter To My Daughter

The world is full of strange men and most of them will want to marry you. I hope you'll be careful. For every girl ruined by a man not marrying her, there are a thousand ruined by the men who do. Villains aren't as easy to spot as they used to be. They once had pointed moustaches, polished manners and a way of getting girls to big cities. They were called snakes. Now they have butch haircuts, bad manners, a way of getting girls into heavily mortgaged bungalows and are often called He men.

He men are supposed to be the opposite of effeminate men. They aren't. He men and effeminate men are both bothered by the same thing: they don't like women. A He man also recognized a third sex- his wife. He sees things simply. Men play poker, have stag evenings, talk politics, operate businesses, run the country, drive cars, laugh at women's hats, understand baseball, fishing, dirty jokes and war. Women wear fancy clothes or none at all, should never be more than twenty-four years of age, are always available and inhabit dreams, sales conventions and pin-up pictures. Wives are wonderful little women. They cook meals, make beds, encourage He men, have no brains, say silly things and can make a housekeeping-allowance go a long way. He men respect them, kiss them twice a day, and forget them from wedding anniversary to wedding anniversary unless they want some laundry done.

The wife who was a sort of happy slave went out with the bison and high-button boots, although there are plenty of women who haven't heard the news yet. I hope you, my daughter, will be more enlightened.

There may have been a day when it was reasonable for a woman to be a household drudge because her husband was too busy clearing the land and doing other things she couldn't do. But the stumps are all pulled up now - and almost every modern task a woman can do as well as a man, and often better. She shouldn't do any more than half of the dirty jobs.

Marriage should be a partnership. There must be two senior partners, sharing the same responsibility, the same salary and the same dull chores. I shall maintain with my last breath that the picture of a man doing the dishes should no longer be funny. It's a serious fact that he belongs at a sink just as much as a woman. Men have proved over and over again that they make wonderful cooks. There's no reason why it should be kept as a party act...

GREEN DRAGON PRESS

Women and work in the 50s

This Bell Telephone ad from 1954, reveals job opportunities available for women at this time. After the war, women were expected to make way for the returning veterans, and therefore had few job options. Bell Telephone had developed dial-up services in the 1920s, and female operators were trained to use this new technology. Women continued as technicians during the war, and continued to find employment with Bell Telephone throughout the 1950s.

THE BUSINESS WORLD

Whether you're the shy, quiet type or ready to begin a career with all the confidence in the world, you'll be looking for "a good place to work" when you finish school.

At the Bell—good pay, a short work-week, and bright, pleasant offices are some of the reasons why girls come to see us about positions. Opportunities for advancement, friendly fellow-workers, and the many other benefits and activities offered our employees are additional reasons why they come and stay!

An organization like ours needs bright, ambitious people to help us grow and succeed—that's why so many girls right out of school find satisfying, rewarding jobs at the Bell.

THE BELL TELEPHONE COMPANY OF CANADA

Reprinted by permission.

- 1953 - Marianna Beauchamp Jodoin is the first francophone woman to be appointed to the Senate.

GREEN DRAGON PRESS

take a fashion tip from a telephone teen

Pat dabs a bit of cologne over her pincurls—it helps her hair dry faster and leaves a sweet fragrance. Like all smart girls, she knows good grooming is important in her job.

Pat's a service representative and talks to telephone customers in the business office. She started as a clerk when she finished school. Her pleasant voice and cheerful manner have helped her advance, and her pay check has kept growing, too.

Take a tip from Pat—with many different jobs at the telephone company, there may be one waiting for you!

BELL TELEPHONE SYSTEM

a good place to work

43

The actual message of the following advertisement is cleverly disguised. What appears to be an ad for cosmetics is in reality an ad for employment with Bell Telephone. Although women worked in the 1950s, it was important to maintain a veneer of femininity. As demonstrated by the prospective Bell employee of this ad, "like all smart girls, she knows good grooming is important in her job."

Reprinted by permission.

• 1954 - Marilyn Bell, a sixteen year-old high school student, becomes the first person to swim across Lake Ontario.

129

Immigrant women played a significant role in the post war economy. They led demanding active lives in their roles in both the paid labour market and their unpaid activities at home. These women faced major challenges in the urban industrial workforce as they struggled to ensure the well being of their families.

Women of colour and immigrant women were mostly segregated into low paying domestic or restaurant work. The discrimination experienced by Chinese and Japanese Canadian women during the war continued long afterward.

"In those days it was difficult to find a job because a lot of places weren't hiring Chinese. Even if you had the training to be a secretary, and you applied for a job in a bank or office, it was very hard especially in a small town like Nanaimo. It was funny how you sort of just accepted it - not being hired because you're Chinese. It was almost futile to really fight for a job when you knew you would never get it anyway. So you either opened your own business or went for higher education. But in those days, very few women went to university. There weren't any Chinese doctors, lawyers and insurance companies - not like today. That's why a lot of Chinese families had their own businesses - restaurants, groceries, laundries, or something like that - create your own employment, in other words.

I worked in the family business. It took up a lot of my time when I was young. Then when I was in my mid-twenties, I decided that I should have a life of my own so I moved to Vancouver in 1954."

Lil Lee, *Jin Guo: Voices of Chinese Canadian Women*, 146.

Between 1951 and 1961 over 250,000 Italian immigrants settled in Canada. Women and children comprised a substantial proportion of this influx of immigrants.

"On Thursday, 16 November 1956, Maria R. and her daughter arrived in Toronto from her peasant farm in Abruzzi. She was met at Union Station by her husband Eneo, who had left a year previously for work in Toronto. After eating dinner with relatives, she was ushered into her new home-a basement flat in a Calabrian's house. Next day, Maria and Eneo, who took the day off from his Royal York Hotel janitorial job, went to Honest Ed's discount department store to shop for household necessities, including an espresso coffee maker and pots for cooking spaghetti. To Maria's delight, next morning the Santa Claus Parade passed by their Dupont Street home. At seven o'clock Monday morning, Maria went directly to work at a nearby laundry where a sister-in-law had secured her a job as a steam press operator at $37 dollars a week. For 20 years Maria worked at many such low-skilled jobs-sewing, cooking, tending a grocery store, and as a cashier-until 1976 when she finally withdrew from the workforce to care for her dying husband."

Excerpt from "Contadina to Worker: Southern Italian Immigrant Working Women in Toronto, *1947-1962*" by Franca Iacovetta, in *Rethinking Canada: The Promise of Women's History*, Veronica Strong-Boag and Anita Clair Fellman eds. 339.

GREEN DRAGON PRESS

Some immigrant women became entrepreneurs. Loreta Chiola and Elisa Fasciani set up their own fresh pasta shop and restaurant, the E & L Pasta Centre.

"Maria Georgekakos and her husband worked and saved to build a family restaurant business.

Maria Georgekakos arrived in Halifax from Greece on December 9, 1958. She came to Canada to marry her fiancé who was already in Canada.

According to the immigration regulations at the time, anyone who came to Canada as a sponsored immigrant intending to get married had to do so within a month. She and her fiancé were married on December 25th because he was working in a restaurant at that time, and Christmas day was the only day the restaurant was closed. They were very poor, and her fiancé could not afford to take another day off to get married. So they spoke to the priest, and the priest said, "Okay, Gus, I'll marry you and Maria and another couple that day." Maria has no trouble remembering the date of her wedding anniversary.

When she arrived, all she could say in English was "good morning." Nevertheless, she found work in a restaurant the Monday after her wedding. Everyone there spoke English; she felt lost and cried when she got home because she couldn't understand anything. She worked behind the counter and helped the waitresses by clearing the tables, or sometimes she served tea or coffee.

She and her husband lived in a big house with a number of other Greek people. Each person had a room - not an apartment - because the rent was cheaper with a lot of people sharing the house. Maria's husband only made $22 a week for seven days' work, ten or eleven hours each day. Maria made $16.75 a week, and she also had to work seven days a week. It was a tiring job; she was not allowed to sit down, even if there were no customers in the restaurant.

She vowed that:

If I have a little bit of money and buy a business, I don't want to treat the employees like they treated me. I want the people who work for me to work with me - we'll all be in this together.

After about a year in the restaurant, she got a job at a dry cleaners. She only had to work six days a week there. She liked to have her Sundays off.

Eventually the time came when she and her husband bought a little business, a corner snack bar. They looked after the customers well, and the business started to grow.

We saved all our money, we never spent anything foolishly. We thought about even spending one dollar.

GREEN DRAGON PRESS

If we had a good reason, we spent it; if not, we didn't. We worked long, long hours. My husband opened the restaurant at 6:00 a.m. and went home at 2:00 in the afternoon. Then he had a nap and went back at 6:00 and stayed until about one or two o'clock in the morning. I went in for dinner and stayed until closing time. I also had to look after my two children, but luckily my niece and my mother helped. Still, I had to prepare everything for my mother and the children because my mother didn't understand anything in this country. I missed going to church, but I didn't have the time to go. Sunday was our busiest day. People liked to go out for dinner after church.

Maria learned about the restaurant business from working in someone else's restaurant and in her own. In Greece she seldom went to a restaurant - just on Sunday afternoons to have some ouzo and octopus. In Canada, her husband learned how to cook, and she learned how to wait on tables, to make banana splits, banana royale sundaes, how to keep the place clean, and generally how to manage the business.

She learned English from the customers. She couldn't go to English classes because she didn't have the time nor the money.

If you're working twelve to fifteen hours a day, you don't have time to go to school. There wouldn't be any time to study, and I don't like to go and have to leave my books in a corner and not study them. I started to learn English with the customers because there weren't any Greek customers. For example, one time someone asked me for crackers, and I gave him a saucer. He said, 'No, Maria, this is a saucer; those are crackers.' So they taught me English. Someone else taught me how to type my menus. She helped me buy a typewriter, gave me a couple of lessons, and then I started to type my menus. Sometimes if I couldn't spell the words, I'd ask a customer, and then I'd write them on the typewriter."

I've Something to Tell You: Stories of Immigrant Women, by Joyce Scane, 53.

Equal Pay for Work of Equal Value

Today many people take for granted the principle of equal pay for work of equal value. In the 1950s though, female employees frequently received a lot less money then men for doing exactly the same job.

To correct this injustice, Margaret Hyndman, president of the Business and Professional Women's Clubs, led the fight to achieve pay equality. Margaret decided her first target would be the Ontario government, then led by Conservative Premier Leslie Frost. Frost was afraid that equal pay legislation would hurt the province's economy. Still, he asked Hyndman to prepare a brief on the issue and draft a bill.

Hyndman immediately sprang into action. In less than a week she and other members of her group had lobbied every member of the Ontario legislature, drafted the bill, and tabled it. On March 8, 1951, the Female Employees Fair Remuneration Act became law in Ontario. By the end of the end of the decade every provincial legislature with the exception of Quebec and Newfoundland had passed similar legislation. On January 10, 1956, the federal government passed pay equity legislation for women working for the government, its agencies or Crown corporations.

Women Changing Canada, Jan Coomber & Rosemary Evans, 44.

GREEN DRAGON PRESS

Notable Women

Eileen Tallman Sufrin

Eileen Tallman Sufrin was a pioneer labour leader. Born in Montreal, she moved to Toronto where she graduated from Vaughan Road Collegiate. Although a good student, she did not go to university, and despite the scarcity of jobs during the Depression, she found work and became aware of the poor working conditions of that period, as well as the lower wages and poorer opportunities for women. She joined a group of young activists who were in the forefront of the Co-operative Commonwealth Youth Movement, an arm of the CCF (later to become the NDP). In the course of her busy life Sufrin organized bank clerks and headed the first strike of bank employees in Montreal in 1941. The following year in Toronto she took part in a campaign led by Steelworkers at John Inglis where half of the 7,000 workers were women. Before she retired, Sufrin spent 19 years organizing women in union movements in Ontario and British Columbia and in the course of her career unionized 15,000 women workers. For Sufrin, despite its ultimate failure, the drive to unionize Eaton's was the highlight of her labour career and she wrote an account of it, *The Eaton Drive: the campaign to organize Canada's largest department store 1948-1952* (Fitzhenry & Whiteside, 1982.) It is a story of one of the longest organizing campaigns recorded in Canadian labour history, and is still used as a teaching tool for union organizers. Eileen Tallman Sufrin pursued her career as a social activist until her death in 1999, aged 86, in White Rock, BC.

For an expanded biography of Eileen Tallman Sufrin go to www.coolwomen.org

Helen Creighton OC

Helen Creighton received a music diploma from McGill University in 1915 and graduated from Halifax Ladies' College in 1916. She worked briefly as a social worker, journalist and children's radio host in Halifax, and as a teacher in Mexico.

While researching for a project on pirates she interviewed Nova Scotians who knew songs and stories from pirate days. She began to collect and transcribe songs and stories around the province, often travelling on foot or by boat to reach isolated communities, pushing her reed organ in a wheelbarrow. In the beginning she recorded on wax cylinders, later switching to acetate discs and tape. Helen collected songs and stories for the Library of Congress in 1943-44 and 1948 and for the National Museum of Canada from 1947 to 1967.

Her collection of over 4,000 songs and stories in English, French, Gaelic, Micmac and German includes some from the 13th and 15th centuries. Many of the songs have been commercially recorded, including Farewell to Nova Scotia. Helen Creighton also published a number of anthologies of stories and songs. She was a Member of the Order of Canada, a recipient of six honorary doctorates and the Canadian Music Council Medal. She died in 1989, age 90.

Dr. Irene Ayako Uchida OC

Born in Vancouver BC in 1917, Irene Uchida was one of many Japanese Canadian citizens who were uprooted from their homes in BC during World War II. She was moved from her home to Christina Lake and later was the principal of the largest Japanese camp school in the Kootenay Mountains. After the end of the war, she moved to Toronto to study at the University of Toronto. She graduated in 1946, and then earned a PhD in Zoology. She began her genetics research career at the Hospital for Sick Children in Toronto looking at the connection between radiation and Downs Syndrome. She is widely respected for her work in cytogenetics (the study of chromosomes in cells).

- 1957 - Prime Minister John Diefenbaker named the first woman into the federal cabinet, appointing Ellen Fairclough secretary of state.

GREEN DRAGON PRESS

Activities
1950 – 1959

"SOMEONE'S WAITING SOMEWHERE", GENDER ROLES, SEVENTEEN, "A LOOK AT TOMORROW."

Obtain a copy of a current Seventeen magazine. Compare and contrast the message sent to young women of today, and in the 1950s, looking specifically at: Advertisements (what products and images sell), and topics of articles.

"HOW TO BE POPULAR"

How did McCall's magazine compile this advice for teens? Is this a reliable source? Based on the advice, create a profile of the "ideal" guy and girl of the 1950s. Create a list of advice in the same format for the new millennium. How does your advice differ from that published in the 1950s?

THE GOOD WIFE'S GUIDE

Compare this guide, p119 to HINTS FOR BRIDES in chapter one, p8. How are they similar, how are they different?

POSTWAR EXPERIENCES

How did the post-war experiences of Canadian women in the 1920s and the 1950s differ?

WOMEN AND WORK

Read the narratives presented on pages 130, 131, 132, and 150. Write a journal entry imagining you are a women newly immigrated to Canada from _____ in the 1950's. Imagine the struggles and emotions that these women experienced in their day-to-day lives.

You are an investigative journalist. In the 1950s much emphasis was placed on woman's role in the home. Yet as these stories reveal, many women worked out of necessity. Write a short article that explores this reality.

Resources

Anderson, Doris. *Rebel daughter: an autobiography,* Toronto: Key Porter Books, 1966. Armstrong, Pat & Hugh Armstrong. *The Double Ghetto: Canadian Women and Their Segregated Work,* Toronto: McClelland & Stewart, 1978.
Iacovetta, Franca, ed. *A Nation of Immigrants: Women, Workers and Communities in Canadian History,* Toronto: University of Toronto Press, 1998.
Peiss, Katy. *Hope in a Jar: The Making of America's Beauty Culture,* NY: Henry Holt & Co., 1998.
Scane, Joyce. *I've Something to Tell You: Stories of Immigrant Women,* Toronto: Green Dragon Press, 1998.

Videos:
A New Life & *Starting Over. Immigrant Women in Canada:* Green Dragon Press.
Too Dirty for a Woman & *Working Mothers:* National Film Board.

GREEN DRAGON PRESS

1960 – 1969

A decade of change

Photo: *Robert Staton*

Milestones

- **1966** - The Committee for the Equality of Women in Canada (CEWEC) is founded in Toronto to "pursue the rights of women in Canada." The Committee immediately begins a campaign for a Royal Commission on the Status of Women.

  Representatives of women's groups in Quebec come together to form a new coalition, La Fédération des Femmes du Quebec (FFQ).

- **1967** - CEWEC founder Laura Sabia threatens a march of 2,000,000 women to Ottawa if a Royal Commission is not established to inquire into the status of women in Canada. Sabia later admitted she was bluffing.

  The Royal Commission on the Status of Women is established by the Liberal Government of Lester Pearson. Former journalist Florence Bird chairs the seven-member Commission, five of whose members are women. The Commission holds hearings in 14 communities in all ten provinces, meets 890 witnesses, and receives 468 briefs and 1,000 letters.

- **1968** - Passage of a comprehensive divorce law by the federal government, enabling many women who had been abused or abandoned to file for divorce.

  The McGill Student Society publishes The Birth Control Handbook, though the distribution of information on birth control is illegal in Canada. It becomes an underground bestseller and is later translated into French.

- **1969** - On June 27, 1969, a Liberal government passes a bill which legalizes contraception. It became law on July 1, 1969. The bill also reformed the law on abortion, allowing it if approved by a hospital medical committee as necessary to preserve the pregnant woman's life or health.

GREEN DRAGON PRESS

1960-1969 Introduction

"At the altar the future splinters furiously into a spectrum of split-level houses filled with appliances, rosy-cheeked children and boyishly handsome husbands. At a time in history when a girl, according to the latest predictions, can live to be a hundred years old, she really only has plans for the first forty years of her life....We're trapping them in a marriage marathon."

From an editorial by Doris Anderson, Chatelaine, July 1962.

In 1960 the Canadian parliament passed a Canadian Bill of Rights and this acted as a springboard for other bills such as the Human Rights Code and the Human Rights Commission. Immigration reforms in the 1960s removed the barriers for non-British citizens to be welcomed into the country and an increase in immigration from non-traditional countries brought a greater diversity to the Canadian population. Major changes were made in the infrastructure in medical health insurance, pension plans, multiculturalism and bilingualism. The 1960s witnessed many political and citizen movements. The civil and human rights movements, counterculture youth movements, the anti-war and women's movement, took active open approaches to change. Canada celebrated its Centennial year with Expo '67, a new national anthem and flag, and The Royal Commission on the Status of Women was established.

Prime Minister Pierre Trudeau spoke of a "just society" and the response was a demand for equity on all fronts. The late 1960s saw the birth of the women's liberation movement. Women gathered across the country to mobilize support for women's rights, service and equal pay. The decade witnessed important amendments to the criminal code dealing with abortion, the sale of contraceptives, homosexuality and divorce.

It also saw the formation of national women's organizations such as the Voice of Women (VOW) that opposed violence and war. Women's groups demanded greater status and control by women of their lives.

There was a rebirth of feminism. Many middle-class women, feeling frustrated and trapped in their isolated suburban bungalows and split-levels began to meet together to discuss their concerns. Sparked by the popular book, *The Feminine Mystique*, by Betty Friedan, thousands of women challenged the stereotypical roles, which they had unquestioningly accepted in the 1950s. Group discussions and consciousness-raising sessions spread like wildfire. Women who had honed their organizing skills in parent-teacher and church groups put these skills to use in the wider community, turning their concerns into action by providing health care services, opening health centres, day care centres and shelters for abused women.

They opened rape crisis centres, and formed self-help groups. Women fought for equal pay for equal work, paid maternity leave, equity in the workplace, elimination of sexual harassment and sexual exploitation. They wrote feminist books and published feminist magazines and campaigned for greater political and legal status. In 1966, la Fédération des

GREEN DRAGON PRESS

Fémmes du Québec (FFQ) was created. Women's organizations in the universities, in the workplaces and at home fought for recognition, greater equality and freedom. Other women though, fought to preserve the traditions of the past and the decade witnessed a division between women fighting for a new identity and those clinging to established roles.

Activist Kay MacPherson OC, one of the founders of Voice of Women, at a meeting with Marc Lalonde, date unknown. Photo courtesy Moira Armour.

GREEN DRAGON PRESS

Social Change
Voice of Women

SPEAKING OUR PEACE

A FILM ABOUT WOMEN, PEACE AND POWER

WITH ROSALIE BERTELL, MARION DEWAR, MURIEL DUCKWORTH, URSULA M. FRANKLIN, DARLENE KEJU, MARGARET LAURENCE, SOLANGES VINCENT, KATHLEEN WALLACE-DEERING. DIRECTED BY BONNIE SHERR KLEIN AND TERRI NASH. EDITED BY JANICE BROWN. NARRATED BY MARGOT KIDDER. PRODUCED BY STUDIO D, NATIONAL FILM BOARD OF CANADA.

National Film Board of Canada   Office national du film du Canada

"A small branch of the Voice of Women was formed in our neighbourhood. We used to meet regularly in our homes for the exchange of ideas and information and to develop lobbying action directed at the federal government. We collected our babies' teeth and sent them off to be part of research about the presence of strontium-90 in breast milk and cows' milk. We prepared briefs, participated in marches, signed petitions, wrote letters to newspapers and politicians - all with the one goal of bringing an end to nuclear testing." Rosemary Brown in Being Brown, 60.

The threat of nuclear war inspired a unique peace organization in the 1960s. A shared sense of urgency led many women to become enthusiastic about doing something - anything - to prevent the world from slipping into a nuclear holocaust. The organizers received hundreds of letters, among them one from a women who wrote, "I don't have a big 'Voice' but I can use it for very prolonged periods of time if I find it necessary, so please give me something do..."As the years went by, national and international events prompted more women of all ages and from all walks of life to join Voice of Women VOW. The nuclear scare intensified in October 1962, when Russia and the United States came terrifyingly close to war over the issue of Soviet missiles in Cuba. In Canada, the debate raged over whether Bomarc missiles deployed under the NORAD agreement with the United States should be fitted with nuclear warheads. The Conservative government of John Diefenbaker, after much argument, refused the warheads. Spurred by the uneasy political climate, VOW spread quickly from the founding group in Toronto to the rest of Canada, and then internationally. The organization had great appeal for women with children. Founders included well-known women such as Kay MacPherson from Toronto, who became president of VOW, and Muriel Duckworth of Halifax. Thérèse Casgrain and journalist and civil rights activist, June Callwood were also active in VOW. Within three years of its founding, VOW had 4,539 members, with affiliations in 17 countries. The members participated in all kinds of activities, and local and regional groups acted independently to accommodate different points of view on the peace issue. They were successful at fund raising - for research projects and organizations like the Canadian Peace Research Institute; to make world trips possible for VOW leaders; to host the first conference of leading women in the western world, held in Montreal in 1962. Members sent children's teeth to Dr. Murray Hunt of the University of Toronto to help him in his experiments to determine if radiation fallout affected children's bodies.

GREEN DRAGON PRESS

Although committed to political neutrality, VOW valued political connections. For example, Maryon Pearson and Olive Diefenbaker, wives of the two leading politicians of the time were invited to become honorary sponsors.

Some members wanted to take a more activist position and on November 1, 1962 at the time of the Cuban missile crisis a "peace train" travelled from Montreal to Ottawa. Some of the women brought small children. They planned to ask members of parliament whether Canada was going to accept nuclear weapons. Some journalists suggested that it was inappropriate for mothers with small children to march on Parliament. The negative publicity raised concerns about the organization's public image both within and outside VOW. Other conflicts arose, conflicting ideas about how to achieve peace, personality conflicts and issues of political judgement. VOW was dealt a serious blow in 1963 when Lester Pearson changed course and supported the acceptance of nuclear warheads. Organization members felt betrayed, unaware that Pearson had seen an opportunity to reveal government indecision. In the next few years political events divided the organization. Although VOW achieved much and still exists today, some observers have said that Canada in the 60s was not yet ready for a peace group that attempted to unite women's concerns with political action.

GREEN DRAGON PRESS

Muriel Duckworth, Peace Worker

An Interview by Christine Ball

Muriel Duckworth is one of the founders of the Voice of Women in Halifax. Since 1962, she has served as a member of the National Council of the Voice of Women/La Voix des Femmes, Canada; as Chairperson of the National Education Committee and as Vice-President and National President of the Voice of Women. She has played a major role in the creation of several organizations, including the Canadian Association for the Advancement of Women and Sport and the Canadian Research Institute for the Advancement of Women. She is a recipient of the Persons Award (1981), and the Order of Canada (1983). The following are excerpts from two interviews with Muriel Duckworth which took place on October 23rd and 24th, 1986, at Kay Macpherson's home in Toronto. Christine Ball, a Ph.D. student at the Ontario Institute for Studies in Education, interviewed Muriel.

How did you hear of the Voice of Women?

I heard about it on the radio because it started off with quite a bang in Toronto. A lot of media women were involved and there was a lot of talk about it but I didn't think of it affecting me. I then heard about it from Peggy Hope-Simpson, who lived in Dartmouth, N.S., at the time. I was 52 years old and I had just taken on the first full-time job of my life working for the Adult Education Division [Department of Education, Province of Nova Scotia] when Peggy phoned me. To back up a little bit, David Hope-Simpson her husband, and she, and my husband and I were involved in an anti-nuclear testing movement at the time...Somebody from Toronto wrote to David Hope-Simpson and said "do you know any women...who would help to organize?"...he didn't think of her doing it and she said "Well, I'd like to be in on that myself." She didn't have much time. She thought of me. I don't think we knew each other, but she

knew something about me. She thought I could organize and she phoned me. We had the first meeting in my living room. I was quite resistant; I had just taken this first full-time job and I said to myself "who needs another organization?"...I wasn't really looking for another organization to belong to. Kay said she had the same feeling.

The same feeling? That was at the time the Voice of Women formed in 1960...?

In 1960. Anyway, we had the first meeting in our house. The living room was packed, about 25 women came. Margaret Colpitts, known professionally as Joan Marshall, who was then a women's morning commentary on the CBC — they used to have them all across the country, 'women's morning commentators' on all kinds of issues — we asked her to chair it and she did. Then we immediately had an issue just dropped in our laps. Word came out that the United States was considering the dumping of nuclear waste off the coast of Nova Scotia into the ocean. People didn't know very much about it but they knew enough to be incensed from a nationalistic point of view that they would think that they could dump nuclear waste in our water and we knew that they were doing it because there would be too much of a fuss for them to do it off the coast of Maine or any other place along the Eastern seaboard. Harold Hathaway, in charge of Public Affairs, at CBC Halifax, got in touch with us about it. Because he was highly incensed, he helped with publicity. We had a good meeting in a school gym, a lot of people, television coverage, and a lot of radio coverage, and in the end they didn't do it. Whether our meeting had anything to do with it or not, of course, we don't know, but they never did do it.

Was this after the first meeting with the 25 women?

Yes. At that meeting, we began planning the public meeting so that was how I first got into [the Voice of Women]... That was 1960. It was founded in 1960 and it spread very rapidly across the country. It was founded in Toronto in response to a crisis in the Peace Talks in Paris. In the middle of peace talks, word came out about the shooting down of the U2 American spy plane with its pilot, Gary Power, over the Soviet Union. Of course, the US denied it. Eisenhower was the President. He denied up and down, which is what they do. We didn't know at the time that's routine; they deny ... [Khruschev] broke up the peace talks and went home. Everybody was very afraid. Everybody thought that meant that there was immediate risk of nuclear war. You understand that by this time, people had begun to realize that, in spite of the terrible destructiveness of the atomic bombs, they were going ahead with planning and making even more powerful nuclear bombs. This knowledge as it seeped out took the place of the feeling that there could never be another nuclear war because it would be too awful. There was this incident in the South Pacific where the Japanese fishing boat was showered with radioactive fall-out and one man died and the Japanese peace movement came alive. Then, the testing, and the risks of testing, became very clear from the testing in the Nevada Desert...My first grandchildren were born in Sackville, New Brunswick in 1959 and the fallout from Nevada was coming across the border as well as causing death and destruction in the United States.

So, these were all the factors around that time that were considerations?

Fallout was a big factor; so was the danger of nuclear war, without a real realization of how terrible it would be but with some sense of it. Then, Lotta Dempsey, a newspaper woman in Toronto, writing [in] *The*

231

GREEN DRAGON PRESS

Toronto Star said "Where are the women? Why aren't the women doing something about this terrible situation? Half the people in the world are women." Then came the organization [Voice of Women]...I had heard that there was the beginning of a women's peace movement in Toronto before that. That women had begun to talk about one and they were almost ready to take off and this gave them a real push...It was Marion Catto who first told me about it. As they met in somebody's house for the purpose of organizing, a question was raised, "What do we call this women's peace movement?" Somebody murmured tentatively, "It has to be called the voice of women;" they latched onto it. You know, from where I sit today, I think that was brilliant, because the problem of women has been their silence. I don't think ... I know that we didn't clearly see it at that time as the problem of women that they are silent, that they don't speak up.

That was three years before Betty Friedan's book The Feminine Mystique...

I got into the women's movement at that point really through the peace movement ... I sort of gradually, gradually became more and more of a feminist.

How long were you involved in the peace movement?

I was involved before the Second World War. In Montreal, we [her husband, Jack, and she] belonged to the Fellowship of Reconciliation which was a pacifist organization.

You're a Quaker. Have you been a Quaker all your life?

No, I haven't. As a matter of fact, I started going to Quaker meetings, partly because of the Quaker peace witness, just after the founding of the Voice of Women. Dr. Helen Cunningham was a psychiatrist and one of the founders of the Voice of Women. [She]

moved with her husband and children from Montreal to Halifax in 1961. They immediately set up a Quaker meeting in their house and they invited us to come. At that time we were active members of the United Church of Canada which did not have any kind of peace witness — it was really pretty shocking. The then Moderator of the United Church was one of the people that the Canadian government took down to Colorado to show them the 'wonderful' headquarters of NORAD. He came back impressed, and he talked about the North, Canada's Northland, as a bargaining chip with the United States. We just couldn't stand that coming from the chief spokesperson of the United Church. So my husband corresponded with him two or three times but he was adamant, he wouldn't back down on this position. For a while we attended both the United Church and the Quaker meetings. Finally, we resigned from the United Church. It wasn't just that. It was also the way the Quakers functioned, the general way that the Quakers functioned which itself leads

to peaceable solutions, the general attitude of decisions by consensus...And it was the simplicity of their belief in the "Inner Light" and their belief "that God in every person." I was with the Quakers for many, many years but I didn't join. Within me, there was this very funny sort of inverted argument. I didn't want people to say "Well, of course she's for peace, she's a Quaker." I resisted that for a long time. I wanted people to accept the fact you didn't have to be a Quaker to be for peace. So, that was one reason I didn't join. Besides, I had an idea that all Quakers were saints and I knew I wasn't one. Finally, when I was 67, it seemed right for me to join. The path my life and thinking had taken seemed to lead to becoming a Quaker. Not something imposed from outside, I just felt comfortable there. They have such a strong social conscience and so much comes out of Quaker thinking into the whole community. Later, at some point in all this I discovered that my ancestor, who came across from the United States in 1792 or 3 and founded the little village of Austen [Quebec] where I was born and where I spend my summers, was a Quaker. I didn't know that when I was growing up.

You said that before World War II you were in the peace movement. When did you begin to be involved in the peace movement?

I think a lot of this [was] partly my whole upbringing, not that my family were [involved in the peace movement], because they supported World Wars I and II. But, I was brought up in the country, and seemed far removed from wars. In the first World War, my brother was too young and my father was too old, and my second cousin was the closest we came to involvement with it. I think what happened more than anything was the Student Christian Movement at McGill when I was an undergraduate. I started at McGill in 1925.

Muriel Duckworth

Photo: NFB

Were you born in Quebec?

232

GREEN DRAGON PRESS

Yes, born on a farm in Quebec, in Austen, lived on the farm, started school in a little one-room school, and then we moved to Magog. I finished school there and then went to McGill. The most important thing that happened to me at McGill was the Student Christian Movement. It was really more important than my courses, looking back at it — being in a discussion group constantly all the time I was there, a religious discussion group. In this group, we supported each other in our attempts to express new ideas, often explored haltingly and tentatively. There was no space for that kind of exchange in the classroom. There was a real trend towards pacifism during that period between the two world wars. Of course, we talked about that too.

Was that where you met Jack?

Yes...He was a strong pacifist. As someone once said, he was the most aggressive pacifist they [had] ever met.

Fighting for peace?

Yes [laughter]. He was really fighting for peace. Then, we went to Union Seminary. We were married in 1929 as soon as I graduated. He was already in theological college. It was not common then to be married as students. We went to Union, to New York together, for one year. Pacifism was very strong around there at that time, that was 1929-30. Then, it became a very discussable question, of course, as World War II loomed up.

Wasn't it overridden by jingoism?

Yes, it was, and by people who felt that *this* war [was] the 'Good War,' this [was] the war that you [had] to fight. The students and the faculty at Union where we went were inclined at that time towards pacifism. Then, of course, came the Depression; the Social Gospel was very strong. We came back to Montreal and worked through the Depression which was really very hard...I remember the year that our first child was born, Jack's salary was $1,800.

What year was that?

'33. We had this child in the bottom of the Depression...People talk now about hav-

ing babies with the threat — the world threat — hanging over them. We certainly had the same feeling: "Should you have babies when things are so, so bad?" There was desperate poverty. At that time, you could see the connection, you could see the buildup towards war which was to solve the unemployment problem You began to see that war was being viewed as a solution to the unemployment problem just as the militarization of industry is now. There was a constant discussion and heated argument between the people who thought that you couldn't have war and social good at the same time and the people who thought "you've got to have war, you've got to defeat the Nazis in order to have a good society. It's absolutely the thing you've got to do."

Did people see peace and social justice as interconnected?

No, I don't think they did. I think [that] they thought the war against fascism had to be fought and won in order to be able to deal with issues of justice everywhere.

How did you see it then? Do you remember?

Yes. It was difficult. I wasn't too certain of myself because so many of my friends who were on the left had said "this is a war that's got to be fought." I remember them getting almost enthusiastic, almost happy, when finally war was declared. "It's got to be done, might as well do it now, it's been put off too long, should have been done sooner, this is all appeasement." My own feeling was often wavering. I found it hard. I wasn't as firm a pacifist as Jack was at that time. But I couldn't get into wartime effort. I didn't really want to and I didn't. I kept on doing work in the church, kept on doing work with young people in the YMCA, and I was aware of criticism. People [were] feeling "well, you're all mixed up; this is not where you should be putting your effort now; your effort should be going into the war."

You were criticized for not supporting the war?

Oh yes. I was aware of that. But, there was no serious suffering about it. I just didn't feel very comfortable about it when I

knew that was what people thought.

What are the milestones of World War II that you remember?

My brother's death was, of course, a *big* thing. The fact that he joined up...[His death] was a hard part of the war.

I was just thinking, during this interview, that my parents discussed what they [had] heard, my mom especially when she was back here, what she had heard about rumours of concentration camps in Europe. She thought [that] they were just rumours.

I remember feeling that, too, because after the First World War, we had been told such horror stories about the Germans. We had these horrible pictures of the Huns and stories of the cutting off of babies' hands, and then came these even more horrible pictures of the Bolsheviks. I was 10 years old when World War I ended and I used to have nightmares about Huns and Bolsheviks. *Terrible* stories of the Bolsheviks with their beards sticking out all over and their hair wild...so you see, it was hard, as your mother said, for some of us to believe what was being said about concentration camps under the Nazis — just impossible, couldn't be.

The thing is that people will talk about concentration camps [now], but I find very few of my parents' generation will talk, or even mention the dropping of the bomb on Japan.

Well, actually, what I remember about it, at that time ... we had no idea how horrendous it was. We knew it had dropped on Hiroshima, we knew it had dropped on Nagasaki, we knew the war had ended, and we all assumed that it had caused the end of the war. But, the Americans deliberately kept information out of people's hands. Journalists were not allowed to visit Hiroshima and Nagasaki. The word began getting out but a lot of it was hushed up. Immediately along came the Cold War. Actually, before the war was over, they knew who the next enemy was going to be, and one of the reasons that they bombed Japan was to keep the Russians from having any share in the victory in the Far East. Russia became the enemy and immediately we were caught up in that...

233

GREEN DRAGON PRESS

[During the time of the Gouzenko case], it was a *terrible* time, everybody was *afraid*; everybody was afraid to talk to anybody and it went on for quite a long time. Many innocent people suffered.

It sort of merged into the whole McCarthy era...

I remember coming from Halifax to a World Mental Health Congress in Toronto. That was 8 years later, in 1955. It was held here because the situation was so bad in the States that the Russians couldn't go to the United States. One of the Russians gave me a Russian cigarette. I didn't smoke but I had it for a souvenir and somebody said "Don't let anybody see you with that Russian cigarette." Everybody was so fearful. Everybody was going through all that. It was still going on when the Voice of Women was founded in 1960. We were called 'Reds,' because we felt that if you're going to talk about peace, you've got to talk to the people on the other side. It's strange just talking to yourself, and so we set out right away to make contacts with other women who had been defined as our enemies. It seemed the logical thing to do.

How did you do that?

Well, we held an international conference of women for peace in 1962 to which we invited them. We arranged exchange visits from women from the Soviet Union and Eastern Europe. We kept in touch.

Muriel Duckworth became the chairperson of the program committee for the Voice of Women's second international conference of women for peace held in 1967 in Montreal. At the end of the conference, during a meeting of the Voice of Women, she became president of VOW/VDF, taking over from Kay Macpherson, who had preceded her as president from 1963 to 1967.

Muriel was the last to serve as president of the Voice of Women (1967 to 1971) before it developed more decentralized (committee) structures.

This article originally appeared in *Canadian Woman Studies/Les cahiers de la femme*, "Women Working for Peace," Vol. 9 No. 1 (Spring 1988)

The Royal Commission on the Status of Women in Canada

In January 1967 a headline in the *Globe and Mail* read: "Women threaten march of millions if Royal Commission (on the Status of Women) isn't granted. Laura Sabia, who led a six-month campaign by a coalition of 32 women's voluntary groups, had promised to bring the women to Ottawa to protest, though later she admitted she had been bluffing.

Prime Minister Lester B. Pearson appointed the Royal Commission on the Status of Women in Canada, on 16 February, 1967. Florence Bird, an Ottawa journalist and broadcaster, was appointed to chair the commission. The RCSW, the first Canadian commission headed by a woman, was given a mandate to investigate and report on all matters pertaining to the status of women in those areas which fell within the jurisdiction of the federal government.

The commission's public investigation began in the spring of 1968, and for 6 months public hearings were held across Canada, including the Far North. This commission attracted extensive public interest, held hearings in 14 communities in all ten provinces, met 890 witnesses, and received 468 briefs and 1,000 letters, all of which attested to widespread problems experienced by women in all walks of Canadian society. The Commission focused attention on women's grievances, recommended changes to eliminate sexual inequality by means of social policy, and mobilized a constituency of women's groups to press for implementation of the commission's recommendations. 167 recommendations were tabled in the House of Commons on September 28, 1970. By the early 1980s most of the 167 recommendations in the RCSW report had been partially implemented and many had been fully implemented. Several controversial recommendations, however, had not been acted upon.

☞ KEY RECOMMENDATIONS OF ☜ THE ROYAL COMMISSION

Women and the Economy:

1. that housewives be permitted to participate in the Canada Pension Plan.
2. that employed women be granted 18 weeks unemployment benefits for maternity leave.
3. that "gender" and "marital status' be prohibited grounds for discrimination by employers.

Women and Education:

4. that training programs offered by the federal government be made more open to women.

Women and the Family:

5. that the criminal code be amended so that the wife may be held responsible to support her husband in the same way that the husband may be held responsible to support his wife.
6. that birth control information be available to everyone.
7. that the criminal code be amended to permit abortion on request by any woman who has been pregnant for 12 weeks or less. (Or for over 12 weeks if a doctor is convinced that the pregnancy would endanger the health of the woman or if there is a risk of the child being born physically or mentally challenged.)
8. that a guaranteed annual income be paid by the federal government to the head of all one-parent families with dependent children.

Women and Politics:

9. that two qualified women from each province be appointed to the Senate as seats become vacant. And that women continue to be appointed until a more equitable membership is achieved.
10. that the federal government name more women judges to all courts within their jurisdiction.

GREEN DRAGON PRESS

The Pill

Birth control became legal in Canada in 1969. Before that it was illegal to sell, distribute or purchase any form of birth control. It was part of the criminal code. In Canada, chemical birth control finally was legalized in 1969, the year after Pierre Elliot Trudeau became Prime Minister. The same law also made abortions legal if approved by a hospital medical committee as necessary to preserve the pregnant women's life or health. Before that, doctors could prescribe it for therapeutic purposes only. It was during this controversial reform that Pierre Trudeau made his famous statement that the "state had no business in the bedrooms of the nation." Many religious groups including the Roman Catholic Church condemned all forms of chemical birth control.

The pill was the brainchild of Margaret Sanger, a lifelong champion of women's rights and birth control. She was born in 1879 in Corning, New York, the sixth of eleven children. She often blamed her mother's death on her frequent pregnancies. In 1950, in her 80's, Sanger met Gregory Pincas, a reproductive scientist. She raised the money to get Pincas started on research that would lead to a universal contraceptive. The Pill became available in the United States in 1960.

The birth control pill became available in Canada in the early 1960s, but was to be prescribed for therapeutic purposes, such as regulation of the menstrual cycles. Around that time Canadian drug companies published several brochures for the general public explaining family planning and describing various types of birth control. Planned Parenthood of Toronto was founded in 1961 with the informal support of the Anglican, Presbyterian, United and Unitarian Churches. During its first year, Planned Parenthood Toronto succeeded in getting the Board of Broadcast Governors to change a rule that birth control could never be mentioned on radio or television without prior permission. There followed a flood of television features, radio interviews, magazine stories, public meetings and letter to the editors and legislators about the subject. In 1966, the Canadian Medical Association recommended the provision of contraceptive information and services. This support was considered necessary for the passage of the legislation that eventually decriminalized birth control.

By the year 2000, the *Canadian Contraceptive Study* published by The Journal of the Society of Obstetricians and Gynaecologists determined that 84% of Canadian women use or have used the Pill. The most recent commercial development is the "morning after" contraceptive pill.

GREEN DRAGON PRESS

Personal Change

"The problem lay buried, unspoken for many years in the minds of...women. It was a strange stirring, a sense of dissatisfaction, a yearning that women suffered in the middle of the twentieth century...Each suburban housewife struggled with it alone...she was afraid to ask even of herself the silent question -"Is this all?" Betty Friedan, *The Feminine Mystique*.

"Someone, I can't remember who, loaned me a copy of *The Feminine Mystique*, by Betty Friedan. Suddenly it was all there, the story of my life - as I read the book, I became more and more agitated; I realized that I was not unique, that there were women all over North America, women of all colours, who were experiencing the same sense of being unfulfilled in their personal lives. Learning this fact should have depressed me further, but it didn't. The effect was the opposite. The fact that I was not alone reassured and mobilized me."
Rosemary Brown in *Being Brown*, 81.

"One day Willie writes a note to the milkman, and is alarmed to read what she has written: the single word 'Help,'" *TV Guide* promo for The Trapped Housewife, with Michael Kane as "The Voice of the Doctor," 1962.

One woman looks back on her experience of suburban living:

Stuck in Suburbia by Pat Staton.

"From 1957 to 1962 my life seemed modeled on an article from *Chatelaine* magazine. I lived in a typical split-level house in a typical suburb on the outskirts of Toronto, with my husband and our three children under four years of age. There was no bus service, no stores within walking distance and for most of that time I had no access to a car. Outwardly I was living the American/Canadian dream. Looking back and considering my own childhood, it still puzzles me how I got to that place in time. My mother certainly went against the grain. In 1941, when I was eight and my sisters six and two years old, she picked us up and left my father, escaping what had become an intolerable marriage. It was the first divorce in the history of our devout Anglican family; her action

GREEN DRAGON PRESS

brought down the wrath of most of her family. I remember being the only kid in my class whose parents were divorced. I was an object of curiosity and pity. As was common in those days, my mother did not share her reasons for the divorce, and for a long time my sisters and I were convinced that if we only behaved better, our father would come home. Our hopes were dampened (though only slightly) when he remarried, and finally completely dashed, when five years later mother remarried.

I think now, that because my mother had always been a rebel and acted outside the norm, often suffering greatly for it, she may have reinforced the stereotypical notions of the ideal life women should strive for, thinking we would have an easier time if we just complied with society's expectations. Certainly my recollection is that print and film media in the post war period focussed on the desirability of creating a home to serve as a setting for a large family. Since low marks in mathematics prevented me from going to university, even if my parents had been willing to help me financially, I settled on art school and then a job in a department store advertising department. My mother naturally assumed I would pay room and board and even though I was now an adult contributing financially, she maintained an extremely tight rein on me - the same rules and curfew as my high-school days. I felt stifled, and resisted at every opportunity. Though now it seems ludicrous to me, it appeared that my only chance to escape and gain independence was to get married. So when this charming, funny person who thought I was perfect, promised to spend the rest of his life making me happy, I said "yes."

Life in the suburbs nearly drove me to distraction. I hated housework, and the conversation of three year olds just did not keep my mind alive. My neighbours positively glowed as they discussed their schedule at our morning coffee sessions. Washing on Monday, ironing and dusting on Tuesday, baking on Wednesday, mending, vacuuming and gardening on Thursday and for a big treat - a grocery shopping expedition to the supermarket on Friday night. I just could not get into this routine. My week went something like this: Monday read a historical novel all day, stopping only to make lunch for the kids, periodically checking they were safe in the sand-box. Tuesday: paint a Disney mural on the wall of the playroom. Wednesday: Build a castle out of 2000 miniature marshmallows with ice-cream cones for turrets and Smarties for the roof. Thursday: read *two* historical novels. On Friday I would rush through the house frantically getting it in shape and crossing my fingers that my mother wouldn't make one of her "surprise" visits to check for dust - something she did quite often. She was convinced that if I didn't keep my house in perfect order my marriage would fail. To pay for this Eden in the suburbs, my husband worked double shifts at the newspaper and was seldom home in the evenings or on Saturdays. For entertainment I watched television, read or played hide and seek with the kids. Everyone in my family told me how lucky I was (lovely home, charming children, devoted husband) I couldn't figure out why I was so miserable. I continued my volunteer work with the Girl Guides and the camping trips were some relief. I got a break from looking after three children and instead got to look after other people's children. Sometimes as many as thirty of them!

Many of the women in my neighbourhood had the same problems I did. Each of them tried to deal with frustration and boredom in different ways. Some drank too much, some took Valium, and some had affairs. I read dozens of books, often one a day, wrote stories that I promptly threw out, painted and gardened and wondered what was

GREEN DRAGON PRESS

wrong with me. There had to be something more, I thought.

I loved my children and my husband but I felt like a cross between Alice in Wonderland and the Wicked Witch of the West. I wanted to get a job, however the children all came home for lunch each day, and there were PD days, spring break and summer holidays to consider. There were no day-care centres within miles and my neighbours all had large families and no interest in looking after mine. Even a mention of working outside the home brought severe opposition from my family. My husband would have agreed to almost anything I wanted to do but it just didn't seem possible. I could see my life stretching before me relentlessly; all mapped out in the *Ladies Home Journal* and *Chatelaine*. Then a series of unrelated incidents changed my life. We decided to abandon our monster mortgage, move to a smaller house in the country so we could have a little financial freedom. I was selected to take a group of Girl Guides to a Jubilee camp in Denmark in the summer of 1962. It was my first time away from home and family in my entire thirty years, and it definitely changed my life. When I returned that fall I read *The Feminine Mystique* by Betty Friedan. What a revelation. At the same time the International Typographical Union struck against all three Toronto daily papers. My husband and most of the men in his union chose to honour the picket line. When it became clear the strike would be a lengthy one, my search for paying work changed me overnight in my family's eyes from a self-centred, whining complainer into a "real little trooper pitching in." And so I began a new phase in my life. It was only later that I realized that while I was living a middle-class idealized dream, and hating it, other women worked all day in factories, worrying about poor or non-existent day care, and came home to face the household chores. Many were trying to raise children on a military pension; others were single and helping support their families.

GREEN DRAGON PRESS

Putting Down Roots in Canada

Idalina Azevedo is a strong and resourceful woman who has played a major role in ensuring her family's success in Canada... Idalina's experiences show that although women often play a key role in guiding their families through the adjustment process, they are rarely given the credit and recognition they deserve.

Idalina was born on Pico, one of the islands in the Azores. Her family were farmers, and life was hard on this rocky island. At twelve years old, with only two years of education, she was sent to work in the fields with her father and brothers...When she was twenty-one, she married... Life did not get any easier... Often the parents went without food so their two boys could eat. Idalina often thought of migrating to Canada to join her older brother. She said:

My brother told me that Canada was a good country and there was work and money to make if you just worked hard... We were so poor, and I thought this was right to go to Canada.

After completing the necessary applications, Idalina and her family left the Azores and arrived ... in the fall of 1962. Their destination was Wawa, a small mining town in Northern Ontario. She describes their first few days in Canada:

We were so tired and hungry after the planes and trains that we took. It seems like we travelled for a long time. I remember my kids asking for food and I was happy that my mother had packed us a basket of roasted fava beans so they could eat. The man on the train came to sell us sandwiches. We felt so strange because we never saw a sandwich in our lives. The kids didn't like it. After many hours we arrived in Sault Ste. Marie to a Portuguese family's house to wait for my brother to pick us up. My God! I felt to cry. The woman was so nice she made us food Portuguese style, chouriccos, eggs, bread and bananas. I never in my life saw bananas so big and bread so soft. Tears were running down my eyes to see my kids filling up their stomachs. I will always remember her.

The first few months in Wawa were difficult...Language and climate had to be adjusted to...During the first few months she felt isolated, and her life centred on the care of her family as she desperately tried to feed, house and clothe them on her husbands meagre salary of $35 a week.

I remember one time going to a French grocery store to shop with my brother. The man seemed very nice to us. I paid him for the food, and he said, "Merci beaucoup" to me. Well, my face turned all red and I told my brother I not go back to that store again because the man had said a bad word to me. I confused the word "beaucoup" with a word in my language, which meant "ass." Then my brother explained to me that the man said "thank you" in French. I felt so ashamed and stupid; now I can laugh about it.

Being pregnant in Canada was something she was completely unprepared for. ...when she was seven months pregnant, [her brother] forced her to visit a doctor...she had never been to a doctor before:

My brother took me to the hospital and said to the nurse, "This is my sister Idalina, she doesn't speak too much English." Then he left for work. I remember the nurse looking at me strange. Probably the way I was dressed. I had a heavy winter coat on and it was summer. Seems they think I'm a crazy person! When you don't understand, they treat you stupid...

Adapted from a term paper for York University, "International Migration" by Nicole Azevedo, Toronto, April 9, 1987. The excerpt selected combines Nicole's perspective with Idalina's unique voice describing her experience as a Portuguese woman. Idalina's story has been published in *I've Something To Tell You: Interviews with Immigrant Women* by Joyce Scane, Toronto: Green Dragon Press.

GREEN DRAGON PRESS

Questioning Gender Stereotypes

In the 1960s many women and some men were beginning to question traditional labels, and what was the more natural role for them in modern society. The debate in the media ran the gamut from serious discussion to articles clearly meant to shock. Advertising, however, lagged far behind, as shown in this advertising copy for a major American airline.

"Old Maid. That's what the other stewardesses call her. Because she's been flying for almost three years now. (The average tenure of a stewardess is only 21 months before she gets married.) But she's not worried. How many girls do you know who can serve cocktails and dinner for 35 without losing their composure? And who smile the whole time like they mean it? (They do) Not too many, right?...Maybe that's why more people fly with us than any other airline. Everyone gets warmth, friendliness and extra care. And someone may get a wife."

Dorothy Sangster, writing in *Chatelaine* in November 1963 described the common vision of "Old Maids."

"You could tell they were Old Maids because they were crotchety little creatures of indeterminate age, or pale wraiths of girls, underweight and unsmiling. A few of them shared homes with kind-hearted elder brothers and their families. But mostly Old Maids lived in small houses with polished brass knockers and starched lace curtains, and took care of their aged mothers. They seldom ventured beyond the front porch, except on Sundays when they went to church." Sangster went on to cite both American and Canadian statistics to support the view that "the spinster is fast disappearing from the scene." In 1940 the United States Population Reference Bureau reported that only 15 per cent of American women in their early thirties were unmarried and by 1960, the figure had shrunk still further to only 7 per cent. In Canada the population of single women in the 35 to 44 age group was less then 10 percent in 1963. Sangster then said "For one reason or another, you hardly ever see an Old Maid these days. What you do see are countless well-dressed career women, holding down important jobs in business, doing well in the professions, recognized in the arts, driving late-model cars, patronizing smart little dress shops, lunching in such expensive bistros as Mr. Tony's in Toronto, or sampling Polynesian dishes in Trader Vic's in Vancouver, or sipping cocktails in the skyline room of Montreal's Queen Elizabeth. Sangster did say that not every single woman was living such an exciting life; many were not that affluent. But, she said, even for them the situation has changed. Because the image has changed"

GREEN DRAGON PRESS

Still, many people continued to cling to rigid gender stereotypes as shown in the following companion articles.

I married
a masculine woman

by GORDON TOLIVER

She liked beer, hockey; hated babies, gossip. She was just one of the boys. That's why I divorced her.

IT'S ONLY NOW, three years after my divorce, that I can look back on my marriage to Ethel with any equanimity.

We were both 22 when we met at night classes at a business school in our native Sudbury, Ont. She was attractive, with a solid, well-rounded figure, and high cheekbones set below wide brown eyes and dark, short-cropped hair—more handsome than beautiful.

It was one of many male traits I was to hate later on, but was too blind to see at the time. Then, she was the ideal girlfriend, "one of the boys" whom I could take on fishing trips in summer, or ski weekends in winter. Strangely, I was entranced with this tomboyishness—something I was to learn is looked on favorably by all men by a husband. For she was popular with the men we knew, and not quite so with their wives and girlfriends. At first, I put it down to natural womanly jealousy of her athletic prowess and popularity.

She was pioneer type — damn it

I WORKED in the offices of the International Nickel Company. Ethel worked as assistant manager of a five-and-dime store in downtown Sudbury. Sudbury, like all communities in Northern Ontario that sprung up around the mine shafts, is a masculine city. The men are tough and robust, and their women are expected to be as tough as they are in some ways.

I don't mean our women aren't as feminine as elsewhere. Only that they can hold their own in a kitchen, on a picket line, or in the nursery. Ethel was both a man's woman, and —I thought—a woman's woman as well. That combination is as rare as catching sunburn in a mineshaft.

During our courtship, we travelled all over the north country, following hockey and baseball teams; sleeping in cabins, motels and flea-bitten hotels; and often on the seats of my car. I felt sorry for those with wives who hated the thought of leaving their nice, warm kitchens. Ethel, to me, was a throwback to the rugged pioneer women who settled the north.

She wanted to fix the sink

SHE COULD drink and smoke like any man. Yet she wasn't cheap; she never got passed-out drunk, or told an off-color story. She could sit up with a bunch of us after the other women had gone to bed, and trade quips and laughter with the best of us.

WIVES who're handy aren't natural.
They should stick to having children.

Liberty

GREEN DRAGON PRESS

I'M NOT WRITING this under my real name, because I'm still married to George after seven years.

It's been a nerve-wracking seven years. George isn't homosexual; in fact, he shows hatred to those who are, probably from a defence mechanism—he knows he's vulnerable to the charge himself. He's the father of our two small daughters, and plays the male role in all but surface manifestations.

No one is wholly masculine or feminine. All of us carry within us the genes of the opposite sex; and it's claimed these rival genes take up as much as 40 percent of the genes balance. Men often do feminine things, and women at times assume the masculine point of view. It's natural and should cause no concern to a normal person. It's only when the delicate balance is tipped towards the opposite gender that it becomes obvious and embarrassing.

He was a whiz with draperies

I MET George when we were both 21. He was a student at the University of Toronto; I was completing a course at Teachers' College in Toronto. A friend, Jean Stanton, invited me to go on a blind date with her, her fiancé and George. I was amazed when George called for me at my boarding house. He was a tall, quiet, polite young man, good-looking in a finely-chiseled manner. Unlike others, he did everything correctly—he presented me with a corsage when we met at the door, and made himself at home with the family.

He had the faculty most men lack—of being able to anticipate a woman's wish. What a change from the men I'd known: a beautiful dancer, a perfect escort, the most gentlemanly. He compared favorably with the crude, ill-mannered boys I danced with throughout the evening.

Jean asked me in the powder room: "What do you think of George?"

"I think he's icky," I answered. "He has exquisite manners."

"Yes, hasn't he?" she said, seemingly disappointed in my assessment.

After he drove me home, he asked for another date and I accepted.

I knew little about men. I'd dated only a few men, and my ideas of what a man should be had been warped by my widowed mother and a spinster aunt. Mother and Aunt Rose judged all men by my dead father, who'd been a drunkard and woman-chaser. To mother, the ideal man never took a drink, never saw any women but his wife and mother. This warped philosophy must have rubbed off on me.

HE DOES DISHES cheerfully. My friends don't sympathize with me.

My husband is too feminine

by SARAH LOGAN

He fathered my children, but he's still effeminate. I wish he'd drink, swear and beat me — like a man.

Women and Work

- *In 1961 women comprised a small proportion of various non-traditional professions in Canada: 0.25% were engineers, 2.64% were lawyers, 4.49% were dentists, 7.33% were physicians.*
- *By 1961 it had become acceptable for married women to be in the paid work force if they were childless, or if their children had left home or were occupied at school.*
- *Women's labour force participation rate had climbed to about 30 per cent by 1961.*
- *In 1967 the average income for men in Canada is $5,331; the average income for women is $2,303, or 43 per cent of the average for men.*

"I was involved with the union right from the start. It was the Service Employees International Union, Local 210. Their office was in Windsor, and they came down to organize us, and I was right in on the organizing from the beginning.

I can remember Mr. Pearce - he was administrator at the hospital. By then a law had been passed that you couldn't stop people from organizing, and they were getting ready to build a new wing. So he called a meeting to show us all what the new wing was gonna look like. Ordinarily, he'd never do this: they don't care if we knew what it looked like or not. And then after he got us into the meeting he started quoting prices - wages, what an organized hospital is getting, and what he was paying. So one of the fellows that was on the organizing with them reported this to the organizer, and the organizer went to their lawyer and told them, "If you don't want that man in jail, you better tell him to stop." So we didn't get any more of that.

We were organized in '67; we got our first contract in '68. I think it was in '72 I became chief steward. They sent me to their seminars - they used to have a seminar every year up near Lake Couchiching - and I went to that for five years. I took all the courses right from steward's training, collective bargaining, how to run a meeting, teach. I was chief steward when I retired in '84."
Grace Fowler, born 1919, in *No Burden to Carry: Narratives of Black Working Women in Ontario 1920s to 1950s*, 192.

"The problem of higher education for girls became a question with high school. All three of us were good students. May wanted to go to college, but our family didn't have the money to send the girls. Some of the older members of the Chinese community thought it would be a waste of money to send girls because it was expected that we would be getting married soon. I remember listening to people tell my father about the futility of sending us to college. This would be about '65 or '66. My father was very much aware of the fact that we were living in a different time and country. He decided that if we could find a way to pay for college ourselves, we could go. He said he'd by able to help us a bit. But basically, if we wanted to go and could pay our own way, that was just fine with him. We knew that our father was under quite a bit of pressure. But at that time, we were not the first girls to ask. Mary Mohammed was ahead of us. There was a big uproar when she wanted to go. So by our time, someone else had at least gotten people used to the idea that the girls might want to go." Linda Lee in *Jin Guo: Voices of Chinese Canadian Women*, 136.

GREEN DRAGON PRESS

70 BEST JOBS
FOR HOMEMAKERS
RETURNING
TO WORK

HELP WANTED
JOBS FOR
OLDER WOMEN

Office Positions
Comptometer operator
calculator operator
posting-machine operator
key-punch operator
bookkeeper
secretary
medical secretary
legal secretary
stenographer
clerk
typist

Food Service
hostess
waitress
kitchen worker

Health Occupations
dental assistant
medical-laboratory
   technologist
medical-record librarian
medical-record clerk
mental-health
   therapist assistant
medical-office assistant
X-ray technician
dietetic aide
nursing assistant
ward aide

Personal Service
hairdresser
cosmetician
manicurist
cosmetic saleswoman
salon assistant
dressmaker
alterationist
decorating seamstress
visiting homemaker
housekeeper
baby sitter

Professional He
teacher
substitute teacher
nursery-school tea
night-school teac
vocational teach
crafts teacher
hobby instructor
day-nursery assistan

Notable Women

Doris Anderson

Doris Anderson was born in Calgary, Alberta. She graduated from the University of Alberta in 1945 and moved to Toronto to pursue a career in journalism. She held a variety of jobs including copy editor for the *Star Weekly*, researcher and writer for radio host Claire Wallace, and copywriter in the advertising department at Eaton's. She travelled to Europe where she wrote and sold short stories to *Maclean's* and *Chatelaine* magazines. Anderson returned to Canada in 1950 and in 1951 began her long association with *Chatelaine* when she was hired to do advertising promotion. Through hard work and determination, Doris advanced to the positions of associate and managing editor. She finally became editor of *Chatelaine* in 1957, a job she held for 20 years. At the time of her marriage to lawyer David Anderson in 1957, she said that "what I wanted more than anything was to be able to look after myself and make sure that every other woman in the world could do the same." She continued to work after her marriage and the births of her three sons. Under her leadership, the content of *Chatelaine* changed dramatically to include serious articles on controversial subjects, as well as practical pieces for working women.

An editorial supported the push for a royal commission on the status of women and other articles examined social issues such as racism and the plight of Canada's Native people. Though some readers disapproved of the more radical focus, circulation increased dramatically from 480,000 when Anderson became editor to 1.8 million by the late 1960s. The content of *Chatelaine* during that period placed it in the vanguard of second wave feminism in North America. Anderson has continued to have a productive career up to the present time.

Kenojuak Ashevak OC (Cape Dorset Artist)

Kenojuak Ashevak was born in 1927, in Ikirisaq, Northwest Territories. She spent her childhood travelling from camps on South Baffin and Arctic Quebec. By the 1950s she was experimenting with carving and drawing. Kenojuak received the Order of Canada in 1967 and was also elected to the Royal Canadian Academy in 1974. Her art includes traditional themes of animals and birds as well as traditional Inuit women's vision of life, as well as spirits. Her art is first and foremost an appreciation of the beauty of the universe and she prefers to tell of her own experiences in her drawings. Although her style has continually changed and developed, her central concern for nature has been a constant in her work. Her wonderful aesthetic sense and enormous artistic talent have contributed enormously to Canadian art.

Honourable Florence Bird OC

Florence Bird was born in Philadelphia in 1908. She studied at Bryn Mawr University and then toured Europe. She married journalist John Bird and moved to Montreal in 1931 where she wrote four novels, all of which were rejected. She then began writing book reviews and short stories. She gave lectures to a peace study group and the Montreal Junior League and the YWCA. This public speaking experience proved to be valuable in her career. During the Second World War Florence was in charge of publicity for the Central Volunteer Bureau. Her broadcasting career began in 1941, using the name Anne Francis. She later worked for the CBC as a broadcaster, producer, interviewer and scriptwriter. She is best remembered though, for her work as chair of the Royal Commission on the Status of Women in Canada. She was made a Companion of the Order of Canada in 1971, appointed to the Senate in 1978, and was a recipient of the Governor General's Persons Award in 1985.

GREEN DRAGON PRESS

Salome Bey

Salome Bey is a Toronto jazz and blues singer, a songwriter, and a playwright. She was born and raised in New Jersey and came to Canada as a young woman. She was interviewed by K. Linda Kivi for *Canadian Women Making Music.*

"I first got involved in music when I was about 14. Wednesday night at the Apollo theatre in New York was a talent show and someone took me over to sing. I won. When you win the talent show, you're supposed to get a week's booking but my father said, "You're too young," so I didn't do it. But that's where I got bitten, so to speak.

How I really started was with my sister and my brother. We had a singing group called Andy and the Bey Sisters. We used to go around and audition for different types of things. We went to New York to audition for these big agents and one of them approached us; he said he could send us to Europe. We were still in school so we were supposed to go for only six weeks; we ended up staying over there for 16 months. That's where our career really started.

George Wein, who has the jazz festival, saw us and brought us back to North America. And we opened at Storyville in Boston. We did an album on RCA-Victor and another two albums on Prestige. He also got us a booking at the Colonial Tavern in Toronto. When we came up to do the show we went to the First Floor

Club to look up the drummer, Archie Aleen. Howard Matthews, who's my husband now, happened to be the owner. When I went into the place and sat there Howard came up to me and said, "You're the most beautiful Black woman I've ever seen." Terrible lines. Afterwards he came to the Colonial to see us and he told my sister, "I'm going to marry her."

That's how I ended up in Toronto. That was a hundred years ago-1964."

Canadian Women Making Music, K. Linda Kivi.
Toronto: Green Dragon Press, 1992, 69.

GREEN DRAGON PRESS

Activities
1960 – 1969

SOCIAL CHANGE

As a class, recreate a rally that might have been organized by the Voice of Women (VOW) in 1962, during the Cuban Missile Crisis.
Create protest signs – what slogans were popular?
Design a pamphlet to distribute. What information would be useful to include promoting and communicating your position?
Nominate four students who will play the role of Thérèse Casgrain, June Callwood, Muriel Duckworth, and John Diefenbaker. These students will prepare a 5-minute speech that speaks to the issue at hand.
Appoint members of the class as members of the press: Prepare questions for the speakers in advance.

ROYAL COMMISSION ON THE STATUS OF WOMEN IN CANADA

Imagine that a commission is appointed today, to investigate the Status of Women in Canada, and that you are invited to participate. In groups of 4-5, appoint a chair. What recommendations would your group put forth today? Are there any women's issues that you believe are necessary to address? Are there any recommendations of the original Commission that have not been yet realized? As a group, write a one-page report.

PERSONAL CHANGE

Create a 15-minute proposal for a TV. Sitcom that would be based in the 1960s.
As a class, vote for the most appealing and true to history storylines.

GENDER STEREOTYPES

Do gender stereotypes still persist today? Explore this issue as a class.
In small groups, brainstorm all the qualities of an ideal woman/wife/girlfriend…man/husband/boyfriend. Are there obvious stereotypes that reappear in each group's list?

Resources

Advisory Council on the Status of Women. Ten Years Later, Ottawa: 1979.
Bird, Florence. *Anne Francis: an autobiography,* Toronto: Clarke, Irwin, 1974.
Friedan, Betty. *The Feminine Mystique,* NY: Norton, 1963, 20th anniversary edition, 1983.
Griffiths, Naomi. *Penelope's Web.*
Kivi, K. Linda. *Canadian Women Making Music,* Toronto: Green Dragon Press, 1992.
MacPherson, Kay. *When in Doubt, Do Both: The Times of My Life,* Toronto: University of Toronto Press, 1994.
Strong-Boag and Anita Clair Fellman, eds. *Rethinking Canada: The Promise of Women's History,* Don Mills, Oxford University Press, 1998.

Video: *Speaking our Peace.* National Film Board of Canada.

GREEN DRAGON PRESS

1970 – 1979

Organizing for change

International Women's Day, 1978.
Canadian Women's Movement Archives/Archives canadiennes du mouvement des femmes.
Photo: Liz Martin.

Women around the world face the common threat of violence in their lives. The first march for Take Back the Night in Canada was held in Halifax in1978, and fifty women took part in the event. Since then, women's groups have marched in numerous cities to educate the public on issues relating to violence against women, as well as to empower women with the right of their own safety.

Reclaim the Night / Take Back the Night

There is perhaps no word as terrifying to women as rape. In an attempt to deal with this horrifying reality, women around the world began to march to "Reclaim the Night." In Halifax the first march, on September 29, 1978, was a direct result of efforts among women in the community—women who were concerned about violence and determined to resist.

The Halifax Reclaim the Night March, now called Take Back The Night, became an annual event (with one exception), and since that first exhilarating walk through the city's streets, so many women and groups have been involved it is impossible to name them.

The first march, organized by the Anarcha-Feminist Reading Group, was left-feminist in orientation and International Socialists, Communists and In Struggle all took part. It started from Red Herring Co-op Bookstore, then considered very "left."

About 50 women marched that night. Due to our rejection of authority, we refused to ask for a march permit, establishing a tradition for all subsequent Reclaim The Nights.

One year there was no march, but women refused to allow the event to die. A group united to make sure women marched the following year because they understood how meaningful and empowering it was.

Worldwide, the march is usually held on the third Friday in September. However, in Halifax the march has been held on a variety of dates—and it has gone beyond educating women about rape and assault to cover such issues as battering, incest and work harassment.

Men are not invited to the march, for our purpose is to empower women and act as a symbol of women's right to safety without male protection. In addition to media coverage, posters and pamphlets are distributed; pickets and banners created. Women and children meet around 8 pm for a short opening rally. Then the group—which has ranged from 50 to 200—marches along streets where women have been raped and through areas particularly dangerous to women.

As the marchers move through the night, slogans, songs of protest and solidarity ring out. The way is lit by candles and flashlights. After the march the women and children gather for refreshments, to collect their thoughts and enjoy—for a few more moments—the safety of each other's company.

For each woman who has marched there is a myriad of images and memories. Here are but a few:

• I remember the brave women living at Bryony House who went on their first march, frightened out of their wits that their husbands would see them in the streets or on TV. Hiding their faces with hoods, they walked together courageously.

• We nailed signs to posts which simply said, "A woman was raped on this spot" but boldly spoke the truth of the march.

• I remember the year we marched in the Natal Day parades in Halifax and Dartmouth, carrying placards denouncing violence against women and handing out pamphlets.

• As the parade moved along Argyle Street, men poured out of the bars and lined the sidewalks taunting us as we passed. Two beer bottles were thrown at us; one bottle was thrown back.

• One year the march ended in the Grand Parade Square. The next day the organizers received a complaint from the "city fathers" that the women had gathered near the Cenotaph, and this was disrespectful of the "war heroes"!

• One march, the largest and the longest, went into the foyer of the police station to express women's concern about the way police handled assault and battering cases.

• The designs and images on Reclaim The Night/Take Back The Night posters and placards will be imprinted on my mind's eye forever. They represent some very compelling feminist art.

• We all remember being touched by the courage and strength of women telling their personal stories of rape. They reminded us why we must Reclaim The Night.

Diann Graham, Diane Guilbault
Verona Singer

Women
RECLAIM THE NIGHT

A Woman's Place
1225 Barrington St.
Halifax, Nova Scotia

September 27. 9:30 p.m.

JOIN WOMEN MARCHING FOR OUR RIGHT TO BE SAFE ON THE STREETS, WITHOUT MALE PROTECTION, AND PROTEST VIOLENCE AGAINST WOMEN.

FREE DAYCARE PROVIDED: 24 HOUR ADVANCE NOTICE
FOR MORE INFORMATION, CALL 429-4063

BRING WHISTLES AND FLASHLIGHTS. CELEBRATION AFTERWARDS AT A WOMAN'S PLACE.

SPONSORED BY: WOMEN AGAINST VIOLENCE AGAINST WOMEN, AND A WOMEN'S PLACE.

(Katherine Kechnie, 1980)

8

Groups Dynamic: A Collection of Nova Scotia Her-Stories. CCLOW, 1990.

GREEN DRAGON PRESS

1970-1979 Introduction

"To have been a woman in Canada during the late 60s and early 70s was to have had the great fortune of witnessing and participating in one of the important struggles for personhood. Not the most important, of course, because that had been won for us by the early feminists of the women's suffrage movement. But after the interregnum that followed the Second World War, the 60s marked an awakening. Those were heady, exciting and challenging times for Canadian women who chose to view them as an opportunity to be independent and equal persons."

Rosemary Brown, *Being Brown: A Very Ordinary Life*.

Feminist movements have always represented different visions of the role and goals of women. All women cannot speak with one voice, however, the challenges of changing public policy on equal rights and women-centred services was a challenge for all women because it benefitted all women. The Liberal government retained power for the 1970s, and the issues of national unity and constitutional changes occupied most of the decade as many Canadians demanded reform. The decade ended with the repatriation of Canada's constitution from Britain. Canada adopted an official Multicultural Act in 1971 and the government placed significant funding for support of ethnic cultural activities. The war in Vietnam ended in 1975 and 80,000 Vietnamese 'boat people' entered Canada as a result of the new Immigration Act of 1978 and our first official refugee policy. Feminist movements were active in all these arenas- knitting thousands of blankets for Vietnamese children (Voice of Women VOW) or as members of Parliament (Flora MacDonald) in the creation of new policies.

Political and social activists along with artists, and environmentalists formed important non-governmental organizations, such as Greenpeace, that advocated for environmental, animal and human rights. The government spent millions of dollars to support Canadian culture and literature. As a result, major feminist writers such as Margaret Atwood and Alice Munro published poetry, novels and literary works that established a stronger voice for Canadian women and raised the stature of Canadian literature internationally. Independent socialist-feminist groups such as the Saskatoon Women's Liberation, Bread and Roses of Vancouver and the International Women's Day Committee played a major leadership role in the feminist movement.

Women's groups focused on labour issues, workplace environment, and childcare and reproductive rights. Women formed feminist unions, and political groups. In 1972 The National Action Committee on the Status of Women (NAC) was formed as a result of the report in 1970 from the Royal Commission on the Status of Women. In 1971 Kay Livingstone, a Canadian journalist formed the Canadian Negro Women's Association by amalgamating groups across the country. As well, women on the west coast formed the South Asian Women's Association in response to their larger presence in Canada.

GREEN DRAGON PRESS

Women Against Violence Against Women (WAVAW) spoke out against sadistic pornography, demanding safe streets for women. These efforts led to the "Take Back the Night Marches" that began in the early 80s. In 1977 the federal government passed the Human Rights Act that outlawed discrimination on the basis of gender and marital status and required that women employed by the government receive equal pay for work of equal value. Women fought on several fronts for further rights and greater power but the wage gap remained a significant hurdle.

In 1975 International Women's Year was proclaimed by the United Nations and major events across the nation celebrated the achievements of all women. Canadian feminist studies were offered in academic institutions and women challenged their legal rights in the courts.

- 1971 The Canadian Women's Educational Press (the Women's Press) was founded in Toronto to recognize the urgent need to publish material "by, for and about Canadian women." Their first project, published the following year was *Women Unite!* a collection of articles from women's groups across the country.

- 1973 The Women's Program of the Secretary of State was created. It became an important source of funding for women's organizations across the country.

GREEN DRAGON PRESS

Women's Organizations

In 1975, The Coloured Women's Club of Montréal looked back on 75 years of community service:

"The Coloured Women's Club of Montreal started in 1900, during the Boer War, as a social club and was founded formally in 1902. At that time there were few social agencies to relieve hardship or to aid the poor of any race, so that it was the Club's aim generally to assist Black people in Montreal in every way it could. Also, during this time there were many immigrants from the West Indies. They were often unprepared for Canadian winters and Canadian discrimination. The Coloured Women's Club provided warm clothing for these newcomers, and a welcome into the community.

During the First World War, when there was a flu epidemic, the Club maintained, as it did for many years after, a bed in the Grace Dart Hospital; it sent its members to look after the homes and children of hospitalized parents, and it provided a plot of land in Mount Royal Cemetery for the internment of members of the community whose relatives could not afford burial. The Club volunteered its members as visiting nurses and mothers' aides and, throughout the Depression between the two great wars, operated soup kitchens for the unemployed.

The Club has always worked closely with the Union United Church, drawing on its own resources to provide the Church with furniture, with its christening font and with its carpeting and linen. On its own and in cooperation with the Church and the Negro Community Centre, the Coloured Women's Club has provided bursaries for Black students, and aided in establishing among the young knowledge of and a pride in its Black heritage by the provision of books for the Black Studies Library at the Negro Community Centre.

The Club is a member of and active participant in the Montreal Council of Women, the National Black Coalition of Canada, the Negro Community Centre, the YWCA, and the Union United Church.

Though the Coloured Women's Club continues to dedicate itself to the well being of the Black community of Montreal, it wishes wholeheartedly to cooperate with any effort to achieve a more enlightened society for all. With this end in view, the Coloured Women's Club organized a large Montreal delegation of women to attend the 1st National Congress of Black Women held in Montreal in 1974, bringing together Black Women from coast to coast and from the United States and from as far away as Africa. After this Congress, they were able to assist in the formation of the Montreal Regional Committee of the National Congress. In 1976, the C.W.C. participated and assisted in the 3rd National Congress held in Halifax, and again in the 4th National Congress held in 1977 in Windsor. The representatives from the various regions have since met and have reached their goal of forming a permanent national body which elected its officers in Toronto in September 1977.

The Coloured Women's Club rejoices that the hopes and aspirations of Black women in Canada, such as those who sought expression 75 years ago in the founding of this club, now has a national voice.

The Coloured Women's Club has now reached this milestone of its 75th Anniversary and intends to commemorate this occasion by establishing a scholarship fund.

Some Missing Pages: The Black Community in the History of Quebec and Canada. Provincal Association of Social Studies Teachers, Quebec Board of Black Educators, Ministère L' Éducation, Quebec, 1996 rev.

GREEN DRAGON PRESS

Black Professional Women's Group

Growing with knowledge together and sharing with others.
Workshop theme, 1977

The Black Professional Women's Group is unique: we are rooted in the many black organizations that have for years struggled for equality.

Teachers and pupils of the segregated schools didn't have the opportunity for educational advancement for many years. Few students completed high school or entered university. In the schools teachers had little to work with; visual aids, reading materials and playground facilities were limited. Knowing what should be done, and how improvements could be made, was discouraging since little assistance was given.

Then in 1954 a group of teachers from eight black communities in Halifax County began to meet every Saturday morning to study and upgrade their qualifications, and to seek ways to improve some of the conditions that existed in their communities. This club was called the "Diogenes Study Club" after the Greek philosopher who, according to legend, searched with a lantern for an honest person.

These teachers believed that black people had a responsibility for the decisions that vitally affected their lives. They had the right to be provided with the education and training that would enable them to become employable, and thus help themselves.

It was not until 1969, however, that changes began to take place quickly. The Black United Front, The Black Educators Association and the Nova Scotia Human Rights Commission were in place to help eradicate segregation and discrimination. People realized the importance of minorities organizing and working together to protect their rights and to establish their dignity as a people.

On September 8, 1969, some dedicated teachers met to pay honour to three faithful teachers who had taught in black communities for more than 15 years: Inez Dymond (Cromwell) from Woodstock, N.B., Georgina Hill (Harper) from Bear River, N.S., and Doris Clements (Evans), Centerville, N.S.

At this gathering the teachers felt there was a great need for professional women to unite and seek ways to improve their status as women of the black race, and to deal with issues pertaining to women socially, culturally, educationally, spiritually and politically.

The Black Professional Women's Group started efficiently and professionally, organizing workshops, bringing in speakers, and setting up the "Inez Cromwell Scholarship Fund."

Many wonderful and interesting events emerged from such discussions as "Women's Role in Politics," "The Progress of the Black Child," "The Women's Liberation Movement" and "The Role of the Black Coalition."

The first Executive of the Black Professional Women's Group was: Alma Johnston, president; Florence Smith (Bauld), vice-president; Doris Evans, secretary; Lalia Grant, treasurer; and Gertrude Tynes, program chairperson. Because meetings were held in members' homes, our membership did not exceed 25.

Members—comprised of teachers, nurses, guidance counsellors, social workers, as well as a family court judge, human rights officers, sales representatives and nurses—have all contributed from their areas of expertise.

Now meetings are held at the Black Cultural Centre on the last Saturday of each month. We have ample space, and are encouraging anyone interested in promoting our aims to join.

We are a non-profit organization and raise money through projects such as raffles, concerts, cookbook sales, fashion shows, fun frolic fairs, teas, bowl-a-thons and bring and buys. Money is also raised by selling membership pins made up of three colours: yellow for prosperity, green for growth and black for our race.

Florence L. Bauld

Some members of the Black Professional Women's Group pose for a portrait in 1977: From left: Carolyn Smith, Connie James Glasgow, Florence Bauld, Carolyn Fowler, Gertrude Tynes, Alma Johnston, Patricia Rowley, Donna Smith, and Judy Barton. (Photo by Henry Bishop)

3

Groups Dynamic: A Collection of Nova Scotia Her-Stories. CCLOW, 1990.

The Case of Sandra Lovelace

The case of Sandra Lovelace is testament to the fact that one woman can effect change within the system – be it legal or political. Her determination to revise the Indian Act to make it equitable and just for Native women is an important milestone in Canadian legal history.

The Indian Act, legislated in 1869, established through law that aboriginal status was determined through marriage. Thus, if a woman born of Indian status married a non-status man, she lost her rights and privileges as an aboriginal according to the act. Section 12 (b) of the Act states that "Persons not entitled to be registered …[include] a woman who married a person who is not an Indian…". Subsequently, she would lose her band membership, property, inheritance, as well as her right to vote on the reserve. If she was widowed or divorced, she would not regain status. Conversely, if a non-status woman married a status male, she would be given the title of "status Indian", and would be entitled to all the rights associated with that title.

This is the document that changed Sandra Lovelace's life. Born on the Tobique Reserve in New Brunswick, 1947, Sandra was a member of the Maliseet tribe. In 1970, she married Bernie Lovelace, and moved to California. When her marriage ended, Sandra moved back to the Tobique Reserve with her children, only to learn that she was not protected by the rights she had previously been entitled to under the Indian Act. Towards 1977, Sandra joined a larger movement of Native women's groups (such as Indian Rights for Indian Women); supported by non-native women's organizations (such as the Voice of Women) lobbying for the removal of the above clause based on the fact that it was discriminatory against women. Part of the larger movement of second wave feminism, these groups used a number of tactics to make their voice heard, and pressure the Canadian government to amend the Act. In July of 1979, the Tobique group of women organized a 100-mile walk of women and children from the Oka Reserve to Ottawa to bring attention to their issue.

The process was slow. At first the Canadian government refused to change the act, stating that in order to do so, Native Peoples of Canada must be in agreement and there was division amongst these groups on the issue of women's status. In 1974, the Supreme Court of Canada upheld the Indian Act.

Sandra Lovelace, however, brought the case before the United Nations, submitting a complaint against the Canadian government in December of 1977. As a result in 1981, the United Nations committee found the Canadian government in breach of the International Covenant on Civil and Political Rights. In 1985, the Canadian parliament passed Bill C-31, amending the Indian Act, ensuring that Native women would be entitled to their status, regardless of marital status. The Indian Act continues to govern the relationship between the Canadian government and the Native peoples of this country.

The document that follows is a selection from the complaint submitted to the United Nations by Sandra Lovelace on December 29, 1977.

GREEN DRAGON PRESS

Sandra Lovelace v. Canada, Communication No. 24/1977 (31 July 1980), U.N. Doc. CCPR/C/OP/1 at 37 (1984).

Submitted by: Sandra Lovelace on 29 December 1977
Alleged victim: The author
State party: Canada
Date of decision: 31 July 1980 (tenth session)

Minorities--Indian Act--Sex discrimination--Right to marry--Protection of the family--Right of residence--Request to author and State party for specific information to enable Committee to formulate views

Articles of Covenant: 2, 3, 23, 27

Interim decision!

1. The author of the communication dated 29 December 1977, supplemented by letters of 17 April, 1978, 28 November 1979 and 20 June 1980, is a 32-yearold Canadian citizen of Indian origin, living in Canada. She was born and registered as a "Maliseet Indian" but lost her rights and status as an Indian, in accordance with Section 12 (1) (b) of the Indian Act, after having married a non-Indian on 23 May 1970. Pointing out that an Indian man who marries a non-Indian woman does not lose his Indian status, she claims that the Act is discriminatory on the grounds of sex and contrary to articles 2 (1), 3, 23 (I) and (4), 26 and 27 of the Covenant. As to the admissibility of the communication, she contends that she w~/s not required to exhaust local remedies since the Supreme Court of Canada, in The Attorney-General of Canada v. Jeanerie Lavell, Richard Isaac et al. v. Yvonne Bddard [1974] S.C.R. 1349, held that section 12 (1) (b) does not contravene the Canadian Bill of Rights and was, therefore, fully operative.

7. The Human Rights Committee recognizes that the relevant provision of the Indian Act, although not legally restricting the right to marry as laid down in article 23 (2) of the Covenant, entails serious disadvantages on the part of the Indian woman who wants to marry a non-Indian man and may in fact cause her to live with her ~anc~ in an unmarried relationship. There is thus a question as to whether the obligation of the State party under article 23 of the Covenant with regard to the protection of the family is complied with. Moreover, since only Indian women and not Indian men are subject to these disadvantages under the Act, the question arises whether Canada complies with its commitment under articles 2 and 3 to secure the rights under the Covenant without discrimination as to sex. On the other hand, article 27 of the Covenant requires States parties to accord protection to ethnic and linguistic minorities and the Committee must give due weight to this obligation. To enable it to form an opinion on these issues, it would assist the Committee to have certain additional observations and information.

10. The Human Rights Committee, accordingly, invites the observations of the parties on the above considerations and requests them, as appropriate, to furnish replies to the following questions:

(a) How many Indian women marry non-Indian men on an average each year? Statistical data for the last twenty years should be provided.

(b) What is the legal basis of a prohibition to live on a reserve? Is it a direct result of the loss of Indian status or does it derive from a discretionary decision of the Council of the community concerned?

(c) What reasons are adduced to justify the denial of the right of abode on a reserve?

(d) What legislative proposals are under consideration for ensuring full equality between the sexes with regard to Indian status? How would they affect the position of Mrs. Lovelace? How soon can it be expected that legislation will be introduced?

(e) What was Mrs. Lovelace's place of abode prior to her marriage? Was she at that time living with other members of her family? Was she denied the right to reside on a reserve in consequence of her marriage?

GREEN DRAGON PRESS

The Bra-Burning Myth

The term "bra-burning" has been used as a reference to female independence. The story was spread that during the 1970s, militant feminists burned their bras as a way of calling attention to their cause and thus raising public consciousness about women's issues. Over time, the term became associated with extreme feminism and by the end of the century it was ridiculed by women who wanted to show that they could be both independent as well as physically beautiful in a traditional way. But it was always a myth!

The bra-burning militant feminist is one of the strongest images of the stereotype – a mental picture of a woman ripping off her brassiere and flinging it onto a bonfire. The memory is constantly reinforced by references in popular culture and has been carried forward from a previous generation into this one. It is entrenched and rarely questioned. But it never happened.

The myth had its beginnings at the 1968 Miss American beauty pageant in Atlantic City, New Jersey. A small group of women picketed the pageant with signs saying "Let's Judge Ourselves as People." They crowned a live sheep, and dumped girdles, cosmetics, high-heeled shoes, and bras into a "freedom trash can". There was no fire and no feminists taking off bras in public and tossing them onto bonfires. The image of bras being thrown into a trashcan was photographed and a flippant print reference then became attached to the photo to create a false memory.

Feminist author Susan Brownmiller was at the event and she has stated:

"That's a myth. It was the time of draft-card burning, and some smart headline writer decided to call it a 'bra burning' because it sounded insulting to the then new women's movement. We only threw a bra symbolically in a trash can."

Between 1968 and 1992 it was assumed that the story was the work of a sensational male-dominated press who were glad to use anything to trivialize the women's complaints. But in the September 1992 issue of *MS Magazine*, contributing editor Lindsy Van Gelder admitted that she had been responsible for the story. Assigned to write a humour piece on the demonstration, she attempted to give credibility to the women's complaints by linking the activity with the burning of draft cards. Her plan backfired when the headline writer saw the possibilities for an image of braless feminists. The subtle comparisons Van Gelder had tried to make between the oppression of women and the oppression of an unjust war were lost to the readers, overshadowed by the mental imagery of braless feminists yelling slogans and waving signs.

- 1972 Nearly 500 women gathered in Toronto for the Strategy for Change conference and founded the National Action Committee on the Status of Women (NAC).

GREEN DRAGON PRESS

Moments in History

Commemorating Women's Role in Canadian History

 Ontario Women's Directorate

2 Carlton Street
12th Floor
Toronto, Ontario
M5B 2M9

Issue 3 February 1993
The third in a series.

International Women's Day — March 8th

On August 26, 1910 at the Second International Conference of Socialist Women in Copenhagen, Denmark, Clara Zetkin, the German socialist champion of the rights of women, proposed that a day be set aside each year as International Women's Day. One hundred women from 17 countries voted to support her resolution.

The women said that having an International Women's Day drew attention to the social, economic, and political injustices to which they were subjected and that it was just the most recent step in their fight against the double exploitation they suffered as women and factory workers.

The Beginning of the Struggle

Women's efforts to draw attention to workplace issues date back to the 1800s. In 1857, women working in the New York garment industry staged a massive demonstration against 12-hour working days, lack of benefits, sexual harassment, sexual assault on the job, and unfair wages.

The women walked off their jobs again in 1908 repeating their demands. This time, they also called for laws against child labour and they wanted the vote.

Their demands went largely ignored.

Then on March 25, 1911, the Asch Building, which housed the Triangle Shirtwaist Company, on the corner of Washington Place and Greene Street in New York City, burst into flames killing 145 women.

The mostly immigrant women who died in the fire worked in abominable conditions. The floors were littered with flammable materials. There were no sprinkler systems. The few fire escapes that existed were unsafe. The doors opened the wrong way and led to narrow dark stairwells. Many were locked to ensure that none of the women would be able to slip out, even for a moment's break, without their employer knowing.

On investigating the fire, authorities claimed that this building was no worse than most others, indeed, far superior to some of the 1,463 such sweatshops in existence in the city.

But New York's Fire Commissioner, who testified before the State Factory Investigating Commission said: "I think that a great many of the fire escapes in buildings today are only put up to be called 'a fire escape.' They are absolutely inadequate and absolutely useless."

The theme for the first International Women's Day in 1911 was "International Female Suffrage." Over the years, the themes have evolved to reflect the diversity of the women's community, women's changing roles and continuing struggle. This year, the theme is "No time to stop...Our struggle must continue."

In 1975, the United Nations formally proclaimed March 8th International Women's Day

197

GREEN DRAGON PRESS

Eighty thousand workers marched through a drenching rain to attend the mass funeral for the women who perished in the fire, while an estimated quarter of a million people watched silently.

And still nothing changed.

Again, on January 11, 1912, textile workers numbering 14,000 went out on strike for better wages and working conditions. With the cry of, "Better to starve fighting than starve working," the women stayed out for nearly three months. Their courage inspired the song that has since become the anthem of the women's movement "Bread and Roses." "Bread" symbolizes economic security; "roses" stand for a better life.

The Canadian Experience

Similar issues existed in Canada. Speaking about wages and women's suffrage in 1893, Ontario's Minister of Agriculture at the time, John Dryden, expressed the prevailing sentiments of the day when he said, "...this same lady tells us that women do not receive equal pay with men for equally good work. How can the ballot correct this? Can you compel by law the payment of a higher scale of wages? So long as women are willing and anxious to work for a lesser wage than men, so long will they be paid less."

There were 1,078 unions in Canada as early as 1902. However, women remained, for the most part, unorganized and unprotected. The fact that women had to work was considered a "social crisis." People felt a woman belonged in the home and that a man should provide for her. Women's work was largely unskilled and so, entirely dispensable.

Unskilled women workers had little leverage or protection against employers. They could be, and were, replaced by other unskilled labour at the whim of their employers at very little cost.

Between 1901 and 1921 there were 287 strikes for better working conditions and a living wage in Montreal alone. In 115 of these strikes, the workers' demands were entirely rejected and often, the strikers were fired and scab labour hired to replace them.

Employers were particularly hostile to women trying to organize. They saw a unionized workforce of women as an end to a ready supply of cheap labour.

Established unions offered little support to women. Despite worker solidarity and policies supporting equal pay, unions often bargained lower increases for poorly paid women workers.

Progress Was Slow

It would take many more years for North American women to achieve some of their demands. Here are some significant landmarks in their struggle for workplace equity:

- Between 1913 and 1929 Canada enacted various pieces of legislation prohibiting child labour.
- Canadian women were given the suffrage to vote in national elections in 1918.

- By the mid-1940s, the average working day had dropped to eight hours.
- Women in Ontario were given equal pay for equal work in 1951.
- Maternity leave was legislated in Canada in 1970.
- The Ontario Human Rights Code was amended to prohibit sexual harassment in 1982.
- Equal pay for work of equal value was legislated in Ontario in 1988.

And yet today, women still have a long way to go before they achieve equality in the workplace:

- In 1990, 60% of all (both full-time and part-time) working women in Ontario earned less than $20,000.
- Average 1991 earnings of women working full-time, full-year, amounted to 70% of men's earnings.
- Women remain clustered in low-paying jobs, often offering little, or no, opportunity for advancement.
- One out of every five women working in Ontario in 1986 worked in a clerical, sales, or service job.
- Women in Ontario made up only 18% of upper-level management in 1986.
- Although union membership can help women secure higher wages, more benefits and increased job protection, only 22% of the female labour force was unionized in 1987.

 Ontario Women's Directorate   Reproduction of this document is encouraged.

Ontario Women's Directorate

198

GREEN DRAGON PRESS

Women and Work

"I warn working women not to give in to rising public pressure from all sides to go 'back to the kitchen' and give jobs back to men. I tell them: 'those are your jobs and you're entitled to keep them."

Grace Hartman, President of CUPE 1975-83. (102,000 members, 40% female.)

Domestic Workers

Throughout history, there has always been a demand for women in domestic service. Canadian women have always found jobs in this field and many immigrant women were engaged in domestic service as entrance level employment in Canada. Women in domestic service worked as caregivers to the young, old and disabled. They worked as cooks, cleaners and house and office managers. Female domestic workers have always faced a number of difficulties. If they are live-in caregivers they often have little privacy, lack freedom, are controlled by strangers, and isolated from their family and friends. They generally work very long hours, engage in large workloads and receive inadequate pay. They are often restricted in terms of providing for their own needs.

In the late 1950s and throughout the 1960s women from many countries came to Canada. They came from Jamaica, Vietnam, Portugal, Italy, Poland and the Philippines. Legislation to regulate foreign domestic workers allowed temporary work permits. Sometimes the permits became invalid once the work contract was dissolved. Immigrant women regarded domestic service as a stepping-stone towards citizenship. Most hoped to eventually find other employment opportunities or marriage and freedom in Canada.

This is the story of one woman who arrived in Canada from Dominica, leaving behind eight children who she supported single-handedly. She left Dominica because the money she earned there was not enough to support the family.

"I am fifty-four years old. I came to Toronto twelve years ago. Sometimes it looks like I only came yesterday. What I mean is that I hardly know anywhere. I don't really go out, ever since I came here it was from work to home, and now it is just from church to home. Since I have been here I have never even gone to a movie…

When I came to Canada in 1971, I wasn't on the work permit. I came up here on an invitation letter from a friend who was here working as a domestic. She write to me in Dominica and told me that she was working as a babysitter and that if I came up it wouldn't be hard for me to get a job. I was glad for the break, because I wasn't doing anything in Dominica. It was hard to find work, and when I did work the money wasn't enough to support my family…In 1971, I came up to my friend and I stayed with her for a while, and I got a job as a chambermaid in a hotel. They didn't ask me for any papers and I was glad for that. It took me about three weeks to find that job. Some places wanted papers, but this place didn't want any so I started working there.

The work was hard and dirty. I stayed it out for a year before I left. I had to leave, not that I wanted to; because out of that money I could send home a little something for my children. But I was given the dirtiest rooms to clean. I began to notice that sometimes when I'm going

GREEN DRAGON PRESS

through four rooms some of the other women working there were just finishing up their first room. They were there longer so I guess they knowed how to operate. Is like they try to break in new girls by giving them the dirtiest rooms to clean and the longest shifts. I even began to notice that I was not getting pay for my overtime and for the holidays that I worked. I remember one day I ask the supervisor about it and she asked me to bring in my papers for her to see. When I got home and told my friend about it, she told me that I mustn't go back to the job, because the supervisor was going to squeal on me. She told me that those hotel people know that most of the girls working there wasn't landed and so they try and overwork them because they know they couldn't go to the law.

I left that job and tried to get one in a factory, but I walk until my foot was tired, everywhere I was told the same thing, that I need Canadian experience. Yet when I worked as a chambermaid nobody ask me for Canadian experience.
I walk and answer a lot of ads in the paper and every time I go for the job interview they said that the job was taken. Eventually, I went back to work in another hotel as a chambermaid. I told

them I had experience working as a chambermaid because I thought would give me more money, but they didn't. They pay me the same pay, minimum wage; and when I worked holidays, they never pay me overtime; sometimes even when I work two shifts they only pay me for the one I work. But I was scared to speak up so I didn't. Eventually I save up my money and bought a suitcase and every week I went to Honest Ed's and bought clothes for my children. Then I bought a barrel at one of the West Indian stores and buy more shoes and clothes and flour and rice, and then the barrel and the suitcase was pack with clothes and food, I bought a ticket and went home. I couldn't take it here any longer, this wasn't the kind of life I was accustom to."

But her decision to return to Dominica proved a failure. Things were just the same so when a friend wrote about a child-care job she returned to Canada. A work permit was arranged and she returned in 1974. At the time of the interview she had been with the same family for nine years and was waiting to hear if she had been accepted as a permanent resident.

Silenced: Talks with working class West Indian women about their lives and struggles as domestic workers in Canada by Makeda Silvera. Toronto: Williams-Wallace Publishers Inc., Toronto, 1983.

Immigrant women entrepreneur.
Vancouver Public Library.

GREEN DRAGON PRESS

In 1977 in British Columbia The Women's Research Team, funded by Canada Works and sponsored by Vancouver Status of Women, was established to determine the degree of provincial implementation of the recommendations made by the Royal Commission on the Status of Women, published in 1970. The team looked at, and made recommendations in four broad areas, labour, education, social services and family law. The team made the following recommendations concerning Equal Pay.

We recommend that the federal Female Employees Equal Pay Act, the federal Fair Wages and Hours of Work Regulations and equal pay legislation of provinces and territories require that:

a) the concept of skill, effort and responsibility be used as objective factors in determining what is equal work, with the understanding that pay rates thus established will be subject to such factors as seniority provisions;

b) an employee who feels aggrieved as a result of an alleged violation of the relevant legislation or a party acting on her behalf, be able to refer the grievance to the agency designated for that purpose by the government administering the legislation;

c) the onus of investigating violations of the legislation be placed in the hands of the agency administering the equal pay legislation which will be free to investigate whether or not complaints have been laid;

d) to the extent possible, the anonymity of the complainant be maintained;

e) provision be made for authority to render a decision on whether or not the terms of the legislation have been violated, to specify action to be taken and to prosecute if the orders are not followed;

f) where someone has presented the aggrieved employee's case on her behalf and the aggrieved employee is unsatisfied with the decision, she have the opportunity to present her case herself to the person or persons rendering the decision who may change the decision;

g) the employee's employment status be in no way adversely affected by application of the law to her case;

h) where the law has been violated, the employee be compensated for any losses in pay, vacation and other fringe benefits;

i) union and employee organizations, as well as employers and employer organizations, be subject to this law;

j) penalties be sufficiently heavy to be an effective deterrent; and

k) the legislation specify that it is applicable to part-time as well as to full-time workers.

Update on the status of women in British Columbia, March 1978.

GREEN DRAGON PRESS

Feminist publications

The women's liberation movement that gained momentum in the late 1960s and gained power and organization into the 1970s, saw the results of their efforts in the feminist publications that materialized during the decade. *Ms* magazine, an American publication, had an enormous impact on the movement as it gave women an important venue in which to access feminist information and gave a voice to problems women faced at work, home, in education and in healthcare. The first issue of Ms magazine launched initially as a "one-shot sample insert in New York magazine" in December 1971, became a landmark institution for women's rights everywhere and set the stage for future publications. The co-founding members of *Ms.* magazine included Letty Cottin Pogrebin and Gloria Steinem, whose names quickly became synonymous with the women's movement. Steinem, for example also help found the National Women's Political Caucus and the Women's Action Alliance the same year. They, and other writers from the magazine, became spokespersons for issues related to women's rights and the treatment of women.

Canadians had their own feminist publications that responded to the issues and concerns of Canadian women. One of these magazines was called *Healthsharing*. It began publication in 1978 and continued to publish with a growing circulation throughout the 1980s. Organizations as well as government committees had been created during the decade in order to deal with the issues related to healthcare. Women demanded greater control in heath issues related to birth control, abortion, and birthing, childcare and general heath advice. The period saw an increase in activists who demanded health alternatives for women and a greater voice in the decision making process. Therefore publications such as *Healthsharing* provided a vital role in providing Canadian women with a venue for information and alternatives. Other Canadian feminist publications included *Resources for Feminist Research*, *Broadside*, *Room of One's Own*, *Briarpatch* and *Bodypolitic*. Although Canadian women also purchased American feminist magazines, they fought hard to create a unique voice for themselves, often developing small independent publishing companies and recognizing the limited revenue available in Canada.

THE OTHER WOMAN

MAY-JUNE '72 TORONTO Vol.one No.one

25¢

A Revolutionary Feminist Newspaper

GREEN DRAGON PRESS

Healthsharing Magazine

"Healthsharing – the concept of sharing health is, for us, a feminist approach to health and healing. It denotes the caring and sense of community, which are the essence of both feminism and healing. The emphasis is upon the positive, the ideal – health. Our concern is with health in all its aspects, as it relates to our bodies, our minds, our common and individual environments. Sharing is the process – the sharing of knowledge, ideas, experiences and responsibility.

The women's health movement has made important inroads into the professional control of health care. Witness the birth control centres, self help groups and women's health collectives, which have sprung up across the country. The 'well woman' and 'self help' approaches to health, originally developed by women, have become popularized. But we in Canada are still working in isolation or in small groups. A women's health movement exists but is scattered and disjointed and all too often, invisible. Our work is important and it's crucial that we develop a strong identity as a movement, supporting each other and sharing with each other.

Before the onset of modern medicine, healing was a traditionally female domain, co-existing with woman's role as mother and nurturer. A fundamental difference between female lay healers and the male-dominated medical profession was in their approach to knowledge. Female lay healers operated within a network of information sharing and mutual support, male doctors hoarded knowledge, restricting access to an exclusive minority. They created in scientific and medical knowledge a valuable and limited commodity to be traded on the marketplace.

We object to the lack of availability of this knowledge and the ways in which it is used to retain power and control in the hands of a few 'experts.' We object to research and technology being directed toward the maintenance of the existing system. The medical profession has long defined health with the male as the norm. Women patients have been subjected to male myths about the female body. As a result, women have been mistreated and ignored by doctors upon whom we have been forced to rely by virtue of the exclusivity of medical knowledge. However, the readily apparent oppression of women is indicative of the inherent oppression of the whole system. It is the whole system which we, as women, are struggling to change.

Our hope for this magazine is that it will become a part of the process of change and discovery in working toward a new vision of health, a vision which we conceive of as a feminist vision. The first step toward creating an alternative is to communicate, to share with one another and to trust one another. We hope that this magazine will provide a vehicle through which women across Canada communicate with each other and share their thoughts, their ideas, their knowledge…their health. We want to take health out of the hands of the experts and return it to our own collective and individual hands."

Healthsharing, Volume 1, Number 1, November 1979.

GREEN DRAGON PRESS

Healthsharing

VOLUME 1, NUMBER 1   NOVEMBER 1979

GREEN DRAGON PRESS

Gender Stereotypes

In the early 1970s, both women and men were beginning to question their traditional roles both in and out of the home. The following article pokes fun at the term "househusband" as an alternative to the traditional "housewife". Society at this point was not ready to accept this role reversal.

According to Doyle

Househusband? Here's A Sure Loser

HOUSEHUSBAND—that's a 12-letter word meaning trouble.

I don't know who dreamed up this masculine equivalent to "housewife" but I wish she (I'm sure it was a she) hadn't.

Originally it was used, I think, only as a term for the occasional man who swapped jobs with his wife by running the home front while she ran around in the business world. But recently I've heard it applied to any man who lends a helping hand with the housework.

It's a fighting word.

You show me a woman who starts calling her mate a househusband and I'll show you a woman who starts doing dishes alone.

Of course "housewife" is a fighting word to many a woman whose running of the home front includes being everything from laundress to chauffeur.

But she's grown accustomed to it. Besides, what's an acceptable replacement for it?

Men won't grow accustomed to being referred to as a househusband, no matter how much housework they do.

These days lots of men lend a helping hand around the home. But they prefer to lend it casually. The male is sensitive in this area, as every veteran housewife knows. He doesn't respond well to a peremptory shout for help. Better to limp a little as you tote that garbage tin. Or, better still, to give him that "you're-so-much-stronger-dear" bit.

Sure it's old-fashioned. Sure it's corny. But it gets the garbage out and it gets *you* in.

Which is where you won't be if you call him that 12-letter word.

Getting A Head Of Myself

This picture shows a couple of housewives who don't mind being called that, even though we work at a few other things besides housework.

It was taken in the back yard of Ella Heagle's Calgary home the day I went there to pick up my head.

Remember Ella Heagle, the button lady?

Last February there was a photograph of her in the column with a couple of pictures she had made from her button collection—one was a clever caricature of our Fathers of Confederation.

When I visited her then, she showed me some needlework portraits she had done, fascinating tapestry work that from a short distance away looked like paintings. To get this effect, she explained, she uses hundreds of different stitches and shadings of color. And all she needs to do a portrait is a photo or a painting to copy or adapt.

"I'll do you a head," she offered.

"Just what I need," said I, "another head."

And that's what I'm holding in this picture, an amusing copy of the photo that's at the top of this column.

Mrs. Heagle is holding her version of a famous head, one of Botticelli's paintings.

Since last February she's been stitching like mad and her needlework portraits have been displayed in museums, libraries and department stores and on television.

Montreal Star Weekend Magazine
Vol. 20, No. 41, October 10, 1970.

The Breadwinner

"WELL, I'VE GOT TO GO TO WORK, EVEN IF YOU DON'T."

Betty Swords, Male Chauvinist Pig Calender, 1974.

The issue of unfair division of labour in the home sparked commentary in Canada and the USA, ranging from cartoon humour to calls for political action. For some women though, society's notions about the value of their work, and the laws that upheld these views had disturbing consequences.

Justice Denied:
The Murdoch case

Irene and James Murdoch were married in 1943 and separated in 1968. Besides performing what the Court referred to as "wifely household duties," Irene contributed substantially to the day-to-day operation of their ranch business. James Murdoch worked away from the ranch for five months every year and Irene did his work in his absence. The work she did included: "Haying, raking, swathing, moving, driving truck and tractors and teams, quietening horses, taking cattle back and forth to the reserve, dehorning, vaccinating, branding... Just as a man would, anything that was to be done." The divorce court ruled that Irene Murdoch had no legal claim to the property that she helped build and support for more that 20 years of marriage. Irene took the case to the Supreme Court who ruled that she was not a partner with her husband in the ranch land and buildings and since her name wasn't on the deed, she was not entitled to benefit. . Irene Murdoch received nothing from the $95,000. gained from the sale of the property and was left with legal bills of $65,000.

The result was a public outcry and inquiry into the state of community property laws and divorce settlements throughout Canada. Women demanded an equal share of the marital property as they had contributed towards it management, operation and maintenance. Within five years all Provinces brought in legislation to overturn the effect of the decision.

The new legislation made it possible to win judgements, however collecting on the judgements was never easy. One of the most tragic cases was that of Rosa Becker. (See Chapter 9.)

The Canadian Women's Movement Archives was founded in 1977 to collect material from the contemporary (post 1960) Canadian women's movement. In 1977 when the newspaper *The Other Woman* closed Pat Leslie took its records into her home and expanded the archival base. Pat was crucial to the founding of the Archives.

Collective members and volunteers of the CWMA were feminist activists creating an independent community based archives, research and resource center. The CWMA collective expanded throughout the 1980's. Women's groups began donating material, organizational procedures and a filing system were established, and the collective raised funds for projects in creative ways, from yard sales and bridge tournaments, to securing short-term grants.

By 1991 it was clear that the Archives had grown to a point that required staff and funds that would ensure long term survival, accessibility and maintenance of the collection. In 1992 the Archives found a new bilingual home, at the University of Ottawa, where it is a part of the Library Network. An advisory committee continues to provide direction and support.

GREEN DRAGON PRESS

Teenagers Speak Out

An article in the *Toronto Star*, March 3, 1977 headlined "School bans students' birth control survey" exemplified the on-going difficulty in dealing publicly with this issue despite the widespread legality and availability of the birth control pill and other means of birth control. Discussion of the topic was considered taboo in many venues. Nevertheless, the comments of Anne Bigwin, an 18 year old in grade 13 suggests that women are knowledgeable about the wider societal implications of the issue. The proposal by two students to conduct a birth control survey was turned down by the principal because he was afraid it might upset parents. The students said they needed the information for a health project on family planning and expressed disappointment that adults did not realize the importance of the subject.

"Statistics show that 12 and 13 year olds are sexually active and we wanted to find out how young people are dealing with the problems that can come from this," Ms Bigwin stated.

The principal responded that there was birth control information available at the school and that he objected to the plan to ask students what methods they were using. He said he didn't understand the need to know what types were being used.

"What difference does it make if they are using a birth control pill or a condom or an IUD – whatever that is" he asked.

Ms Bigwin said that she believes that many young people don't know about the different methods and that parents are often unwilling to talk with their children about the issue. She said that she understood the delicate nature of the subject but felt strongly that sweeping it under the rug would not cure the problem.

In the 1970s, *Liberty* Magazine provided a forum for youth expression – the For Teen-Agers page. The attitudes and perspective of young Canadian women and men are voiced in these letters to the editor. The topics include a number of issues: the role of parents, authority and dating.

TEENS SPEAK OUT

Let's Rough It

Teen-agers today are too sheltered.

We've all heard our parents tell us: "You're too young. I don't think you should go. You'll just end up in some kind of trouble."

They probably mean well, but do they realize they could be doing more harm than good? Eventually, we will meet problems we must face alone. We might as well begin now.

We should be allowed to experience life gradually—both its joys and heartaches—and decide for ourselves the difference between right and wrong. To become mature citizens, we need the experience of making our own decisions, thereby proving to our elders we're grownup enough not to let them down.

Linda Schrader, 17
Okla, Sask.

Girls Aren't Dirt!

Boys have a lot of habits that make me angry.

They think it's good manners to blast the car horn out front, instead of coming in to get me like a gentleman. They think a big necking session goes with every date, just like dessert goes with supper.

Well, I'm fed up with the way boys treat girls. Like other girls, I'm sick of having to fight and argue and coax to keep boys in line. On the whole, boys treat girls like dirt. They make us feel we're just bodies, with no minds, no emotions, no anything. I'm tired of boys acting like we're just necking machines. We're whole people, with minds and feelings as well as bodies.

Inez Brophy, 17
Daniel's Harbor, Nfld.

We've Got Ideas, Too

Just because we're teen-agers, does that mean we haven't got any brains, any good ideas?

Some parents look down on teen-agers when they try to give advice, as if teen-agers can't possibly have a good idea because they haven't lived long enough. Parents look at us and say: "We're older and have a lot more experience." They're right to some extent, but that doesn't mean teen-agers' ideas should be sloughed off like water from a duck's back.

Just because parents have had more experience doesn't mean they shouldn't heed a little advice once in a while. They should remember they're setting the example for the parents of tomorrow.

Gary Burke, 17
New Glasgow, N.S.

Liberty awards prizes every month for teen-agers' opinions. Let's hear what you think, in a letter 300 words or less, on any subject which might interest other teen-agers. Prizes are $25, $10 and $5 respectively for the month's three best letters. Send as many entries as you wish to TEENS SPEAK OUT, Liberty, 55 York St., Toronto.

GREEN DRAGON PRESS

The 1970s Recalled

For many young women, to be young and female in the 1970s meant being a part of the very vocal women's liberation movement. This movement challenged the status quo. Women wanted equal rights and equal pay, and they were now willing to fight for this outcome through higher education, through the workforce and through union work. Crusaders such as Gloria Steinem, and publications such as *Ms. Magazine* provided important role models for young women.

Young women discussed issues of equality and civil rights in their schools and their homes and joined numerous organizations in order to make their voices heard. They also listened to music that supported their political and social beliefs. This awareness was an essential part of the 1970s anti-war, human rights movements.

The following is a brief list that defined the life of one teenager during this decade.

Ten Memories about being in High School in the early years of the 70s.

1. It meant wearing clothes just like my older brother: jeans, shirts and comfy shoes, and protesting in school, with 'sit-ins' to demand that we be allowed to wear jeans to class.

2. It meant marching in peace protests down Yonge Street, singing songs.

3. It meant wearing lots of buttons on my jackets to indicate my support for a clean environment, saving the whales, women's rights to abortion and government supported daycare.

4. It meant going to coffee shops to hear folk music, music with a message, and leaving with more buttons.

4. It meant going to the reception houses where young and frightened American draft dodgers were staying, giving them support.

6. It meant Bob Dylan, Leonard Cohen, Joan Baez, The Doors and The Stones: playing music in my bedroom and believing in their political messages.

7. It meant writing letters of concern or protests about injustices around the world, purchasing Diet for a Small Planet and then deciding to become a Vegan because it was better for my body as well as the earth's body.

8. It meant having a boyfriend who was an artist and photographer, a family that was loving and supportive, and the excitement of knowing that more doors were open to women of my generation than had been open during my Mother's early years.

9. It meant believing that the future would be more peaceful and more equitable.

10. It meant being proud to be a Canadian and not an American.

Rose Fine and a friend. 1972, *Forest Hill Collegiate Year Book.*

GREEN DRAGON PRESS

Notable Women

Rosemary Brown 1930 - 2003

"We must open doors and we must see to it they remain open, so that others can pass through." Rosemary Brown, 1972.

Feminist, writer, lecturer, and social activist Rosemary Brown was born in Jamaica on June 17, 1930 into a family of politically active, dynamic female elders. Her early years shaped a passionate sense of obligation and responsibility for social and racial justice. She came to Canada to study. Following graduation from McGill University, she married and moved to Vancouver, where she obtained an MA from the University of British Columbia. A social worker, she served as ombudswoman for the Vancouver Status of Women, entered politics and won a seat in the BC provincial legislature, the first Black woman to be elected to a Canadian legislature. She ran for the leadership of the federal New Democratic Party in 1975, coming a close second. In 1986 Rosemary continued her work on the national and international level through organizations such as MATCH International. From 1993 to 1996 she served as Chief Commissioner of the Ontario Human Rights Commission. She was the recipient of the Order of Canada and the Order of Distinction, Jamaica. That was the public Rosemary Brown, who spoke out on women's rights, poverty, human rights and race issues, with commitment and passion. The private Rosemary Brown cherished her family and friends. She had a wonderful sense of humour. She loved gardening, opera, orchids, line dancing, crocheting, reading and everything that was beautiful or joyous.

Rosemary Brown followed her own advice; opening doors and keeping them open so that we could pass through them too.

2004 Black History Poster
Green Dragon Press
www3.sympatico.ca/equity.greendragonpress

Joyce Wieland 1931 - 1998

Joyce Wieland was a Canadian artist. She was a proud feminist and a strong willed, independent person who expressed her strong beliefs through her art in a very unique way. Joyce Wieland was born in Toronto in 1931, the elder daughter of British immigrants. She attended Central Technical School where she studied commercial art and was taught by Doris McCarthy, a landscape painter who was instrumental in encouraging Joyce's talents. Joyce practiced art and filmmaking and became one of Canada's most prolific and influential artists. A filmmaker, painter, and assemblage artist, she was actively involved with early Pop Art work. Wieland and artist husband Michael Snow lived in New York between 1962 and 1972 before they returned to Toronto. After returning to Toronto, Joyce Wieland became the first female to be the subject of a retrospective at the National Gallery of Canada. The show, entitled "True Patriot" highlighted the significance of her contribution of feminism, nationalism and ecological issues into Canadian art. Since then she has been the subject of a number of other large-scale exhibitions and retrospectives. Most recently, the Cinematheque Ontario held a film retrospective and published a book of theoretical writings on her films which was edited by Kathryn Elder." She

GREEN DRAGON PRESS

believed in democratizing art by blurring the line between crafts and high art, and "serving her country as an artist. Her work Young Woman's Blues was reproduced and discussed in Lucy Lippard's early survey book, *Pop Art*.

In 1971 the National Gallery organized the first solo exhibition of the work of a living Canadian woman, Joyce Wieland.

Kay Livingstone 1918 - 1975

Kay Livingstone is best known for her role in organizing the first National Congress of Black Women in 1973. Her life was devoted to social activism - as a member of many groups, including the Canadian Negro Women's Association. Kay was born in 1918 to James and Christina Jenkins of London, Ontario. Her parents were themselves active in the Black community, founding the newspaper *Dawn of Tomorrow*. She showed an early interest in the performing arts, studying first in London, then at the Royal Conservatory of Music in Toronto, and later at the Ottawa College of Music. During the Second World War, Kay worked at the Dominion Bureau of Statistics in Ottawa, where she married George Livingstone in 1942. It was in Ottawa that she began a career as a radio host with "The Kathleen Livingstone Show" a career she would continue with their move to Toronto, where she hosted programs on several stations including the Canadian Broadcasting Corporation (CBC). She also became a leading amateur and professional actress. Her involvement with the Canadian Negro Women's Association (CANEWA) began in late 1950, when she joined a Toronto women's social club then known as the Dilettantes. Kay lost no time in changing both the name, and the club's focus. As the new organization's first president, she encouraged the other

members to take up service projects. An early CANEWA undertaking, and one which would continue throughout the group's existence, was the provision of scholarships to deserving Black students. Later activities included the organization of the Calypso Carnival (forerunner of the Caribana Festival) as a fundraiser for other service projects.

Kay served as the president of CANEWA from 1951 to 1953, although she continued to act as a strong influence in the group for many years afterwards. She was the guiding force behind CANEWA's most public success: the first National Congress of Black Women, which was held in Toronto from April 6 to 8, 1973. Eighteen months in the planning, the Congress brought together 200 women from across Canada. Workshops were held on subjects such as education, single parents, and senior citizens, and resolutions on many subjects were passed. Perhaps most importantly, the Congress inspired the delegates to maintain close ties with each other, leading to further conventions at Montreal in 1974, Halifax in 1976, Windsor in 1978, and Winnipeg in 1980. It was at the Winnipeg meeting that the Congress of Black Women was formed, an organization which today has over 600 members and is one of Kay Livingstone's legacies.

In the last years of her life, Kay worked as a consultant to the Privy Council of Canada, travelling the country in preparation for a conference on visible minorities in Canada (a term with which she is credited with coining). One of the people she met on these travels was Carrie Best; it is a credit to Kay Livingstone's influence that after her death in 1975, Ms. Best formed the Kay Livingstone Visible Minority Women's Society in her honour.

GREEN DRAGON PRESS

Activities
1970 – 1979

FEMINIST PUBLICATIONS

As a class, produce a "feminist" publication as it may have appeared in the 1970s.
Create artwork for the cover.
Write short articles that report on key women's issues of the 1970s. Use this chapter for ideas.
Assign a creative student to write a poem or short story.
What advertisements would you include?

THE CASE OF SANDRA LOVELACE

Create a "heritage minute" for Sandra Lovelace, p165.

ORGANIZING FOR CHANGE/WOMEN'S ORGANIZATIONS

Form small groups. Vote on an issue that is important to bring to the attention of the class. Create the framework for an organization that would champion this cause. Consider the following:
What would the name of your organization be?
How would you structure this organization?
What activities would you plan to promote your cause and educate the public?
Write a manifesto for you organization detailing its objectives and philosophy.
As a concluding activity, discuss as a class the difficulties women may have encountered forming and running these clubs/organizations.

INTERNATIONAL WOMEN'S DAY

On March 8, as a class, prepare a display for the school, which highlights the history of International Women's Day, p168, and women's achievements and struggles on a global level.

Resources

Adamson, Nancy, Linda Briskin & Margaret McPhail. *Feminists Organizing for Change: the Contemporary Women's Movement in Canada,* Don Mills: Oxford Univer. Press, 1988.
Briskin, Linda and Lynda Yanz. *Union sisters: Women in the Labour Movement,* Toronto: Women's Press, 1983.
Brown, Rosemary. *Being Brown: A Very Public Life.* Toronto: Random House, 1989.
Hewitt, Marsha & Claire Mackay. *One Proud Summer,* Toronto: Women's Press, 1981.
Kechnie, Margaret & Marge Reitsma-Street. *Changing Lives: Women in Northern Ontario,* Toronto: Dundurn Press, 1996.

www.coolwomen.org - Rosemary Brown

Poster: Rosemary Brown: Daring to dream the impossible. Toronto: Green Dragon Press, 2004.
www3.sympatico.ca/equity.greendragonpress

GREEN DRAGON PRESS

1980 – 1989

Fighting for charter rights

WOMEN IN HEALTH

Staff of Immigrant Women's Centre

Immigrant Women's Shelter

The Immigrant Women's Centre is a community-based health service which promotes health among immigrant women. It has adopted a holistic approach focusing on well-being, not just on the absence of disease. Dionne Brand, a counsellor at the centre says they do not just "give the women information and services but also that these services are designed specifically to empower immigrant women to take control of their bodies."

Counsellors at the centre identify language, culture and race as vital components to be considered in any communication or education process.

Accordingly, staff is multilingual and multiracial.

The IWC was established in 1975 to fill the need that existed among immigrant women for proper health care. Services are used mainly by women of Caribbean, Chinese, Spanish, Italian, Portugese and Vietnamese backgrounds. Counsellor Patricia Hayes states that immigrant women did not and still do not have access to professional health care, not only because of language barriers but also because of their specific jobs. "Immigrant women," she says, "tend to be concentrated in service occupations or as textile and garment workers. These jobs tend to be among the lowest paid and women are reluctant to take time off to have routine examinations. After the working day is done, medical services are relatively unavailable."

Many of the counsellors have backgrounds in community health. Some are nurses. The centre operates a clinic every Tuesday evening staffed by a doctor, usually a woman. Hayes says the centre provides counselling, information and referrals on a variety of health matters — detection of breast

and cervical cancers, pregnancy and childbirth, gynecological infections, family planning, good nutrition, stress management, patient rights. "We stress the concept of preventive health care," she says, "since many women seek medical attention only in crisis situations." On average, about 200 women use the clinic each month.

Although the centre was very successful, staff realized that many immigrant women were not and could not make use of the services. They were unable to take time off work, and after work had to rush home to attend their families' needs. In an attempt to bring health services to these women, a mobile clinic was opened by the IWC in January 1984. Like the centre, the Mobile Health Unit places emphasis on reproductive and preventive health care.

When a work site is selected, the major language group or groups are identified and the appropriate counsellors travel with the clinic. Before the mobile clinic sets up, IWC counsellors come to the factory or shop and, in lunch break presentations, tell the women what the clinic is and does,

1980-1989 Introduction

"Notwithstanding anything in this Charter, the rights and freedoms referred to in it are guaranteed equally to male and female persons."

Section 28, Canadian Charter of Rights and Freedoms."

The decade began with a major referendum in Quebec in which 60 % of the population voted "Non" and 40% voted "Oui" on the question of sovereignty association. Women in Quebec gathered in massive rallies called the "Yvette movement" and challenged the separatist movement's position on the status of women. The Clark government fell and Pierre Elliot Trudeau regained power. He began steps towards constitutional changes. The Canadian Charter of Rights and Freedom (1982) included a universal declaration of human rights. Women in Canada fought aggresively to ensure that their rights were included in this important document. Women's groups continued to lobby for change. One of these groups was the National Action Committee on the Status of Women (NAC). The NAC grew into a major lobbying group with over 500 member groups by 1984, representing over five million Canadian women by 1988. Bertha Wilson made history by being the first woman to be appointed to the Supreme Court in 1982. Trudeau appointed Jeanne Sauvé as first speaker of the House of Commons and established major societies for women such as the society for Canadian Women in Science and Technology (CWST) and the Canadian Association for Women in Sports and Physical Activity (CAAWS) Jeanne Sauvé was then appointed first woman Governor General of Canada.

Women continued to gain status. In 1985, the federal government revised the Indian Act and responded to concerns by Native women's organizations and in that same year both the Disabled Women's Network (DAWN) was founded as well as the Women's Legal Education Action Fund (LEAF). In 1987 Prime Minister Brian Mulroney appointed Madame Justice Claire L'Heureaux-Dubé as the second women Justice of the Supreme Court of Canada and in 1989 he appointed Madame Justice Beverly McLaughlin, who would become Chief Justice in January 2000.

The increased influx of women into the paid labour force changed the face of the workforce, concerns over childcare, and impacted on the union movement. By the mid-1980s, women represented 35 per cent of union membership in Canada. This shift in the gender balance in the labour movement saw women gradually, and often in the face of male opposition, begin to assume more prominent positions in union locals, labour councils, and the workforce. Women brought important issues to the bargaining table: maternity leave, child care, sexual harassment, and equal pay to women workers for work of equal value. More women became active in politics, in positions of responsibility in corporate boardrooms, and as administrators in hospitals and in universities. The baby boomers were having babies of their own and Canada was about to embark on the domination of the country by big business.

During the 1980s there was a change in the diversity of immigrants coming into Canada, as almost 50% of immigrants were of Asian and Middle Eastern origin. (This is compared with 90% of immigrants before 1961, who were born in Europe) This impacted on all areas of the economy as well as social issues. The concerns of South Asian women and Southeast Asian women were now added to the voices of all Canadian women.

GREEN DRAGON PRESS

The assassination of John Lennon, musician, political activist, artist and author represented to some, the end of the very public human rights movement in both the United States and Canada. The decade embraced a conservative administration that resulted in free trade between the two countries. Student protests continued throughout the world, in Tianamen Square in China, in the Solidarity movement in Poland, and in the anti-free trade movement here in Canada. The decade reflected a move towards the democratization and corporatization of the world. The 1980s celebrated corporate and materialistic excess. Television shows like Dallas glorified the products and rewards of a capitalist society. This was manifested in a Free Trade agreement (NAFTA) that resulted in Corporations gaining a greater control of goods in the North American market. Native women formed associations to fight control and assimilation and by 1985 the Indian Act was changed to remove discriminatory clauses against women, and women regained their status in marriages to non-Aboriginal men.

Audrey McLaughlin became the first female party leader in Canada and it was clear that by the end of the decade, women had increased their political and legal positions in Canada and feminist organizations had expanded to represent a more diverse representation of Canadian women's voices.

However, anti-feminist sentiment permeated some elements in society, resulting in the horrific death of fourteen engineering students in 1989. The Montreal Massacre of these young women enrolled in the engineering department of Montreal's Ecole Polytechnique shocked all Canadians. Women participated in Take Back the Night Marches from coast to coast in Canada. The marches were organized locally, but made a national statement about our collective vision, and our will to name and end violence against women. The decade also exposed the country to a new terrifying plague: AIDS.

> • 1981 Society for Canadian Women in Science and Technology (CWST) and Canadian Association for Women in Sport and Physical Activity (CAAWS) founded.

GREEN DRAGON PRESS

Women Challenge the Constitution

Women's involvement in Canadian constitution making was a mass involvement – not the undertaking of a handful of women. Women achieved success in their constitutional goals - notably, entrenched equality in Section 28 of the Charter of Rights - because of collective action that incorporated a well organized strategy of both experts and reformers working together to achieve equity for all Canadian women in the future. The Charter was to incorporate the equality clause already present in the 1960 Bill of Rights. Women's groups were well aware that this clause had never been interpreted to women's benefit and that further constitutional reforms were needed in order that equality for women be entrenched in the new Charter.

There appears to be three stages of women's involvement in the constitution-making process. Before December 1981, the participants tended to be the legally knowledgeable members of the established women's organizations. These women had a clear understanding of the law and were able to successfully lobby the government. The second stage drew a wider membership from women's groups who came together under the single-issue umbrella of the Ad Hoc Committee of Canadian Women on the Constitution. The first two stages of the women's lobby were essentially negotiating phases within which expertise on the issues and demonstrations of strength were critical. The third phase, in November 1981, by contrast required little or no specific knowledge of the issues except that "equality" was under attack. Large numbers of women received that message and perceived it as a threat at a rock bottom level. Women responded at both an individual and group level using whatever channels were available. The common message was "I've never been involved before but this time, I'm in and I'm furious!"

After the battle women were victorious in obtaining guarantees under the law through the passage of both s.28 and s.15 of the Charter. With s.28, Canadian women won an important new tool with which they would be able to force unwilling governments to help them take their rightful places as equal partners in the workforce, the bureaucracy, the professions, and the government. Equal benefits and protection of the law. Were guaranteed under s15. These achievements were the result of thousands of women who participated in the women's constitutional lobby. Women such as Laura Sabia, Michelle Landsberg, Doris Anderson, Rosemary Billings, Flora MacDonald, Marilou McPhedran, and others organized successfully, lobbied government and private individuals in order to effectively create social change. As Linda Ryan-Nye said after s.28 was reinstated, "Women will never again take equality for granted, or take governments' word for what's best for women."

The Taking of Twenty-Eight: Women Challenge the Constitution by Penney Kome. Toronto: Women's Press, 1983.

The repatriation of the constitution as well as the introduction of the Charter of Rights and Freedoms in 1982 was preceded by numerous proposals by active women's groups. The following is from the National Action Committee on the Status of Women, taken from a special NAC Memo, Toronto, November 1980. Proposed changes appear in bold block letters.

GREEN DRAGON PRESS

The Charter of Rights and Freedoms

"The Proposed Resolution Regarding the Constitution of Canada"

1. 'Equality before the law' – the wording proposed in the federal government's Charter of Rights, has been interpreted to mean only that laws, once passed, will be equally applied to all individuals in the category concerned – the law itself can treat women unequally, and that's acceptable. Thus the Supreme Court of Canada decided against Lavell and Bedard, two Indian women who lost their status on marriage to non-status men. If the wording as presently proposed is passed, there is no guarantee that Indian women will not continue to be denied equal rights with Indian men.

- NAC RECOMMENDS AMENDMENT SO THAT EQUALITY IN THE LAWS THEMSELVES, AS WELL AS ADMINISTRATION OF THE LAWS, IS PROVIDED
- Further, we deplore the three-year moratorium on the Charter's application, and RECOMMEND THAT IT BE DELETED.

2. Entrenchment of rights means that the courts, and ultimately the Supreme Court of Canada, will decide on what rights Canadian women will enjoy. Yet it was the Supreme Court of Canada that decided
   - women were not persons – the famous 1928 Persons' Case;
   - that discrimination against Indian women in the Indian Act does not violate 'equality before the law';
   - that Stella Bliss was not discriminated against because she was a woman, but a pregnant person;
   - and that, again in the Bliss case, there was no discrimination because not all pregnant women were denied benefits under the Unemployment Insurance Act.
   - Can we reasonably expect that, without fair representation of women in the courts, including the Supreme Court of Canada, women's rights will be understood and protected?
   - NAC RECOMMENDS AMENDMENT TO GUARANTEE THE APPOINTMENT OF A REPRESENTATIVE NUMBER OF WOMEN TO THE COURTS, INCLUDING THE SUPREME COURT OF CANADA

1. Vague wording in the section on affirmative action makes us nervous – will we have to spend years in court proving that an affirmative action program for women does not constitute discrimination.
- NAC RECOMMENDS SPECIFYING WOMEN AS A DISADVANTAGED GROUP REQUIRING AFFIRMATIVE ACTION. BETTER STILL, THERE SHOULD BE A STATED OBJECTIVE OF ACHIEVING EQUALITY.

Women and the Constitution Conference
Speak With Their Own Voices: A Documentary History of the Federation of Women Teachers' Associations of Ontario, Pat Staton and Beth Light, Toronto: FWTAO, 1987.

GREEN DRAGON PRESS

Women's Legal Education and Action Fund

www.leaf.ca

In the early 1980s when the Canadian Charter of Rights and Freedoms was being drafted, thousands of women from across Canada worked tirelessly to ensure strong and effective equality guarantees. Their efforts succeeded. When the Charter came into effect, it offered Canadians an extraordinary opportunity - to build a fairer and more equal society.

The women who founded the Women's Legal Education and Action Fund (LEAF) knew that the strong words of the Charter would mean little if they were not tested in the courts. LEAF was established to undertake precedent-setting cases, which would turn the promise of equality into reality.

Since then, LEAF has been involved in more than 114 legal cases and has played a key role in persuading Canadian courts to develop a just definition of equality. LEAF has broken new legal ground, presenting a clear and consistent vision of equality based on the reality of women's lives.

LEAF has helped the courts to understand the gender-based inequality experienced by women cut off social assistance because they lived with men, women refused registration as status Indians, women who could not pass on their names to their children, pregnant women denied benefits, domestic workers refused overtime pay, and sexual assault survivors brutalized by the accused at sexual assault trials. LEAF has won positive decisions for all these women and more. (LEAF)

"What feminists do in the legal system is to expose its previously unseen maleness and attempt to deconstruct it, in order to make room for the viewpoints, the concerns and the experience of women." Mary Eberts, lawyer and author.

Persons Day, October 18

Persons Day celebrates the Persons Case decision of October 18, 1929. The Persons Case only came about because of the commitment of five women – Judge Emily Murphy, Nellie McClung, Irene Parlby, Louise McKinney and Henrietta Muir Edwards – and their supporters. They challenged a law that symbolized how women were seen and treated – the law said that women were not "persons" and could not be appointed to the Senate of Canada. The "Famous Five" won, and the case influenced many that came after. It was a beginning, not an end. Women and girls still must look to the law and the courts to ensure their full civil, political, economic, social and cultural rights. Every year thousands of women and men celebrate Persons Day at LEAF fundraising Breakfasts across Canada.

LEAF (Women's Legal Education and Action Fund)

LEAF advances the equality of women in Canada through litigation, law reform and public education using Canada's *Charter of Rights and Freedoms*. Since 1985 it has helped women win landmark legal victories in areas such as violence against women, pregnancy discrimination, sexual harassment, sex bias in employment standards and social assistance, unfair pensions, and reproductive freedoms. LEAF is the only women's organization in Canada that focuses primarily on court action to bring about social change. LEAF participated in 5 of the 20 Supreme Court of Canada Charter decisions that the *Globe and Mail* cited as being the most significant of the last 20 years.

LEAF
2 Carlton Street, Suite 1307, Toronto, ON M5B 1J3
Tel: (416) 595-7170 Fax: (416) 595-7191
www.leaf.ca

LEAF Toronto
PERSONS DAY BREAKFAST
October 17, 2003

- 1982 Bertha Wilson was appointed the first woman to serve on the Supreme Court of Canada.

GREEN DRAGON PRESS

LEAF
(Women's Legal Education and Action Fund)

LEAF advances the equality of women in Canada through litigation, law reform and public education using Canada's Charter of Rights and Freedoms, particularly sections 15 (1) and section 28:

15.(1) Every individual is equal before and under the law and has the right to equal protection and equal benefit of the law without discrimination, and in particular, without discrimination based on race, national or ethnic origin, colour, religion, sex, age, or mental or physical disability...

28. Notwithstanding anything in this Charter, the rights and freedoms referred to in it are guaranteed equally to male and female persons.

Since 1985, when section 15 of the Charter came into force, LEAF has helped win landmark legal victories for women and girls in areas such as violence against women, pregnancy discrimination, sexual harassment, sex bias in employment standards and social assistance, unfair pensions, and reproductive freedoms. LEAF participated in 5 of the 20 Supreme Court of Canada Charter decisions that the *Globe and Mail* cited as being the most significant of the last 20 years.

Inequality is a continuing state for many different groups in society. Women, as a group, compared with men as a group, still experience widespread discrimination. Women who are oppressed on the basis of, for example, their race, class, sexual orientation, religion or disability, experience inequality of different kinds and degrees. Laws that do benefit women, such as those governing maternity leave and all aspects of sexual assault, are often challenged. The law can be an effective tool for change, although it is not the only tool. And sometimes the law is needed to save things that benefit women and girls and that would otherwise be dismantled.

LEAF is the only women's organization in Canada that focuses primarily on court action to bring about social change. Every year, women from countries around the world come to LEAF to learn about Canada's Charter and how we use law and litigation to advance equality. LEAF developed and advocates the principle of "substantive equality" – that these Charter guarantees are intended to benefit individuals and groups that historically have had unequal access to social and economic resources. LEAF works to ensure that the Charter is applied to improve the day-to-day lives of all women and girls.

Cases come to LEAF's attention in a variety of ways: through regular examination of reported court decisions; through an informal network of lawyers, academics and women's organizations; and, through the hundreds of inquiries LEAF receives from the public each year. LEAF is a registered charity that raises money from the public to pay for its legal work.

LEAF
2 Carlton Street, Suite 1307, Toronto, ON M5B 1J3
Tel: (416) 595-7170 Fax: (416) 595-7191
www.leaf.ca

GREEN DRAGON PRESS

Throughout the 1980s, Native women fought for rights to their homeland. Feminist organizations, like the National Action Committee on the Status of Women (NAC), joined them in their protests. These Innu women are fighting to save Nitassinan in 1989.

White women's response to the call for help from Innu women to save Nitassinan, their homeland, from military destruction is another example of mainstream feminist organizations hearing the cry for help against injustice uttered by the heavily disadvantaged... Protected until more recently by their isolation, the Innu of Labrador have only become, in the last forty years, the target of genocidal practices. First, more than ten large hydroelectric projects undertaken by the provincial governments of Quebec and Newfoundland/ Labrador flooded vast tracks of the hunting and fishing lands of the Innu...including their burial grounds. The Innu were persuaded to abandon their traditional nomadic existence with the promise of houses and Canadian social benefits if they took up residence in settlements. Year-round life in settlements, however, involving as it has the abandonment of their traditional way of life, has had a devastating impact on the Innu. Colonization has robbed them of their sense of identity and self-worth. In the 1980s, the situation of the Innu worsened as Canada's military presence in Nitassinan escalated. The Canadian government stepped up its efforts to attract a North Atlantic Treaty Organization (NATO) base to Goose Bay and turn the Quebec-Labrador peninsula into a testing ground, complete with bombing ranges for the training of

An Innu woman protests outside a Goose Bay police station in 1989 in support of Innu Indians arrested on charges of public mischief for demonstrating against low-flying NATO test flights.

NATO pilots of low-flying jets. Bombing practice nearby and low-flying jets overhead have had a horrific effect on Innu of all ages, but particularly on children and pregnant women. The military maneuvers have also taken their toll on the animals hunted by the Innu. Innu women began to take a prominent role in the struggle of their people to regain their homeland and to protest against its militarization. In 1989, the NAC subcommittee on peace invited a group of Innu women to attend NAC's annual general meeting in Ottawa in May. On the second day of the conference, three Innu women presented a workshop on the Innu struggle against annihilation. They mentioned in particular the sexual exploitation suffered by Innu women, such as increase in rape and in the birth of babies, called "souvenir babies", fathered by British, American and West German military personnel. The workshop was well attended and word of its powerful impact spread. The next day, the three Innu women were asked to lay their concerns before the six hundred women assembled in the final plenary session of the NAC conference. The delegates unanimously passed a resolution requesting the Canadian government to demilitarize the Innu homeland immediately. They also took up a collection to help the Innu pay some of the legal costs of their struggle.

GREEN DRAGON PRESS

Gender Roles

The excerpt on the next page is from an article that appeared in the February 1983 *Redbook*. The article was written in reaction to a revealing study of gender roles and male and females perceptions of one another. The results of this study suggest that in 1983, many gender stereotypes persisted.

The authors also question the impact of the 1970s women's movement, as the frightening conclusion of the study seems to suggest a "fundamental contempt for females – held by both sexes."

- 1982 Bertha Wilson was appointed Canada's first woman Supreme Court judge. Among decisions to which she contributed was the 1988 striking down of Canada's abortion law. "If women lawyers and women judges through differing perspectives on life can bring a new humanity to bear on the decision-making process,," she said, "perhaps they will make a difference."

- 1984 Jeanne Sauvé was appointed first woman Governor General of Canada on May 14th.

- June 1985 DisAbled Women's Network DAWN was founded to offer support, information, and resources to women with disabilities.

GREEN DRAGON PRESS

How Would Your Life Be Different If You'd Been Born a Boy?
By Carol Tavris, with Dr. Alice I. Baumgartner

In essence it was a comparison between the lives of men and women that launched the movement for women's rights. As women realized that their lives would be not only different but also better – in status, income, advantages, freedom – if they were men, they began seeking ways to eradicate the inequities between the sexes. Anyone who has lived through the last decade knows what a bumpy ride it has been: a little progress here, a little relapse there, but over-all, a steady improvement.

Or has there been? The clearest measure of progress may be found not in the generation that struggles for change but in the generation that should be the beneficiary of change – the children of the pioneers. For ten years, public-school teachers and administrators have been trying to eliminate sex bias in the counseling they provide to children…To measure the effect of this effort, Dr. Alice I. Baumgartner and her colleagues…came up with a startlingly simple method…. They simply asked one question: If you woke up tomorrow and discovered that you were a (boy) (girl), how would your life be different?

The answers were sad and shocking, for they show how little has in fact changed in children's attitudes in the recent years of social upheaval. Dr. Baumgartner did not find that boys and girls think there are benefits and disadvantages to being either sex. What she found was a fundamental contempt for females – held by both sexes.

The elementary school boys, for example often titled their answers with little phrases such as "The Disaster", or "The Fatal Dream," or "Doomsday". Then they described how awful their lives would be if they were female: "I wouldn't like having a little pink dress or anything about a girl. It wouldn't be fun"(fourth grade boy). "If I were a girl, I'd be stupid and weak as a string"(sixth grade boy)…"If I were a girl, everybody would be better than me, because boys are better than girls" (third grade boy). And this one, succinctly: "If I were a girl, I'd kill myself."

But the girls wrote repeatedly of how much better off they would be as boys. "If I were a boy, I would get treated better. I would get paid more and be able to do more things" (fourth grade girl). "I could do stuff better than I do now" (third grade girl) "People would take my decisions and beliefs more seriously" (11th grade girl). "If I were a boy, my whole life would be easier" (sixth grade girl). And this poignant response from a third grade girl: "If I were a boy, my daddy might have loved me."…

Is women's work as valued and valuable as men's work? Don't you believe it, said these children…Their general view is summed up in the words of a boy who said 'Girls can't do anything that's fun' and the depressing words of a girl who said her expectation as a female was 'to be nothing'.

Girls continually pointed out that they would have more or different career choices if they were male: "I could run for President"; "I want to be a nurse, but if I were a boy, I'd want to be an architect"; "I would consider work in math or science"; "If I were a boy, I could do more things"; "If I was a boy, I'd drop my typing class, and start taking really hard classes…". The boys felt they would lose choices if they were female: "I wouldn't be able to keep my job as a carpenter"; "I couldn't be a mechanic." One adamant young man, though, said he would "refuse to work as a secretary or something stupid like that."

When the boys even considered the possibility that as females they could marry and work outside the home (for most boys, these were mutually exclusive categories), the jobs they listed most often were secretary and nurse. Other possible "female" occupation included cocktail waitress, social worker, airline stewardess, interior decorator, receptionist, model, beauty queen – and prostitute. "Boys still see women's work as serving others and providing support," says Dr. Baumgartner, "instead of being in charge."

To the girls, the thought of being male liberated their imagination. The career they mentioned most often as a possible choice if they were male was – ready? – professional athlete. This was followed by a much longer list of possibilities than the boys see for girls: mechanic, construction worker, pilot, engineer, race-car driver, forest ranger, dentist, architect, stunt man, coal miner, geologist, farmer, sports commentator, draftsmen, and so on.

But there is a glimmer of good news. Four occupations that were once nearly all male are now (the children say) open to both sexes: truck driver, computer programmer, doctor and lawyer…

GREEN DRAGON PRESS

In July 1980, Chatelaine magazine published a focus section entitled "Women in Canadian Politics". The articles featured updates on the presence of women in government office, as well as a survey of women who would be potential candidates for the highest political office – the Prime Minister of Canada. The following is an excerpt from this feature.

☞ A CANADIAN WOMAN PRIME ☜ MINISTER? WHY NOT!

Is Canada ready to elect a woman, first as leader of a party, then as prime minister? And if so, is there anyone among our current crop of women politicians with proven leadership qualities, who is ready to toss her hat in the ring?

By Judith Timson

On the evening of February 22, 1976, when Flora MacDonald lost her bid for the leadership of the Progressive Conservative party, her executive assistant Hugh Hanson bitterly offered up a conclusion that…was rife in the air: "The Progressive Conservative party proved today it hasn't got the [nerve] to elect a woman leader."

Today, nearly four and a half years later, the country has whirled through two general elections and their accompanying dramas-the rise and fall of Joe Clark (who starred in Prime Minister for a Day) and the resurrection of Pierre Elliot Trudeau (The Bionic Politician)"-but we still don't know the answer to the question: Is Canada ready to elect a woman, first as leader of a party, then as prime minister? Some seasoned male observers think decidedly not: "Canada is a more conservative country than Britain," maintains political columnist Allan Fotheringham, "and look what they're doing to Margaret Thatcher over there, calling her Attila the Hen." Here, he says, a woman wouldn't even get that far. "Oh, there will always be women mentioned and the media will latch on to someone who's chic and charming."

…The closest any women in this country every came to winning a national party leadership was when Jamaican-born British Columbia MLA Rosemary Brown scared the pants off Ed Broadbent, force-marching him to a fourth-ballot victory at the 1975 NDP leadership convention. But even she does not see the same circumstances happening again.

Clearly times have changed. The smoke has lifted from the '70's, which were, according to the Progressive Conservative's Jean Pigott, a "watershed decade, in which so many myths about women died." And the '80's are a whole new ball game, with just about everyone agreeing that, politically, it's hardball they're going to be playing. Issues are getting tougher – energy, defense – and the most attractive commodity any man or woman can bring to the public arena is probably guts, says Pigott. Forget sensitivity. And forget, to a certain extent, on-the-job training. Canadians proved emphatically last February they didn't feel like being Joe Clark's lab assistants in his great political experiment. They wanted competence, tried and true.

Although it still remains a rougher ride for women, the criteria for political leadership, male or female, will be the same…

GREEN DRAGON PRESS

Women's participation in the military has always been a contentious issue. Not until the late 1980s were women allowed to take combat positions in the Canadian Armed Forces, and acceptance to this idea is slow. Many people find it difficult to reconcile ideas of femininity with military combat, and many feminists are opposed to the idea due to their firm support of anti-violence and peace issues.

Canada Successfully Allows Women to Serve in Combat Positions

Isabelle Gauthier just wanted a chance to drive a jeep. "I've got my license and all that," she explained…In 1981, she had fulfilled all the major requirements to be in the Regiment de Hull, a reserve armored division of the Canadian Armed Forces (CAF). During the three months of training, she held her own in target practice, strength tests, and drills. But after the initial training ended, the men were tooling around in jeeps, and she was behind a desk, shifting papers.

Gauthier could never be in the driver's seat, because rules preventing women from engaging in military combat put operating jeeps, tanks, and rifles off limits. Worse, after only seven months, she got fired. Not for incompetence or insubordination, but because the regiment had its 10 percent allotment of women.

Gauthier fought back by suing the forces in 1981, and in 1989 she finally won. The Canadian Human Rights Tribunal, which hears cases of discrimination against federal employees, ruled that all combat positions must be opened to women, and no restrictions may be placed on their numbers. So for the first time, qualified women can be fighter pilots, tank commanders, and naval officers – serving everywhere except in submarines where privacy needs preclude mixed gender crews…

The progress is real-albeit slow-but nothing would have happened without two decades of outside pressure. In 1970, the Royal Commission on the Status of Women noted that the military employed women in a small number of positions, such as nursing and personnel, and recommended opening up more opportunities…Then the 1978 Canadian Human Rights Act (CHRA) forced complete reassessment of military policy. The act stipulated that there should be no discrimination against women, except under bona fide occupational requirement….with the CHRA, the armed forces had to demonstrate why it was not possible for women to go into combat…

A far bigger problem may be changing macho attitudes. "Nobody would come up and say that they didn't want women because they were women," said Anne Trotier, attorney for Gauthier. "But there was a lot of reluctance."

But the military isn't expecting armies of women to flood recruiting centers either. "There are not many women who want to get into this kind of employment," said [Judith] Harper [director of CREW – Combat Related Employment of Women]. "You can take an ordinary man and make a soldier of him, but you have to have an extraordinary woman to be a soldier."…

Feminist groups are divided about the ruling. "We had an ambivalent reaction to it," said Lynn Kaye, president of National Action Committee on the Status of Women. "We take a very strong pro-peace position, and we are very concerned about the militarization of our economy."

Women in the Military: Current Controversies Series, by Mary Suh. Greenhaven Press c 1991. Greenhaven Press Reprinted by permission of The Gale Group.

Work

Women 46 per cent of working poor in 1986

BY SEAN FINE
The Globe and Mail

As women have entered Canada's work force in greater numbers, thousands have wound up in jobs that leave them in poverty, a report from a federal government advisory body indicates.

Between 1971 and 1986, the number of poor women who held full- or part-time jobs more than doubled — to 599,000 from 230,000, said the report, commissioned by the Canadian Advisory Council on the Status of Women.

Women made up 46 per cent of the working poor in 1986 — a proportion slightly above their 43 per cent share of the labor force. In 1971, they made up 30 per cent of the working poor, slightly below their 34 per cent part of the work force. (The figures do not include women whose total family incomes were above poverty levels.)

The report, written by Morley Gunderson and Leon Muszynski, was based on data compiled by Statistics Canada.

The council, pointing to what it called "the feminization of working poverty," said the number of working poor women had increased by 160 per cent from 1971 to 1986, while the number of working poor men increased by 28 per cent.

It cited generally low-paying areas in which it said women are over-represented: clerical jobs (78.9 per cent women), sales (45.4 per cent) and service jobs such as waitresses (54.9 per cent).

"Working poor women in general are worse off than working poor men because they experience job segregation and discrimination as well as lower wages and more unstable employment," the council said.

It called for pay-equity laws, which would require equal pay for jobs of equal worth; employment equity, which would require hiring and promotion targets; higher minimum wages, indexed to inflation; improved job training and literacy programs; and increased unionization, especially for low-wage workers.

It also urged improvements to child-care, and greater earnings supplements for single mothers.

About 21 per cent of the women whose jobs left them below unofficial StatsCan poverty lines held full-time jobs, while 37 per cent of working poor males held full-time jobs. About 28 per cent of those women who worked part-time did so involuntarily, because they could not find full-time work, the report said. The authors also said raising children prevents some women from working full-time.

"Part-time work is the evil of our time," the report quoted an unidentified retail clerk at a department store in Ontario. "There are 12 people working in my department for a 22½-hour week . . . there are no benefits . . maybe they could hire fewer people for more wages."

Most working women who are poor have one or more of the following characteristics: They are under 25, a recent immigrant, unattached or a single parent, live outside Ontario, have less than a Grade 9 education.

"The children of these women are poor, so child poverty is on the rise," Glenda Simms, president of the council, said in an interview.

The *Globe and Mail,* Wednesday, June 6, 1990

Cleaning fish
United Fisherman Allied Workers Union

126

F O C U S O N

Racial Minority Women

INTRODUCTION

The combined issues of racism and sexism are barriers most likely to affect racial minority women. In the workplace, racial minority women are often judged by their color and race rather than their experience or capabilities. This profile discusses some of the social and economic issues affecting the employment status of racial minority women in Ontario's labour force. Information about labour force participation, occupational representation, education and earnings of racial minority women are included as well as employment barriers and suggested remedial measures.

Racism exists when individuals, because of their race, are: i) denied access to services or oppressed; ii) excluded from decision-making processes; iii) treated differently and negatively; iv) described or depicted as inferior; v) affected negatively by policies, programs and practices; and vi) subjected to direct or indirect harassment. (For an explanation of some of the terms used in this profile, see the Glossary of Terms, page 7).

The term racial minority refers to people of color who are visibly different from the dominant group and who are non-white or non-Caucasian in race. For the purpose of this document, the term racial minority will include the term visible minority, defined as "persons who are, because of their race or color, a visible minority in Canada."[1]

Data for this profile came from a variety of sources. The primary sources were the 1986 Statistics Canada Census and the Ministry of Citizenship Ethnocultural Data Base.* Wherever possible, data are included to compare racial minority women and men, as well as racial minorities and the rest of the population. These comparisons are not intended to create an ideal model for racial minority women. They are intended to compare the social and economic status of racial minority women with the rest of Ontario's labour force.

WOMEN IN ONTARIO'S LABOUR FORCE

Women make up 51 per cent of Ontario's population. In 1986, there were 4,633,900 women in Ontario and 4,467,795 men.[2] Although women have always participated in the paid labour force, an unprecedented number have joined the workforce in recent years. In 1975, for example, only 48 per cent of all women over age 15 were working outside the home. By 1986, 59 per cent of all women over 15 had joined the paid workforce.[3]

If current trends continue, by the year 2000, women are expected to total 50 per cent of the labour force. Also, Ontario's diverse population, with men and women from over 100 ethnic and racial backgrounds, is now being reflected in the workplace.[4]

Despite the strong participation of women in the labour force, there are still many barriers to women's equality in the workplace. Employment barriers have caused women to be concentrated in a narrow range of occupations, such as clerical, retail sales and service jobs, which contribute to their lower earnings. In 1986, women earned on average 65 cents to every dollar earned by a man. Bridging this wage gap has been very slow. Income data indicate that women in Ontario in 1989 "earned on average 67 per cent of men's earnings."[5] In other words, for every dollar a man earned, a woman working the same number of hours earned 67 cents.

---

* The Ethnocultural Data Base uses visible minority instead of racial minority and non-visible minority for the rest of the population.

WOMEN
IN THE
LABOUR
MARKET

Ontario
Women's
Directorate

GREEN DRAGON PRESS

RACIAL MINORITY WOMEN

RACIAL MINORITY WOMEN ARE NOT A UNIFORM GROUP.

R acial minority women are not a uniform group. They come from a variety of racial and ethnic backgrounds. "In 1986, approximately 30 per cent of Ontarians who belonged to a racial minority group were Canadian-born,"[6] while the remaining 70 per cent were born outside Canada in places like Asia, the Caribbean, and South East Asia. Many racial minority women speak English as a second language. Their traditional native languages include Amharic, Spanish, Somali, Vietnamese, Laotian, Cambodian, Hindi, Punjabi, and others.

The 1986 Statistics Canada Census showed that 69 per cent of Ontario's racial minority residents were between age 15 and 64. Less than five per cent are over 65 compared with 11 per cent for the rest of Ontario's population. These statistics show that, as a group, racial minorities are younger than most of Ontario's population.[7]

In 1986, 49 per cent, or 775,250, of Canada's racial minority population lived in Ontario, accounting for nine per cent of the province's population.[8] Blacks and people of Asian origins, such as Chinese, Filipinos and South East Asians, form the largest number of racial minorities in Ontario. The following chart shows the population composition of Ontario's racial minority groups.

Composition of Racial Minority Population, Ontario 1986

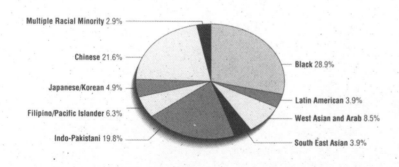

Multiple Racial Minority 2.9%
Chinese 21.6%
Japanese/Korean 4.9%
Filipino/Pacific Islander 6.3%
Indo-Pakistani 19.8%
Black 28.9%
Latin American 3.9%
West Asian and Arab 8.5%
South East Asian 3.9%

Source: Statistics Canada, 1986 Census of Canada

RACIAL MINORITY WOMEN—LABOUR FORCE PROFILE

T he data presented in the following statistical tables show a pattern of low earnings, high unemployment and occupational segregation for racial minority women. "As a result, the central issues for visible minority women, as they relate to full and equal participation in the Ontario labour force, are the added barriers of racial and sexual discrimination."[9]

Despite these barriers, the labour force participation rate for racial minority women is slightly higher than for women as a group. Their higher participation rate may be due to harsh economic realities which require a greater number of racial minority women to seek paid work. Tables 1 and 2 compare the labour force composition and participation rates of racial minority women and men with the rest of the population.

Table 1:
Ontario Labour Force Composition 1986

	In the Labour force (thousands)	Composition rate (in the labour force) (%)
Total population of Ontario	4,795	
Men	2,701	56
Women	2,094	44
Racial minorities	403	
Men	215	4.5
Women	199	4.0
Rest of the population	4,392	
Men	2,487	52.0
Women	1,905	40.0

Source: 1986 Census, Statistics Canada. Distributed by: Ministry of Citizenship Ethnocultural Data Base (Table P3462T7)

Table 1 shows that racial minorities totalled approximately 8.5 per cent of Ontario's labour force in 1986. Also, the percentage of racial minority men and women in the labour force was relatively close: 53 per cent for men and 47 per cent for women.*

Although racial minority women have a higher labour force participation rate (80 per cent) than the total female population, Table 3 shows that job ghettoization and occupational segregation are a problem. Racial minority women are under-represented in middle and upper-level management positions, over-represented in the manual field, and, like women as a group, are heavily concentrated in the clerical field.

Racial and sexual discrimination have also influenced earning differences. There is a noticeable difference between the income of racial minority women, and men and women in the rest of the population.

Income and employment differences are particularly important to note, given the educational skills of racial minority women. "The skill levels of minorities vary, but the number with higher qualifications is above average."[10] For example, in 1986, 18.5 per cent of racial minority women in Ontario's labour market had a university degree, compared with 13 per cent of Ontario women in the rest of the population.

Over 14 per cent of racial minority women who are clerical workers have university degrees compared with four per cent of women in the rest of Ontario's population. This shows how systemic discrimination in employment can present barriers to opportunity for racial minority women. Twenty per cent of racial minority male clerical workers have degrees compared with only seven per cent of the rest of the population. Table 5 shows the percentage of workers by occupation with a bachelor degree or higher.

*The percentages were reached by dividing the number of racial minority women (and racial minority men) by the total racial minority population in the labour force and multiplying by 100.

Table 2:
Unemployment and Participation Rates 1986

	In the Labour Force (thousands)	Unemployment Rate (%)	Participation Rate (%)
Total population of Ontario	4,795	6.2	75
Men	2,701	5.4	83
Women	2,094	7.2	68
Racial minorities	403	6.4	84
Men	215	6.1	89
Women	189	6.9	80
Rest of the population	4,392	6.1	75
Men	2,487	5.3	82
Women	1,905	7.1	67

Source: 1986 Census, Statistics Canada. Distributed by: Ministry of Citizenship Ethnocultural Data Base.

Table 3:
Occupational Distribution: Ontario 1986 Census

	(%) Racial minority		Rest of population	
Occupational category	Men	Women	Men	Women
Upper management	1.6	0.4	2.6	0.7
Middle management	6.7	3.8	8.6	5.8
Professional	13.9	13.4	10.6	14.2
Semi-prof. and technicians	4.6	5.0	4.1	5.1
Supervisory	2.7	2.8	2.3	2.9
Foremen/forewomen	2.4	0.5	4.2	0.5
Clerical	9.3	30.0	6.7	31.4
Sales	6.1	6.0	7.2	8.6
Service	10.3	11.8	6.4	12.0
Skilled crafts and trades	7.8	1.1	11.5	1.1
Semi-skilled manual	10.5	2.5	13.5	3.1
Other manual	19.5	17.7	18.8	11.0
Occupation not stated	4.6	5.0	3.5	3.6
Total:	**100.**	**100.**	**100.**	**100.**

Source: 1986 Census, Statistics Canada (Ministry of Citizenship, *Ontario: A Diverse and Changing Society*, Ethnocultural Data Base Materials - Series III, Special Report, #5).

GREEN DRAGON PRESS

Table 4: **Average Income By Occupation**
Ontario 1986 Census (Full-time/full-year workers age 15+)

| | ($) | | | |
| | Racial Minorities | | Rest of the population | |
Occupational category	Men	Women	Men	Women
All occupations	28,055	19,187	32,176	20,550
Upper management	48,814	33,880	63,898	35,366
Middle management	32,166	24,721	39,603	25,254
Professional	42,217	28,624	43,876	29,220
Semi-prof. and technicians	28,793	20,752	31,226	21,477
Supervisory	23,942	18,823	30,596	19,502
Foremen/forewomen	28,399	17,108	32,346	19,623
Clerical	22,483	18,512	24,483	18,114
Sales	25,357	16,765	30,808	18,050
Service	16,590	12,262	24,882	13,229
Skilled crafts and trades	26,836	16,259	27,683	17,037
Semi-skilled manual	23,945	15,717	25,853	17,009
Other manual	20,788	13,595	24,337	15,666
Other occupations	23,132	18,127	24,994	18,015

Source: 1986 Census, Statistics Canada. Distributed by: Ministry of Citizenship Ethnocultural Data Base.

Table 5. **University Graduates By Occupation**: Ontario 1986 Census

| | (%) | | | |
| | Racial minorities | | Rest of the population | |
Occupational groups	Men	Women	Men	Women
All occupations	27	18	16	13
Upper management	55	36	36	32
Middle management	37	29	25	20
Professional	75	46	64	46
Semi-prof. and technicians	31	27	16	17
Supervisory	21	14	10	6
Foremen/forewomen	13	8	3	4
Clerical	20	14	7	4
Sales	25	15	13	8
Service	7	4	3	2
Skilled crafts and trades	8	5	1	3
Semi-skilled manual	8	11	1	4
Other manual	6	3	1	0.5

Source: 1986 Census, Statistics Canada. Distributed by: Ministry of Citizenship Ethnocultural Data Base.

Tables 4 and 5 show that even in occupations where women and men have similar education levels, men's earnings far exceed women's. For example, although 36 per cent of racial minority women and 36 per cent of men in the rest of the population in upper-level management are university graduates, men earn approximately 53 per cent more than racial minority women. Similarly, when earnings of racial minority women are compared with racial minority men in upper-level management, there is a notable earning difference of 44 per cent. The earning difference between racial minority women and women in the rest of the population in upper-level management is four per cent.

Similar patterns of earning differences between racial minority women and men with university degrees are evident in clerical, sales and semi-skilled manual fields. In the clerical field, where 14 per cent of racial minority women and seven per cent of men in the general population have university degrees, racial minority women earn approximately 32 per cent less.

The statistical data in this profile give a picture of the labour market status of racial minority women. Some of the factors which have contributed to the disadvantaged employment status of racial minority women suggest the existence of systemic and racial discrimination.

Who Gets the Work: A Test of Racial Discrimination in Employment, a study by the Urban Alliance on Race Relations and the Social Planning Council of Metropolitan Toronto, 1985, reported: "the results of this study clearly show there is substantial racial discrimination affecting the ability of racial minority groups to find employment."[11]

GREEN DRAGON PRESS

What You Can Do To Stop Mulroney's Trade Deal

The trade agreement doesn't take effect till 1990, so it's not too late to stop it. But there's no time to spare. The actions we take in the next few months can make a critical difference.

CANADA
does not belong to these two men.

CANADA
belongs to all of us.

- Write your MP and MPP. Sign petitions. Send in postcards.
- Join in any rallies, lobbies or days of protest against the deal.
- Seize every opportunity to express your views against the deal; by writing letters to the editor, phoning in to radio hotline shows, and talking to as many people as you possibly can.
- If and when an election is called, get actively involved. Help make sure that the Mulroney Trade Deal becomes the number one issue.
- Join your local Women Against Free Trade Campaign or form one in your community (15 Gervais Dr., Don Mills, Ont. M3C 1V8) or join your provincial Coalition Against Free Trade and take part in its activities:

B.C. Coalition Against
Free Trade
#203 — 1104 Hornby
Vancouver, B.C. V6Z 1V8

Cape Breton Coalition
Against Free Trade
84 Union Street
Sidney, N.S. P1P 4X5

Coalition Québecoise
d'opposition au libre échange
2236, chemin Ste-Foy
Ste-Foy, Québec G1V 4E5

Manitoba Coalition Against
Free Trade
57 Maralbo Avenue East
Winnipeg, Man. R2M 1R3

Ontario Coalition Against
Free Trade
1260 Bay Street
Toronto, Ont. M5R 2T1

Saskatchewan Coalition for
Social Justice
2267 Albert Street
Regina, Sask. S4P 2V5

Victoria Coalition Against
Free Trade
Office of Social Justice
Suite #1 — 4044 Nelthorpe Street
Victoria, B.C.

Metro Halifax Coalition Against
Free Trade
2277 Brunswick Street
Halifax, N.S. B3K 2Y0

Newfoundland Coalition for
Equality
Office of Social Action
Box 986
St. John's, Nfld. A1C 5M3

New Brunswick Coalition
Against Free Trade
P.O. Box 1135, Station A
Fredericton, N.B. E3B 5C2

P.E.I. Pro-Canada Network
81 Prince Street
Charlottetown, P.E.I. C1A 4R3

Pro-Canada Network
c/o 90 Parent Street
Ottawa, Ont. K1M 7B1

During the 1980s women were concerned with the impact that free trade might have on their lives and the lives of all Canadians. It was suggested that NAFTA might destroy more jobs than it created, depress wages, worsen poverty and inequality, erode social programs, undermine democracy, and greatly increase the rights and power of corporations, investors, and property holders. Many of these challenges were presented by women's groups who took their position to the street through their participation in public protests or by writing to the various media venues.

Healthsharing, Fall 1988

GREEN DRAGON PRESS

Health

In the 1980s many immigrant women still did not have access to professional health care, as they tended to be concentrated predominantly in the service occupations or as garment workers. They could not afford to lose wages by taking time off during the day. Shelters and health care centers opened to provide services to immigrant women in the evenings, providing assistance in different language groups.

Public March and Rally
Saturday, Sept. 19, 1987

Assembly at: **11:00 a.m. in front of 400 University Ave.**

March begins at: **11:30 a.m.** (we will march to Queen's Park)

Rally/Program at: **12:30 p.m. at Queen's Park.**

* Speeches * Songs * Poetry * Skits

bring your family and friends. Let us all reach out to one another and work together ! !

GREEN DRAGON PRESS

Backlash!

Rosa Becker's loss

Rosa Becker has killed herself. After 19 years of working with her common-law husband to buy land and develop a business, after six years of battling him in court for a share of those assets, after six years of trying to enforce a favorable court ruling, she has left a suicide note calling her death a protest against the legal system.

She did not need to die to make that protest; the facts spoke for themselves. But her suicide has underscored the pain she must have felt as every note of optimism faded and every triumph evaporated.

The story began in 1955, as she and Lothar Pettkus began to live together. They remained together until 1973, living off her money in the early years as he saved his to buy property for a bee farm. They bought land, always in his name. In 1973 they separated; he asked her to come back; she did. In 1974, they split up permanently. As Mr. Justice Brian Dickson of the Supreme Court of Canada later described their relationship, Mr. Pettkus "had the benefit of 19 years of unpaid labor, while Miss Becker has received little or nothing in return."

She went to court. The Ontario Court of Appeal, overturning a lower court decision, ruled that she was entitled to half the property and revenue from the beekeeping business. It invoked a doctrine known as "constructive trust," which says that both partners in a relationship have a right to expect each other to deal fairly and reasonably with them.

The Supreme Court of Canada upheld the ruling, applying it to common-law spouses. Judge Dickson wrote, "I see no basis for any distinction, in dividing property and assets, between marital relationships and those more informal relationships which subsist for a lengthy period... The equitable principle on which the remedy of constructive trust rests is broad and general; its purpose is to prevent unjust enrichment in what-ever circumstances it occurs."

Rosa Becker stood to receive an estimated $150,000. In an editorial at the time, we wrote, "Although there will undoubtedly be other battles fought on this ground ... Miss Becker at least has won her case. She has received her fair due."

As matters progressed, it became clear that her fair due was a long way off. To enforce the court's judgment, Miss Becker's lawyer, Gerald Langlois, applied to the Registrar of the Ontario Supreme Court for an order specifying how the property was to be divided. Lothar Pettkus fought against it. When the court finally ordered in 1984 that two pieces of land be sold, Mr. Langlois seized the entire proceeds of $68,000 for legal fees incurred during the 11 years he had worked on the case. At her death, Rosa Becker had yet to receive a penny.

Her case raises troubling questions, as she knew it would. Was hers an isolated episode, or has it become a feature of Canadian justice that people who receive judgments in their favor from the highest court in the land may fight for six years without realizing them? Would her task of collecting the money have been any easier if Ontario's Family Law Reform Act of 1978 had included common-law spouses in its provisions requiring the division of property following a marriage breakup? (That act, like the Family Law Act which replaced it this year, includes common-law partners only when dealing with support payments.)

In 1974, the Supreme Court denied Alberta farm wife Irene Murdoch a half-interest in the farm she had worked on for 25 years; the resulting outcry caused several provinces to adopt laws on the division of matrimonial property. Rosa Becker's defeat should have the same effect on laws governing the enforcement of judgments. No one should have to go through what she did in pursuit of a recognized claim.

The Globe and Mail. Thursday, November 13, 1986

Rosa Becker

In 1980 the Supreme Court of Canada ruled that Rosa Becker was entitled to half the farm and bee-keeping business she had built up with her common-law husband of 17 years. Overruling an earlier decision, the Court supported an Ontario Court of Appeal decision. Becker's ex-husband fought the award through a variety of means. She eventually collected $68,000 from the sale of property, but it was applied in its entirety to expenses incurred by her lawyer in his 11-year fight on her behalf. In November 1986, bitter, distraught and destitute, Rosa Becker took her own life. Her death revealed to the public the need to reform laws that would enforce equity judgments.

GREEN DRAGON PRESS

March 30, 1989 Madame Justice Beverley McLachlin was appointed to the Supreme Court of Canada. She became Chief Justice of Canada on January 7, 2000. Photo: Phillippe Landreville

GREEN DRAGON PRESS

Growing up in the 80's

In the early 1980s, my grade seven teacher assigned a creative writing project entitled "If I were Prime Minister". In reponse to this challenge, I wrote a one page article stating my intent to promote only women to fill what would be my all-female cabinet. In what was then the Cold War environment, I outlined my plans to develop stronger diplomatic relations with the USSR; to ensure peace in a world threatened still by nuclear war.

Stephanie Kim
Gibson

Recently, in 2003, I came across this short piece of writing and I was struck by what I read, by the force of conviction in the words. I clearly remembered thinking I could be Prime Minister, or anything else I wanted to be, for that matter. I could see clearly, from my perspective today, that I was a product of the second wave feminism movement.

Girls of the late seventies, early eighties were different from their predecessors in that they felt the sky held no limit (although clearly it did and still does). We grew up wearing corduroy bell bottoms, and wooden clogs, watching as the older women in our lives, our role models, questioned their world, their decisions. Our role models as little girls were different: Wonder Woman, the Charlie's Angels, the Bionic Woman... Although clearly sexualized from our perspective today, these women were strong, took charge, and spoke their mind. I was mesmerized by them. Blondie, Joan Jett, and of course, Madonna, were women whose music we loved and identified with: clear messages of strength and power.

All of these changes in society and culture had an enormous impact on young women. If I can speak for many girls of the eighties, I would say that we felt we could have it all. Looking to our future, we felt confident that we would have professional careers in law, politics, medicine, education, science... I, myself, questioned the need for marriage or children at all. My mother reinforced this belief, expressing her hopes that I would be a successful individual before I committed to any relationship, she herself having given up University for marriage. I felt that my future belonged to me. I took part in "Take Back the Night" marches. I wore a button on my jean jacket that stated "never again" in reference to the pro-choice position.

Most importantly, I believe, I was proud to call myself a feminist. This word, I used often. I felt it defined who I was, what I believed, and what I wanted. It gave me power.

Nevertheless, as I grew older, the obstacles became more apparent. Many traditional views of women and marriage still abounded. I was told by a math teacher that I could not succeed "because I was a girl". I was disillusioned. The message became contradictory: You can have it all, but it may make you miserable. There were clearly defined limits.

Today, these limits are fewer, the path is clearer, but there are obstacles nonetheless. I can look back and appreciate how I benefited from the struggles of the second wavers. There is less pride today in young women to declare themselves "feminist". This I feel we must try to change.

GREEN DRAGON PRESS

The Montreal Massacre

"Violence against women is part of a continuum of sexist power relationships which define our roles in the home, workplace and society. Inequality, poverty and alienation spawn further violence and make women more fearful…which in turn causes them to limit their right to participate fully in city life.' "The Safe City" METRAC, Metro Action Committee on Public Violence Against Women and Children, Toronto".

On December 6, 1989, fourteen young women at the engineering department of Montreal's Ecole Polytechnique were shot to death by a man, who singled out women students to kill, ordering the men present to leave, and screaming that he hated "feminists." The murderer then shot himself, leaving a letter claiming that women had ruined his life and blocked his entry into the engineering school. In the aftermath of shock and grief women and men vowed to keep the names of the fourteen women alive and work to prevent violence again women. Memorials, vigils and marches were held; discussion escalated around the need for gun control, and initiatives, both individual and community-wide were planned in response to the tragedy. In 1991, the Canadian government proclaimed December 6 a National Day of Remembrance and Action on Violence Against Women. Every year, across Canada, events are held to remember these young women, murdered because they were female.

Geneviève Bergeron, 21

Hélène Colgan, 23

Nathalie Croteau, 23

Barbara Daigneault, 22

Anne-Marie Edward, 21

Maud Haviernick, 29

Barbara Maria Klueznick, 31

Maryse Laganière, 25

Maryse Leclair, 23

Anne-Marie Lemay, 27

Sonia Pelletier, 23

Michèle Richard, 21

Annie St-Arneault, 23

Annie Turcotte, 21

GREEN DRAGON PRESS

NO

means

NO

...IT'S THE LAW

December 6 is a national day of remembrance and action on violence against women. Each of us can end violence in our communities. We can break the silence and provide shelter. We can also call on all governments to:

- enact strong gun control
- enforce the No Means No law
- provide more funding for shelters and crisis centres
- fund education

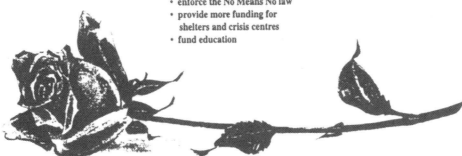

Ontario Federation of Labour Women's Committee

GREEN DRAGON PRESS

A Sample Case: R. v. Ewanchuk
– sexual assault and consent

Do you think women play hard to get? Do you think that women say "no" to sexual advances, that they are really saying "yes" or "try harder"? Do you know what, in law, a woman needs to do in order to communicate that she does not wish to begin, or to continue, sexual activity with a man? Do you know what a man needs to do when a woman says "no"?

Sexual assault is a crime in which gender plays a clear role. Statistics indicate that 90 per cent of the victims of sexual assault are women, and 99 per cent of the perpetrators are men.

The case of "B".
Steve Brian Ewanchuk, was interviewing a 17-year-old woman –(B) – in his van, for a job in his woodworking business. She left the van door open, as she was hesitant about discussing the job offer in his vehicle. After the interview, Ewanchuk invited B to see some of his work, which was in the trailer behind the van. B left the trailer door open, but Ewanchuk closed it in a way that made B think that he had locked it. Ewanchuk started to touch B, although she clearly said no. He stopped his advances on each occasion when B said no, but persisted shortly after with an even more serious advance. On returning home, B called the police who charged Ewanchuk with assault under section 265 of the Criminal Code of Canada.

What happened at Ewanchuk's trial?
Although the trial judge found B to be credible (believable), he acquitted Ewanchuk. The judge said that Ewanchuk was entitled to believe that B had given "implied consent" to the sexual assault. Even if she did not consent by her words, B could be taken to be consenting by her actions? The Crown appealed to the Alberta Court of Appeal. A majority (2 out of 3 judges) agreed with the trial judge. A third, dissenting, judge, said that "Once a woman says "No" during a course of sexual activity, the person intent on continued sexual activity with her must then obtain a clear and unequivocal "Yes" before he again touches her in a sexual matter. The Crown appealed again, to the Supreme Court of Canada.

What happened at the Supreme Court of Canada?
LEAF (Women's Legal Education and Action Fund and DAWN Canada (DisAbled Women's Network) were given leave to intervene at the Supreme Court of Canada. This means that we could make arguments to the Court on how the Court should interpret and apply the law. LEAF and DAWN Canada argued that issues regarding the definition of consent and other questions of sexual assault law raise equality issues for women, including women's right to equal protection of the law as stated in the Canadian Charter of Rights and Freedoms. They argued that to endorse the notion of 'implied consent", in the face of evidence that there was in fact no consent, presumes men's sexual access to women and trivializes all persons' rights to autonomy, physical safety and personal choice.

The Supreme Court of Canada, in a unanimous decision, rejected the defence of "implied consent" and took the unusual step of convicting Ewanchuk (rather than sending the case back to a new trial). The Court was very clear that an accused cannot say that he thought "No" meant "Yes".

GREEN DRAGON PRESS

Notable Women

Claudette MacKay-Lassonde P.Eng.

When Claudette MacKay-Lassonde graduated in 1971, a job placement officer informed her that she would be wasting her time trying to get a job in engineering. Because "they don't want women." She ignored the advice and went on to a successful career. She also worked to improve the status of women in engineering, organizing the first Canadian convention of women engineers and founding Women in Science and Engineering. Galvanized into action by the 1989 murder of 14 women engineering students at Ecole Polytechnique in Montreal, MacKay-Lassonde helped establish the Canadian Engineering Memorial Foundation in memory of the women.

Justine Blainey.

By the time Justine Blainey was ten years old, she was playing hockey in a woman's league and had made the all-star team. To develop her stick-handling skills, Justine went to a boys' hockey school and then decided she wanted to play on a boy's team. What seemed like simple goal to her, resulted in a series of five court battles, beginning in 1985, to win the right for a girl to play on a boys hockey team. In June 1987, the Supreme Court of Canada ruled in her favour. In 1988 she played her first minor-bantam league hockey game.

Mary Two-Axe Early

Mary Two-Axe Early was born in 1911 at Kahnawake, Quebec. When she married a non-Aboriginal man, she immediately lost her Indian status, but returned every year to visit the reserve where she had grown up. In the 1966 the band council refused to allow another woman who had lost her Indian status to be buried in the reserve cemetery. Mary was so upset she founded Equal Rights for Indian Women. After Mary's husband died in 1967, she moved back permanently to the Kahnawake reserve. She continued the fight for re-enfranchisement and in 1985, Parliament passed Bill C-31, which removed the part of the Indian Act that took away a woman's status if she married a non-Aboriginal. Mary became the first woman to have her Indian status officially restored. She died in 1996.

Fran Reid Endicott

Fran Endicott was born in Jamaica and came to Canada in the 1950s. She was a research officer at the Ontario Institute for Studies in Education where she was a pioneer in the development of multicultural curriculum resources. She became a Trustee of the Toronto Board of Education, representing Ward 7 for eight years and served on the Race Relations, Status of Women and Labour Education Committees. Fran was responsible for pushing the Toronto Board of Education to develop leading edge programs on anti-racism, affirmative action, Holocaust studies, literacy and de-streaming. After she left the Toronto Board of Education Fran was appointed Chief Commissioner with the Ontario Human Rights Commission. She served only three months of her term before her death at the age of 48 in 1992.

Activities
1980 – 1989

WOMEN IN THE MILITARY

What kind of debate would ensue between a Voice of Women (VOW) member, and a woman who has won her right to serve in the army? OR ...between a senior military officer who holds the traditional view that women do not belong in the military, and a woman who is considering joining the army. Divide the class into partners. Each partner should choose a role, and research the position assigned. Write a dialogue where the two characters confront each other with their respective points of view.

THE MONTREAL MASSACRE

As a class, create a memorial display for the 6th of December and/or an awareness campaign regarding violence against women. Research current statistics. Educate your school and your classmates. Distribute white ribbons.

CONSTITUTIONAL EQUALITY

As a class, examine the Charter of Rights and Freedoms. Find "loopholes" in the wording, where the charter could be applied unequally to different groups and/or men and women. Look specifically for vague language. Propose revisions.

INNU WOMEN

Read the article about the struggle of the women of Nitassinan, p191. Research their struggle in depth if possible. Write a public declaration, which clearly outlines their grievances, and their demands for change. Begin with "We the women of Nitassinan..."

HOW WOULD YOUR LIFE BE DIFFERENT IF YOU'D BEEN BORN A BOY/GIRL?

Each member of the class should ask a sample of five girls, and five boys this question, and record the responses. Compare and contrast the results with those presented in the article, p193. Discuss the implications of sampling different age groups, as well as the length of time (approximately 20 years) that have passed since the original study.

Resources

Andrew, Anne Marie. "The Government of Mischief" and Hurley, Mary Martha. "Life on the Edge of a Bombing Range" in Byrne, Nympha & Camille Fouillard. *It's Like the Legend: Innu Women's Voices.* Toronto: Women's Press, 2000.
Guberman, Connie & Margie Wolfe. *No Safe Place: Violence Against Women,* Toronto: Women's Press, 1985.
Kome, Penney, *The Taking of Twenty-Eight: Women Challenge the Constitution.* Toronto: Women's Press, 1983.

Video: *After the Montreal Massacre:* National Film Board of Canada.

www.coolwomen.org - Feb. 14, 1981 – Women's Constitution Conference.

GREEN DRAGON PRESS

1990 – 1999

Are women equal yet?

The January 21, 1998 Gable cartoon poked fun at the monument to the five Alberta women who fought successfully to have women declared persons. The names and images of the popular "Spice Girls" are substituted (Sporty, Posh, Baby, Ginger, Scary) Reprinted with permission from *The Globe and Mail*.

A Great Event: Dr. Roberta Lynn Bondar - Canada's first female astronaut, selected in 1983, became the first Canadian woman in space in 1992 on the Shuttle Discovery.
Seven years later, in 1999 Bondar was followed by Julie Payette who was part of the crew that re-supplied the International Space Station. Payette was the first Canadian to participate in an assembly mission and board the Station.

Photo: Endicott Centre.

1990-2000 Introduction

"Answering questions from politicians or corporate leaders on standard feminist goals-equal pay, for instance-taught me that most people thought about women's advancement as a zero-sum game. If women gained equal pay, there would be less for men. No one considered the fact that better use of women's talents would be a source of productivity. To most people, changing the segregated workforce and giving women opportunities to learn and advance over a lifetime career wasn't a productivity issue, it was just a transaction in a zero-sum game. I'd try to get people to see how the abolition of slavery and a free market for labor had enhanced productivity in earlier stages of capitalism, and what would be lost in the emerging knowledge-based society if women's intellectual abilities were underutilized. Jill Ker Conway, A Woman's Education, 121.

The decade began with a public demonstration for women's rights as the National Action Committee on the Status of Women (NAC) led a national campaign to persuade the Canadian government to proclaim December 6 a national day of Mourning and Action on Violence Against Women. Brian Mulroney, and his Conservative government tried to re-criminalize abortion in Canadian but the bill failed to receive passage from the senate. This was due to major objections by Feminist Conservative Senator Pat Carney, who did not support the government. The move towards the right in North America permeated the early 1990s and witnessed the emphasis on conventional family life and traditional roles for women. This was revealed when a major comedy show featuring a newspaper reporter named Murphy Brown, gave birth to a baby boy out of wedlock on public television. She had the choice of two fathers but rejected them both and decided to raise the child alone. The next day the Vice-President of the United States criticized her decision, stating that unwed mothers violated "family values." Canadians addressed the issue of working mothers when Ontario Premier Mike Harris announced a $5-million government program to finance school breakfasts in November 1977. Such a program was necessary, he said, because times were changing.

Thirty years ago, he averred, "It seemed to be that Mom was in the kitchen with the hot breakfast cooking as everybody woke up in the morning. That's not the normal situation today." When several female MPPs from the New Democratic Party challenged his remarks in the legislature later that day, a male backbencher from Mr. Harris' Progressive Conservative government yelled out to one of them. "Go home and take care of one of your own kids." It seemed that in some quarters, a turn-of-the-century mindset still prevailed. (In 1914, the *Albertan* reported on a debate at the local council where someone warned: "The women of today were shirking their proper responsibilities and the day would come the men would have to cook the meals, while the women were out legislating.") Many women wondered how far they had really advanced in the struggle for equity.

Canadian women, however, had few plans to return to their kitchens as greater numbers of women entered the workforce and into positions of power. Rita Johnson, for example, became the first woman provincial Premier in Canada (of the province of British Columbia) and in 1993, Kim Campbell, also of British Columbia, became the first female Canadian Prime Minister after Brian Mulroney stepped down.

GREEN DRAGON PRESS

1990 The Ontario Women's History Network/le Reseau d'histoire des Fémmes en Ontario (OWHN-RHF) was founded to encourage the study and further the knowledge of women's history in Ontario and Canada. Since the proclamation of Women's History Month in 1992, OWHN has sponsored a series of posters celebrating the achievements of Canadian Women. Themes have included Work, Technology, Education, the Arts, Sports, Law, Inventions, Women Writers, and Native Women in the Arts.
OWHN: 2267 Lake Shore Blvd. West, #1009.
Toronto, On M8V 3X2
Posters available through: www3.sympatico.ca/equity.greendragonpress

Senator Joyce Fairbairn was appointed to the cabinet as the first woman leader of the government in the Senate and Dr. Jean Augustine became the first African Canadian woman elected to the Parliament of Canada. In 1995, the Supreme Court ruled that sexual orientation must be included as a prohibited form of discrimination under the Charter of Rights and under the provincial Human Rights Codes. Women were demanding laws and status that recognized their greater role in the economic and political life of the country. In 1997, Sharon Carstairs (Manitoba) was named Deputy Leader of the Government, the first woman to hold this position. In 1998 Vivienne Poy became the first Asian woman appointed to the Senate and in June 1999, after harrowing years collecting evidence of war crimes for the UN, Madame Justice Louise Arbour was appointed to the Supreme Court of Canada. That same year, the Supreme Court of Canada acknowledged same-sex marriages. There were many women who helped place Canadians into the international forum. Dr. Roberta Bondar became the first Canadian woman in space and Julie Payette flew the Space Shuttle Discovery in May-June 1999, one of the crew that re-supplied the International Space Station. She was the first Canadian to participate in an assembly mission on board the Station. Finally, thousands of Canadians joined politicians and dignitaries on Parliament Hill, Wednesday October 18, 2000 to honour a group of women known as the "Famous Five." When Canada's Supreme Court said women couldn't sit in the Senate because constitutionally, they weren't considered people, Henrietta Muir Edwards, Louise McKinney, Emily Murphy, Irene Parlby and Nellie McClung took the fight even further. They took it all the way to the Privy Council in England and on Oct. 18, 1929, they won the right for women to be recognized as "persons" under Canadian law. Their achievement was marked with a bronze monument on Parliament Hill. "This monument is a source of joy and strength, of comfort and inspiration. It is beautiful and it is powerful," said Frances Wright, president of the Famous Five Foundation. The century came to a close with the celebration and recognition of the achievements of Canadian women.

- 1990 Rachel Zimmerman at age 13, developed a printer for Blissymbolics, an international pictograph language which permits people with disabilities to communicate by computer.

- Canada wins the first Women's World Hockey Championship.

Political Action

Despite the progress made in the 1980s towards recognizing the issue of violence against women, it was clear that there was much reform still needed to create an equitable judicial system to protect women who have been victims of assault. Federal Justice Minister Kim Campbell, proposed a number of reforms, including the rape shield law and the issue of consent.

(see Regina vs Ewanchuk in Chapter Nine)

"New Sexual Assault Legislation a Step Forward"
Toronto, January 1992[8]

"The proposed sexual assault legislation, introduced by Justice Minister Kim Campbell on December 12, is an important step forward in making sexual assault law more responsive to the problem of sexual violence against women," said Helena Orton, LEAF Litigation Director.

LEAF was one of a number of women's organizations which met with Ms Campbell and Department of Justice staff to urge a major review of sexual assault laws. "It is clear that Justice Minister Campbell listened to the input from women's organizations," said Ms Orton. "There is a recognition that women have constitutional rights at stake, as well as the accused."

The proposed amendments to the Criminal Code (1) define the notion of consent to sexual activity, and (2) provide guidelines and procedures in determining admissibility of past sexual history as evidence.

Consent

The proposed legislation defines consent as "the voluntary agreement of the complainant to engage in the sexual activity in question." As well, it outlines specific situations which do not constitute consent by the complainant, such as when there is incapacity to consent due to intoxication, when agreement to sexual activity is extracted by someone in a position of authority, when initial agreement to sexual activity is revoked.

"The definition of consent will help deal with some of the stereotypes and myths about women's sexuality which have traditionally infused the laws of sexual assault," said Ms Orton, on first reading of the Bill. "It makes clear that no means no."

The legislation leaves open the defence of honest belief in consent but requires that the accused has taken reasonable steps to ascertain consent. Similarly the law makes clear that wilful blindness, self-induced intoxication or recklessness cannot be used to excuse a failure to recognize that a woman was not consenting.

"These are important equality-promoting developments," said Ms Orton.

Past Sexual History

The Bill says that past sexual history of the complainant with the accused or any other person cannot be used at trial to suggest that the complainant is more likely to have consented to the activity or is less worthy of belief.

In addition, evidence that the complainant has engaged in other sexual activity will not be allowed unless the judge determines, according to a legal test which balances relevance, fairness and other considerations, that the advantages of admitting the evidence outweigh the disadvantages.

Helena Orton said, "Significantly, the Bill recognizes that sexual history evidence is inherently prejudicial and that judges need guidance for considering whether to admit this evidence."

"By further defining consent, the legislation should minimize the circumstances in which past sexual history evidence could be considered relevant," said Ms Orton.

The Bill sets out procedures which must be followed for admissibility of sexual history evidence.

"LEAF will be examining the Bill in detail over the next month," said Helena Orton. "While there are clearly areas in which we would like to see improvement, such as recognition in the preamble that sexual assault victimization is not gender or race neutral, we are nevertheless greatly encouraged by the equality promoting steps that we see."

Women's Groups Meet with Justice Minister

After the rape shield law was struck down, LEAF and other women's groups sought meetings with the Department of Justice staff to discuss the need for a new law which would not only take account of the fair trial rights of those accused of sexual assault, but would take account of the Charter guarantees to the women and children of Canada who are, as a group, the victims of sexual assault.

Women's organizations met with Justice Minister Kim Campbell to urge her to consider the issue fully. "We made the point that more consultation was necessary to ensure that the new law meets the needs of all women survivors of sexual assault who want to use the courts, including women of colour, women with disabilities, aboriginal women, immigrant women and domestic workers who are particular targets for sexual assault," said LEAF Executive Director Christie Jefferson.

8. *LEAF Lines* 4, no. 4 (January 1992), 1, 4.

GREEN DRAGON PRESS

Throughout the century women's talent for organizing to fight for change has been a key factor in gains for equality. The National Association of Women and the Law produced this useful pamphlet describing how to start a women's group.

Getting Started: Organizing a Women's Group and Your
Responsibilities as a Director
Ottawa, 1986[13]

How to Organize

1   First, you should draw up a constitution, or governing document. Consider what the purpose of your organization is, and how you wish to provide for the day-to-day operation of the group if that is necessary. Make provision for the internal workings of the group, how executive members will be elected, how often meetings will be held and how the decision-making process will be carried out.

2   Call a meeting. To attract supporters, you could advertise throughout your community with flyers, place notices in community centres and other women's centres or groups, or call your local radio station and inquire about free public announcements. Word of mouth can also be successful.

3   At the first meeting have a copy of the constitution for all present. You may wish to appoint a Chairperson to conduct the initial meeting. You will also need someone to take complete and legible minutes of the discussions that take place, including the date, time and place of the meeting and the names, addresses and telephone numbers of all who attend.

4   While you may not wish to be too formal, it will be helpful to review Roberts' *Rules of Order* or Bourinot's *Rules of Order*. They provide simple guidelines for conducting a meeting. Most meetings will run smoothly if all members are considerate of the others present. If the group is a large one, a list of meeting procedures covering issues like time limits for individual discussions on a topic or how to introduce an item for debate may be helpful.

5   After the meeting is called to order, the constitution should be discussed. All proposed changes should be noted and voted on. The results of the vote should be recorded. When there are no more changes to discuss, the constitution as a whole should be adopted by a vote of all those present.

6   Executive members should then be elected according to the procedure set out in the constitution. At the very least you will need a chairperson and a secretary/treasurer. You may wish to expand your executive committee to include a vice-chairperson and individuals in charge of "special issues" like fundraising or social gatherings if your group is a large one.

7   Depending on the nature of your group, you may wish to consider incorporation.

8   Now you're ready to go ahead and discuss the policies and activities in which your organization is going to engage ...

Directors Have Responsibilities
Executive committee members or "directors" of non-profit organizations have a responsibility to their members and to the public at large. They have an obligation (duty) to conduct the activities of the group in accordance with the law. They must also accept the blame if things are not done in accordance with the law. In other words, they are liable for damages suffered by other individuals, or for losses sustained by the organization if it is not incorporated.

When someone accepts the position of a director or executive committee member, she commits herself to acting in good faith, and in the best interests of the organization. She must take care to avoid any conflicts of interest which may arise between her personal activities and those goals or objects of the organization. She cannot act for personal gain or profit in her capacity as a director, but must always act on behalf of the organization itself.

A director is responsible to see that the internal operation of the organization runs smoothly. This would include bookkeeping and controlling the finances of the organization; taking and distributing minutes or meetings to other members; setting the agenda and organizing meetings; ensuring that the goals (policies) are being met through the organization's activities; maintaining effective communication with other directors and members of the organization; notices to members of meetings, resolutions or special activities.

Directors' Liabilities
In addition to the responsibilities that a director owes to her organization, she is also exposed to liabilities. She may be held personally responsible for damages or losses to the organization, or others, if the organization is not incorporated.

A director is not, however, responsible for mere errors of judgment. In the absence of fraud, negligence or acting for personal gain in a conflict of interest situation, a director will not be held personally liable. The director is held to a standard of loyalty and good faith in her dealings with, and on behalf of, the organization.

In order to avoid personal liability, a director should fully and frankly discuss problems and issues with other directors and members and, where possible, seek approval and ratification of actions or expenditures prior to undertaking them.

13. National Association of Women and the Law, Pamphlet, Ottawa, 1986. CWMA file: National Association of Women and the Law.

GREEN DRAGON PRESS

Women and Work

By Rose Fine-Meyer

Domestic Labour in Canada

By the 1990s Canada took the majority of domestic immigrants from the Philippines. The Live-In Caregiver program was enacted in 1992. The program increased educational and skill requirements.

Although the end of the century brought washing machines, dishwashers and electronic devises to make everyday life easier, domestic workers were still needed as the majority of Canadian women worked full time. But faced with workers who once brought into Canada would change jobs and leave domestic service, the government decided to implement more restrictive controls. In fact these restrictions force workers to remain in abusive and often violent environment. Their temporary status makes them vulnerable to their employees as well as the system. The LCP program gives temporary work permits to workers and caregivers coming into Canada with the understanding that landed status and citizenship must be achieved over time and through proper participation of the program. Specific conditions imposed by the LCP involve separation from family, live-in requirements and having to fulfill 24 months of full-time work in a 3-year period. Temporary status leaves domestic labourers with more regulations to follow and in a vulnerable state with greater risk of being deported. Often through no fault of their own, many domestic workers are unable to meet the requirements of the LCP program and as workers are dependent on employers for employment records, the continued legality of their employment, and eventually a chance for permanent status.

In response, organizations such as INTERCEDE in Toronto and Vancouver, the Committee for Domestic Workers, and Caregivers' Rights were formed to provide a comprehensive advocacy and action group where members can find legal advice, support, job opportunities and friendship. The migrant women who come to Canada as domestic workers make valuable contributions to Canadian society. After much hardship and difficulties, they eventually become full citizens and are able to fully participate in Canadian society.

The following is from Women and Society, Yesmim Ternar, *Tiger Lily: Journal for Women of Colour*. It is a reduction of a much longer article.

"The French couple who employ Saliha Samson are very nice people. They leave for work early in the morning, as soon as she arrives. They know she is a conscientious worker and that she doesn't slack off like some of the other cleaning women. Madame Rivests tells Saliha to eat whatever she wants from the refrigerator. She knows that Saliha likes to snack on strawberry and blueberry yogurt so she makes sure that there is some in the refrigerator for her. The Rivests live a long way off from where she lives but the trip is worth it because some of the people she works for close to home treat her so badly that she'd rather lose an hour and work for Madame and Monsieur Rivest. The wash is done in one of the machines. She opens a dryer and transfers the load there. Just as she starts the dryer, the other two machines go off. She puts those loads in the dryers, too, and feeds quarters to the machines. It's time to go up and vacuum, the Rivest's bedroom.

GREEN DRAGON PRESS

Saliha notes that the dryers must have completed their cycle. She finishes her work in the bedroom. She takes along the yellow plastic laundry basket to carry the wash. She gets unlucky going down. A young housewife and her son step into the elevator on the second floor and ride with her to the main floor.

Saliha tries to act oblivious to the woman's presence, but she winks surreptitiously at the little boy. The boy responds with a blank face. Saliha is relieved when they get out. In the basement she quickly piles all the wash together in the laundry basket and she goes up to the Rivest's apartment to sort the clothes.

Saliha remembers about life in Turkey. After she finished her primary education with distinctions she went to teacher's college to become a primary teacher. After teaching in remote Anatolian villages where she gained the awe and respect of the peasants, she came to Canada to join her brother who is an auto mechanic in Montreal. She is presently enrolled at Plato College to learn English and French. Saliha folds the towels and linen neatly. Only some light dusting remains to be done. Then she will clean the bathroom. Saliha cleans for two spinster sisters on Thursdays. They always follow her around and check how much detergent and soap she uses. They never offer her much at lunchtime. On Fridays she cleans the old man's home. He is a kind and quiet man who doesn't demand much from Saliha. She cooks a couple of light dishes for him.

Madame Rivest returns from work. She informs Saliha that she will call her next week. She gestures as if she was dialing and holding onto the receiver of an imaginary phone. Of course, Saliha can understand Madame Rivest without the added jestures. Madame Rivest gives Saliha her earnings in an envelope.

Saliha replies "merci beaucoup, Madame Rivest." In the elevator going down, Saliha is alone. She checks the contents of the envelope. She has enough for the week's food and cigarettes. Last week, she paid the last instalment for her tuition at Plato College. She is tired but life is under control. We come here to speak like them, she thinks; but it will be a long time before they let us practice."

- 1990 Canada wins the first Women's World Hockey Championship.

- 1995: 57.4 per cent of all Canadian women were either working or looking for work (Statistics Canada.)

GREEN DRAGON PRESS

Garment Workers

The woman in the photograph sewing clothing at home for retail sale could be working anywhere in the world. She happens to be in Canada. For many women, working at home means that we can take care of their own children. Wherever they work, garment workers tend to be poorly paid, often at or below subsistence level. Many must work long hours to meet production deadlines. In factories, women & children often work in appalling conditions, with little or no protection from health hazards; homeworkers face injuries & chronic conditions.

Even in countries like Canada where there are laws setting out minimum requirements, industry standards often fall significantly below these requirements. For example, homeworkers and those working in small shops set up by contractors - sweatshops - are usually paid "piece-rates" (a certain amount for each sewing step). Highly experienced homeworkers who are fast sewers often cannot even make the minimum wage. Yet there are factories supplying major brand names & contractors employing homeworkers who follow the law.

Around the world, women are organizing to try to improve their working situation. We as consumers can support them by demanding that the clothes we buy are produced under decent & fair conditions, including the right to a living wage, the right to organize, the right to safe & healthy working conditions. The story begins & ends with the retailer. The retailer determines the price of production, and therefore must take responsibility for the wages and working conditions of the women who sew its clothes.

Here are some questions we can ask the store manager the next time we buy clothing:

- ☐ do you know how the workers who made this garment were treated?
- ☐ does your store have a code of conduct for all workers that make the clothes you sell?
- ☐ is the code of conduct posted in every factory and given to every worker?
- ☐ does it forbid child labour and protect the human rights of workers?
- ☐ does it specify living wages?
- ☐ is there an independent monitoring agency to make sure that everybody lives up to the code?

The Labour Behind the Label Coalition, a working group in Canada of labour, women, church & economic justice organizations has organized the WEAR FAIR CAMPAIGN to raise public awareness

GREEN DRAGON PRESS

Maria's Comments

It is a good thing that consumer power works, because corporate responsibility is a few centuries behind. Why is that? The profit motive, you tell me. I accept that, but I think there are other important reasons. Making cloth, sewing cloth has always been women's work, although depending on their economic status many women can choose to buy rather than produce. There is lots of evidence, historical & before our very own eyes, that women's work is treated differently than men's work in all kinds of ways. I'll do my part as a consumer, but I want to see employers (men and women) act decently and fairly of their own accord too. Why should we always have to ask?

Photographs reproduced with the permission of the Ontario District Council of the union of Needletrades, Industrial & Textile Employees(UNITE).

Soukenya

www.coolwomen.org

GREEN DRAGON PRESS

Soukenya's Comments

Consumer power works. We need to remember that the next time we are standing in front of a cashier, perhaps nervous or shy about asking about that retailers' commitments to its workers & its customers. The GAP recently signed a groundbreaking agreement allowing for independent human rights observers to monitor conditions at contractors' plants where GAP clothing is made. This was the result of a campaign by a broad coalition of labour, religious, women, student, consumer and grassroots groups from Canada and the US. Woolworth, the US company which owns the clothing stores Northern Reflections, Northern Traditions & Northern Getaway, has agreed to carry out an investigation of some of its contractors' practices in Canada in response to publicity and other actions undertaken by people supporting the WEAR FAIR CAMPAIGN. Take a deep breath, & ask those questions.

Photographs reproduced with the permission of the Ontario District Council of the union of Needletrades, Industrial & Textile Employees(UNITE).

GREEN DRAGON PRESS

WERE YOUR CLOTHES MADE IN A SWEATSHOP?

Chances are they were.
Maybe in Honduras or China.
Or right here in Canada.

SWEATSHOPS ARE NOT A THING OF THE PAST!!

There are hundreds of sweatshops in Canada, and tens of thousands around the world...and they make **huge profits for retail stores** by paying workers pennies to sew the clothes we wear. These workers, mostly women, face exhausting hours, sub-minimum wages, arbitrary discipline, unsafe workplaces and all forms of harassment.

We are all hurt by sweatshops. Some big companies in the garment industry...just like in other industries...are looking all over the world for the cheapest labour. They say we have to compete with sweatshops to keep our jobs.

UNITE says they are wrong and that we have to take a stand against sweatshops...to ensure better jobs and working conditions for all.

Join UNITE in our campaign to stop sweatshops...let the retailers and major labels know that they are responsible for the working conditions under which their products are made!!

UNION OF NEEDLETRADES, INDUSTRIAL
AND TEXTILE EMPLOYEES
15 Gervais Drive, Suite 700
Don Mills, Ontario M3C 1Y8
tel:(416) 441-1806 fax:(416) 441-9680
email: nosweat@unite-svti.org

A poster distributed by the Union of Needle trades, Industrial and Textile Employees during their campaign to stop sweatshops in Canada: Reprinted by permission.

GREEN DRAGON PRESS

Northern Group Fails the Test

In 1996, the Homeworkers' Association discovered that homeworkers and contract shop employees in Metro Toronto who were sewing apparel for the Woolworth Corporation's Northern Reflections, Northern Traditions and Northern Getaway labels were being paid $4.50 an hour, 65% of the minimum wage. Some workers were being paid as little as $2.50 an hour. In heavy production periods, workers were toiling 12-hour days with no overtime pay. They were not receiving vacation pay or statutory holidays. Woolworth contractors were not making contributions to the Canada Pension Plan or Employment Insurance. After meeting with the workers, Woolworth agreed to carry out an investigation. However, against the wishes of the Homeworkers' Association, Woolworth suspended future orders with one of the contractors, rather than working with the contractor to improve labour practices. As a result, workers are now afraid to bring forward complaints, because they fear doing so would result in a loss of employment. More than three years later, Woolworth (since renamed "Venator") still refuses to release any information on the findings of its investigation.

Indentured Labour in Saipan, an island in the US Northern Mariana Islands

In January 1999, two class action suits were filled against 18 major US apparel companies, charging them with using indentured labour under sweatshop conditions in the US Commonwealth of the Northern Mariana Islands. The class action suits were filed on behalf of more than 50,000 "guest workers" recruited from China and other Asian countries. The predominantly women workers were forced to work up to 12 hours a day, seven days a week without overtime pay in unsafe, unsanitary and abusive conditions. They were required to repay "recruitment fees" of between US$2,000 and $7,000, which were deducted from their pay cheques. To date, nine of the 18 companies named in the class action suits have agreed to a settlement that includes the prohibition of recruitment fees, and acceptance of independent monitoring of factory conditions. Companies that have not yet agreed to the settlement include the GAP, Sears Roebuck, Tommy Hilfiger and Wal-Mart. "Made in Saipan" and "Made in the Northern Mariana Islands" labels have been found on Eddie Bauer, Tommy Hilfiger, Calvin Klein and Dockers garments sold in Toronto, Vancouver and St. John's.

For more information, contact:
Maquila Solidarity Network
606 Shaw St., Toronto, ON M6G 3L6
Tel: (416) 532-8584 • Fax: (416) 532-7688
perg@web.net
http://www.web.net/~msn/

In the 90s a number of organizations spoke out against the oppression of women through sweated labour both in Canada and abroad. A June 1999 study by University of Toronto professor Roxanna Ng confirmed that many Toronto area home workers were not receiving the minimum wage or statutory benefits.

Home workers interviewed were being paid as little as $2.00 per hour and on average between $6.00-8.00 per hour. At that time the minimum wage in Ontario was $6.85, but, to compensate for their overhead costs, home workers were legally entitled to a minimum wage of $7.54 per hour. Almost half the workers interviewed worked 10-12 hours per day. Most of the home workers interviewed were not being given labels to sew on to garments, probably because labels have been used to identify retailers whose products the home workers were sewing in order to bring pressure against them to take responsibility for labour rights violations.

GREEN DRAGON PRESS

Remembering the Montreal Massacre

On December 6, 1989, a man entered the School of Engineering at Ecole Polytechnique, University of Montreal. He went to several classrooms, saying: "You [women] have no right being here" and separated the women from the men. He then systematically murdered 14 young women. In his suicide letter he wrote: "...I have decided to send the feminists, who have always ruined my life, to their Maker."

12 of these women were engineering students, one a graduate student and instructor. The other 2 women were an administration staff worker and a health sciences student.

As physicist Professor Ursula Franklin said to engineering students in 1995: "This event has become a benchmark for all of us - because so much changed in the wake of this tragedy; it changed perceptions and interpretations of the climate and the realities of life for women in engineering. In light of the sudden, horrible realization of what had happened in Montreal, it became possible - likely for the first time in Canada - to say, 'this could have happened at OUR university, it could have happened in MY class.' There was a quantum leap in reality recognition across this country."

- 1991 December 6 was established as a National Day of Remembrance and Action on Violence Against Women, by parliamentary consensus. This National Day commemorates the tragic deaths of 14 young women on this date in Montreal in 1989.

Ursula Franklin. Scientist, social justice activist.
Photo: Peter Bregg.

GREEN DRAGON PRESS

Women and Music

Lilith Fair: A Celebration of Women in Music
A History of the Festival Tours of the late 1990's

The true origins of Lilith

"After the Holy One created the first human being Adam, He said, it is not good for Adam to be alone. He created a woman, also from the earth, and called her Lilith." (From the Alphabet of Ben Sira 23)

The most ancient Biblical account of the creation relates that God created the first man and the first woman at the same time. Jewish legends tell us that this woman was Lilith. Lilith, we learn, felt herself to be Adam's equal (We are both from the earth) but Adam refused to accept her equality. Lilith, determined to retain her independence and dignity, chose loneliness over subservience and flew away from Adam and the Garden of Eden. God sent 3 angels to bring her back but she refused to return. Her punishment is that one hundred of her children will die every day. She is then associated by many with that of a demon or witch. Lilith is clearly a powerful female and the myths that surround her image reflect her independence. Her strength of character and commitment to self is viewed as either inspirational or rebellious.

The festival tour: "Lilith [Fair] was a great example of strong women out there doing something they love, doing something really positive." (Sarah McLachlan 1996)

The story of Lilith is evidently one of determination to be independent and free. The name Lilith could not be more appropriate as the title of the first all-women festival tour, conceived of and realized by Sarah McLachlan, perhaps one of Canada's best-known and celebrated female musicians.

In 1996, McLachlan was inspired to create a venue for women artists through a personal experience. Discussing a potential tour with concert promoters, she suggested that Paula Cole open the show for her. The promoters balked at this idea, stating simply "Who would pay to see two female musicians".

Angered and inspired by this refusal, McLachlan began to experiment with the idea of concerts featuring all-female performers, and in 1997, the first Lilith Fair was born. This first all-women festival featured such talent as Tracy Chapman, Suzanne Vega, the Indigo Girls, Sheryl Crow, Jewel, and of course, Sarah McLachlan herself. As one of the philosophies behind Lilith Fair was helping others, 50% of the proceeds from the CD were donated to charities such as RAINN (Rape Abuse Incest National Network) and LifeBeat (AIDS benefit).

Proving all critics wrong, Lilith Fair went on in 1997 to be the top grossing festival tour, male or female. When the media announced this the "year of the woman" in the music industry, Joni Mitchell responded with "Is that all we get?". In fact, there would be two more highly successful Lilith Fairs in the late 1990s, all featuring talented women songwriters and musicians. The impact was astounding, for example guitar companies began marketing more aggressively to women.

GREEN DRAGON PRESS

Nevertheless, into the new Millenium, the focus seems to once again have shifted, as the "folksy" and "earthy" sound of the women musicians has been replaced by the "glossy pop" images of highly manufactured pop artists, as well as anti-women lyrics. It appears there is still very much a niche and a need for the inspiration, rebellion and spirit of "Lilith".

• 1992 The Federal Government proclaimed October Women's History Month.

"www.coolwomen.ca was founded because history books don't tell the whole story. Women in Canada, in all their diversity, are making change here in all sorts of ways, big and small. We want our stories to be visible, accessible to others. We also want to think about our history and our future from a woman's perspective - we want to explore the links between individual choices, group actions and social change. We picked a web-based project so that we could do this learning and exploring together, and with the hope that our stories would find their way into classrooms and media across the country. We want women and girls to make more history."

• 1994 Myriam Bedard became the first woman to win two gold medals in the Winter Olympic Biathlon.

Patricia Hy-Boulais, two time Canadian tennis champion, singles and doubles.
Photo: Canadian Tennis Association.

Joanne Marshall, veteran Special Olympics competitor.
Photo: Canadian Special Olympics Inc.

Charmaine Crooks, five-time Olympian, silver medalist 1984, member International Olympic Committee since 1999.
Photo: Claus Anderson.

GREEN DRAGON PRESS

The first woman ever to play in a major professional hockey game by starting in goal for the National Hockey League Tampa Bay Lightning team against the St. Louis Blues in 1992.

Manon Rheame

GREEN DRAGON PRESS

Women and Sports

Canadian women's right to participate in competitive sports has been neither automatic nor easily won. They have had to contend with medical concerns about their "femininity," opposition by self-appointed moral guardians of society to the idea of women performing in front of male spectators, dress restrictions, inequities in funding and facilities, and lack of support even in their own athletic associations. All these obstacles conspired to exclude women, especially in high performance sports. Winning the right to compete at the Olympic Games was especially difficult.

In the 20s and 30s women became more visible, and this period was the golden age of women's sport. The success of the "Matchless Six," the 1928 Women's Olympic track team (Ethel Smith, Myrtle Cook, Jean Thompson, Bobbie Rosenfeld, Ethel Catherwood and Jane Bell) resulted in a huge outpouring of public interest - echoed today in the interest in the successes of Canadian women Olympians in hockey, curling, speed skating, biathlon, skiing, swimming and track and field.

Throughout the century the public responded to the outstanding achievements of women athletes such as skater Barbara Ann Scott, swimmer Marilyn Bell, rower Silken Laumann, wheelchair racer Chantal Petitclerc, first Olympic downhill medallist Lucille Wheeler, mountain biker Alison Sydor, swimmer Elaine Tanner, outstanding track athletes Charmaine Crooks and Angela Chalmers, double gold biathlon medal Olympian Myrian Bedard, rowers Marnie McBean and Kathleen Heddle, speed skaters Catriona LeMay Doan and Susan Auch and women's hockey and curling medallists. Individual women, such as Alexandrine Gibb, founder of the

Women's Amateur Athletic Federation and the founders of the Canadian Association for the Advancement of Women and Sport and Physical Activity (CAAWS) gave women an official voice and worked to overturn the obstacles. Over the years, many advances were made. In a one hundred year period, participation the Olympic Games grew from no women in Athens in 1896 to 3,800 of the 10,000 athletes in Atlanta in 1996. The International Amateur Athletics Federation (IAFF) proclaimed 1998 The Year of Women in Athletics. Much has changed since female tennis players had to contend with the dress code at the Rideau Club in Ottawa. At the first women-only tournament in 1881, women were instructed to wear "a ground-length dress of wool or coarse silk, well-flounced, with decorative sleeves, high neck and nipped waist, over corsets and petticoats."

Women's Hockey in Canada

Ice rinks around the country were dealing with an increase in female hockey teams demanding ice rink time. Ice rinks that had traditionally rented to male hockey players were concerned about the loss of their rink time. Should women have the right to equal participation in Canada's national pastime? Megan Williams, a journalist, addressed these concerns in an article on Women's Hockey. She pointed out that competition as well as lack of facilities is often a reason cited to explain why many young women leave sports. One women recalled: "I can recall having to walk one and a half hours to get a chance to skate in an outdoor rink as a girl. Then I'd have to put on those skates with picks on the toes that I was constantly tripping over. We girls were sort of like Bambi - shoved to the margins of the rink while the boys skated and played their games in the middle." Greater numbers of women were participating in the sport. Between 1990-1995 female participation in hockey rose 200% with a total of 25,000 registered players. Attitudes towards female hockey players were beginning to change in response to demands for equal access to equipment and facilities. Another issue was whether boy's teams should allow girls to participate. Exceptional female hockey players have traditionally seen their opportunities restricted as they were denied access to participation in male teams where the level of play was more in their league. Several court cases challenged this position. In each case the organizations attempted to bar girls from boy's teams, claiming they were following the Amateur Hockey Association rules that limit members to "every male person" In 1986, 12-year-old Justine Blainey challenged the Ontario Hockey Association (OHA) over their refusal to allow her participation in a boys' hockey team in Toronto. The Blainey case resulted in the elimination of the exemption in the Ontario Human Rights Code that had allowed sports organizations to discriminate against girls by not allowing them to participate in all its programs. Still, private sports organizations were not subject to these provisions and therefore could choose to have exclusive male teams. The court cases and the demands by young female players have changed attitudes towards the female athletes. Blainey said, " I used to watch my brother's games and practices and realized that he was playing twice as

often and getting more practices. My practices would be at 5 a.m. and his were at 11 a.m. My tournaments would be a four-hour drive away, and his would be close by. Mine would be outside; his would be inside. And there was a huge difference of what was expected in terms of quality" Girls continued to demand the right to their place in Canada's national sport and to challenge existing restrictions and discrimination.

GREEN DRAGON PRESS

A Parent's Wish For Her Daughters

by Marg McGregor

Une mère nous fait part des espoirs et des rêves qu'elle entretient pour sa fille. Elle imagine sa fille dans un système sportif sain où elle aurait du plaisir et où les filles seraient soutenues et respectées.

I want my daughters' sporting experience to be fun and joyful, helping them to develop self-confidence and leadership skills. I want them to discover that excellence, not winning at all costs, is what matters.

As I choose activities for my young daughters, activities which will help them to learn and to grow, I have a huge menu from which to choose. Appealing possibilities include sport programs, piano lessons, painting, Brownies, ballet, choir, computer camp—there is no shortage of options. Before I choose sport over the others, it first has to demonstrate that it offers the values, the positive experiences, and the learning opportunities that I am seeking for my daughters.

Exactly what am I, as a parent looking for? Well, for starters I want to encourage them to pursue sporting activities which offer them the opportunity to make choices, and then supports them in the choices they make. Let's say Kristy wants to be a pole vaulter. I want to know that she will receive moral support and encouragement to pursue that choice, even though it is not a traditional "female" pursuit. On the other hand, if the lesson of that choice teaches that "it's OK for girls to pole vault for fun, but competitive pole vaulting is for boys," then it is not an activity I could wholeheartedly support and encourage.

I want my daughters' sporting experience to be fun and joyful, helping them to develop self-confidence and personal leadership skills. I want them to learn to work cooperatively with others. I want them to discover that excellence, not winning at all costs, is what matters. I want my kids to look around and see women and men who are valued in the sport system.

I want my daughters to be taught and coached by qualified and certified women, and to be officiated by women as well as men so they learn that women can be leaders, not simply spectators or chauffeurs. I want their coaches to hold female values and to understand what it is like to be an eight- or a 12- or a 16-year-old girl. I want their coaches to understand the position of power that coaches hold—and to respect and not abuse their power.

I want my daughters to be part of a sport system that is deeply rooted in the values of fair play, safety, and equity. I want a sport where Kaleigh does not have to compromise her personal health and safety in order to excel, or where the only way to stay competitive is to perform manœuvers which put her at great risk. There must be no possibility that she will be pressured, from her coach or from her peers, to take performance-enhancing drugs or alter her hormones in order to perform better.

I want my children to play and compete alongside athletes with a disability so that Kristy and Kaleigh gain understanding and respect. I want them to feel that the sporting environment is friendly and comfortable, and gives them so much satisfaction that they choose lifetime involvement as a participant, and by contributing leadership as a coach, an official, or an administrator.

Should one of my daughters choose to be a high performance athlete, I want the sport organization to respect her as a total person, not merely as a gifted athlete, recognizing that she has needs beyond the sporting field. The support may take the form of ensuring that her education needs not be sacrificed while she pursues her sporting goals, that she will be supported during maternity leave and while making her comeback, and she will be assisted when she retires from competitive sport.

I want an equitable system, one which acknowledges that the needs of girls and boys are different, that values these differences, and that strives to satisfy those differing needs. I want a system in which women and men, girls and boys, share the responsibility, share the rewards, and share the pleasures, working hand in hand to build sport for all.

Sport is about so much more than learning raw athletic skills. To a parent, sport's appeal lies in learning solid values and carrying them with you every day of your life.

This article is adapted from one which originally appeared in The Way Ahead for Canadian Women in Sport: The Report of the 1992 IDPD Tour *(a publication of the Tait McKenzie Institute, Canadian Sport and Fitness Administration Centre, 1992).*

Marg McGregor is Executive Director for CAAWS. She is the proud mom of two active daughters. She is committed to getting girls and women out of the bleachers and cheerleading uniforms, and into the pools, gyms, rinks, locker rooms, and board rooms of Canada.

Canadian Woman Studies/les cahiers de la femme, Fall 1995, Vol. 15, Number 4, p11.
Reprinted with permission.

Notable Women

Sandra Schmirler

Three-time Canadian and world curling champion, Schmirler was a dominant force in her sport, leading her rink to victory in the 1998 winter Olympics in Nagano, Japan - capturing the first gold medal in Olympic curling history. She was admired for her curling skills and for her commitment to her family. Sandra Schmirler fought cancer with the same determination she had always shown on the rink but it was a battle she could not win. She died on March 2, 1999.

Sylvia Hamilton

Born in Beechville, Sylvia Hamilton is a filmmaker and writer who lives in Halifax, Nova Scotia. Through her work as a filmmaker and artist, she has brought the life experiences of African Nova Scotians to the mainstream of Canadian arts. Her first film, Black Mother Black Daughter, has been seen in over forty film festivals throughout North America and Europe, and her films have won awards at festivals in Canada, USA, Europe and the Caribbean. Speak It! From the Heart of Black Nova Scotia received both the 1994 Maeda Prize awarded by the NHK-Japan Broadcasting Corporation, and a 1994 Gemini Award. Hamilton's writing, both literary and non-fiction has appeared in many Canadian journals and anthologies.

Judy Rebick

Judy Rebick was born in Reno Nevada and grew up in New York City, Toronto and Montreal, where she received a B.Sc. from McGill University. Her years of activism in the women's movement have made her a household name and face to Canadians. From 1990 to 1993, she was president of the National Action Committee on the Status of Women, Canada's largest women's group with more than 500 member groups. In 1993, she led a grass roots opposition to the Charlottetown Accord and during the time she was president, NAC helped to win refugee status based on gender persecution, a stronger rape law and the defeat of a new abortion law. She was appointed a lay member of the Ontario Judicial Council, the body responsible for adjudicating complaints against provincial court judges in Ontario and she has been an active supporter of people with disabilities. She is also a nationally known writer and political commentator.

Doris McCarthy OC

"If you want a good life, be an artist. It's never dull. You're never finished, you can take it to the grave, you don't have to stop, ever."

Born in 1910, Doris McCarthy is one of Canada's most celebrated artists. Since first exhibiting one of her paintings in the Ontario Society of Artists (OSA) 1931 annual exhibition, she has exhibited across Canada and throughout the world. Her many achievements include: receiving the Order of Canada in 1986; being appointed the first woman President of the OSA; becoming President of the Canadian Society of Painters in Water Colour; and graduating from the University of Toronto in 1989 at the age of 79. She has produced more than 5,000 works, creating landscape paintings that capture the total feel of the land. A dedicated teacher of art for more than 40 years at the Art Gallery and the Art Department of Toronto's Central Technical School, her students recall her energy, enthusiasm and teaching skills. McCarthy has continued to live an amazing life into her 90s, travelling all over the world to paint, seeking new challenges and sharing her experiences with students.

GREEN DRAGON PRESS

Activities
1990 – 1999

DOMESTIC AND GARMENT WORKERS

List in your own words, all the issues/inequalities that women domestic and garment workers face. For each problem, propose a possible solution.

WERE YOUR CLOTHES MADE IN A SWEATSHOP?

Ask the class to examine the labels of the shoes, and shirts they are wearing. On the board record all the brand names, and the countries where the clothes were made.

As a class project, research the issue of sweatshops in these countries, and possible controversy surrounding the company that produced the garments.

Make connections between what we wear, and the experience of the women and child garment makers who are exploited. Research and read their stories.

REMEMBERING THE MONTREAL MASSACRE

Do a quick, unannounced survey in the class. How many students are able to write down, unassisted, the date of the anniversary of the Montreal Massacre? Alternately, write "December 6, 1989" on the board and ask students to identify the significance of the date. How many can identify correctly this event? Discuss why remembrance of such an event is crucial to all of us.

WOMEN AND MUSIC

Since Lilith Fair, how have women been doing in the world of music? Have the class identify all the different genres/types of music that are available. How many girls in the class are involved in "girl-bands"?

Resources

Canadian Woman Studies/les cahiers de la femme, Fall 1995, Vol. 15, Number 4.
Caldicott, Helen. *If You Love this Planet: A Plan to Heal the Earth,* NY: W.W. Norton, 1992.
Childerhose, Buffy. *From Lilith to Lilith Fair.* Madrigal Press, 1998.
Fitzgerald, Judith. *Building a Mystery: The Story of Sarah McLachlan and Lilith Fair.* Quarry Press, 1997.
Long, Wendy. *Celebrating Excellence: Canadian Women Athletes.* Vancouver: Polestar Books, 1995.
McCarthy, Doris. *A Fool in Paradise: an artist's early life.* Toronto: Macfarlane Walter & Ross, 1990.
McCarthy, Doris. *The Good Wine: An artist comes of age,* Toronto: Macfarlane, Walter & Ross, 1991.

Videos: Black Mother Black Daughter and Speak It! From the Heart of Black Nova Scotia. National Film Board of Canada.

GREEN DRAGON PRESS

2000 and beyond

The challenge ahead

Dragon Boat team made up entirely of breast cancer survivors.
Photo: Christopher Grabowski

- Statistics Canada's 1998 report - Family Violence in Canada: A Statistical Profile, which analyzed data provided by 154 reporting police agencies, shows that:
- Women continue to outnumber men nine to one as victims of assault by a spouse or partner;
- In 1996 half of all family homicides involved spouses;
- Between 1977 and 1996, three times as many women were killed by their spouses as were men killed by their spouses;
- Girls are at greatest risk of sexual assault by a family member while between 12 and 15 years of age;
- In 1996 nine of ten crimes committed against older adults by family members were physical assaults.

Cardiovascular disease is the major cause of death and disability among Canadian women. The number of deaths from CVD is just about equal for Canadian men and women. In 1996, 40,037 men and 39,924 women died of CVD.

- Two in three women have one or more of the major risk factors for heart disease;
- In 1996, CVD in women accounted for over 2,569,333 hospital days, a greater number than that reported for other conditions, including cancer, pregnancy and neurological ailments;
- In 1996, 26% of women aged 15 and over smoked. Forty-eight percent of women smokers aged 18 to 24, and 23% aged 25 to 34 also take oral contraceptives, thus significantly increasing their risk for CVD;
- Thirteen percent of Canadian women have high blood pressure, and 45% have elevated blood cholesterol.

Women are under-represented in heart health research and prevention studies. The lack of data and the consequent difficulty of determining appropriate preventive interventions for women hamper their ability to deal with heart disease.

Statistics Canada

GREEN DRAGON PRESS

2000 and beyond: The challenge ahead

Introduction

"I need to speak further about this problem of women, how they are dismissed and excluded from the most primary of entitlements. But we've come so far; that's the thinking. So far compared with fifty or a hundred years ago. Well, no, we've arrived at the new millennium and we haven't "arrived" at all. We've been sent over to the side pocket of the snooker table and made to disappear. No one is so blind as not to recognize the power of the strong over the weak and, following that, the likelihood of defeat."
Carol Shields, Unless, 2002.

As Canadian women enter the 21st century their fight for equality is not over. Although the women's movements of the past have helped bring about important legislation that created greater recognition of women's right within society, there is still much to be done. There are still significant issues that need to be addressed especially in areas such as domestic violence, sexual assault, inequity in the job markets, restrictions in job promotion, assessment and management training and job placement, and women's health. Statistics indicate a rise in violence and abuse against women. Women are still the dominant care providers for children and seniors and an increasing number of men leave their spouses to raise their children alone. Over 78 per cent of single parent women head families and 76 per cent of court ordered family support payments are not received. The largest numbers of individuals living in poverty are single mothers and our current level of child poverty in Canada has been openly criticized by the United Nations. There seems little hope that governments will address these issues in a significant way within the near future unless significant pressure is brought to bear. The 1999 Statistics Canada indicated some disturbing trends. In Canada, 92 per cent of men work in full time jobs compared to only 77 per cent of women. Women are still dominant in industries related to health care, sales, administration and domestic service, jobs that traditionally have lower incomes. And Canadian men are more likely to be employed in management and technical occupations and in highly self-directed workgroups where they become managers and professionals. Women are still clustered in occupations with lower than average training opportunities. At the end of the 20th century, women earned between 8-15 per cent less than men, depending on the workplace conditions. They also worked lower numbers of full-time hours, greater numbers of part-time hours and had fewer opportunities for promotion. In an effort to be included in the male dominant work place women have often not been in a position to exchange or establish shared duties but rather doubled their own workloads. Over time, studies have revealed that many women are now burdened with the double task of childcare and demanding work responsibilities outside the home often resulting in the "superwoman" label, a term which reflects the present situation for women. However, this trend has serious health consequences and as women increase their work on all levels, they increase their levels of stress on both their physical and emotional bodies, which can result in significant increases of health related problems. For example, Statistics Canada revealed in 1996 that cardiovascular disease is the major cause of death and disability among Canadian women.

GREEN DRAGON PRESS

The number of deaths from CVD is just about equal for Canadian men and women now. In 1996, 40,037 men and 39,924 women died of CVD. Clearly women need to establish a more equitable balance between work, home and childcare. As well, women in Canada continue to outnumber men nine to one as victims of assault by a spouse or partner. Women will not be free from violence until they achieve equality with men, and equality cannot be achieved until violence and the threat of violence are eliminated from women's lives. It is still an issue that young Canadian women must face both at home, within their workplace and in society as a whole. These are all issues that young women need to address in the 21st century, as trends can easily become the norm. Like the women in past generations, young Canadian women must refuse to accept inequities and be willing to mobilize support for change, so that trends do not become the norm. This way, they will ensure that their children, the future generation of Canadians, will not face the same challenges, as they work and live in a more equitable society. There are important ways to ensure that women's issues are addressed.

One way involves placing more women in positions of responsibility. More than eight decades after women won the right to vote in Canada, men still run the country. By 2004 the House of Commons is still only 21 percent female. In legislatures, and on municipal councils, women make up only a fifth of those elected to office, and lately the number is dropping. In 2003, the United Nations called on Canada to do something about our ranking (36th in the world according to the number of women elected nationally.) According to this trend Canadian women will have to wait several generations more to see gender equity in their political institutions and clearly this will impact on other issues related to health and welfare of women in Canada. Statistics: www.coolwomen.org

GREEN DRAGON PRESS

Women and Work

Work or Family: Is there a Third Option?

The women's movement helped open doors to the world of education and work for women but has failed to provide a path for balancing the demands of a career with those of parenthood. For many working mothers today, this is still the principal struggle. Statistics show, that although there is an increase in the participation of men in terms of childrearing, women still carry the greater load of household duties, especially with babies and young children. As a result, many women must put their successful and rewarding careers on hold.

Many women are rejecting the work or family option and looking for a third choice. In the rigid corporate world women are examining options or dropping out. In an article in a recent *Maclean's* magazine," Kids vs Career," the author examines the lives of several women, some who chose motherhood over careers. All the women state that they are torn between the choices and feel forced to make compromises, especially in terms of their own careers.

"For Kim Gray, for example, the last straw came in December. The mother of a boy who turns three next week and a six-year-old girl, she had to leave halfway through her daughter's kindergarten Christmas concert to get to work. "That was after prying off my son and distracting him into staying with the babysitter so I could run out of the school," recalls the Calgary resident. A journalist who, pre-kids, filed stories from Bosnia and had written for most major western Canadian newspapers, Gray agonized over her decision. On the one hand, she loved the buzz and excitement of her career; on the other, she'd begun thinking of her children as management issues, and her work life was

intruding too much on the home front. "I love, love journalism, says Gray. I was thinking about it even when I wasn't at the office." But her son was not thriving emotionally. "All the feminist politics aside, it just wasn't sitting right." Gary quit her job as a part-time feature writer with the *Calgary Herald* and keeps a foot in journalism by freelancing." ("Kids vs. Career" by Katherine Macklem, *Maclean's*, March 15, 2004, volume 117, #11.)

Women still face conflicting messages. If you stay at home you have no status and risk jeopardizing future career options; if you work and must spend time away from your children, you are seen as someone who has abandoned your motherhood responsibilities.

Although many women love their children and being a mom, they also find a great deal of self-satisfaction in their work and worry about getting back into similar senior level positions later in their lives. These are justified concerns. Studies found a striking difference in the career paths of men and women who had graduated from the same prestigious schools. Women with MBAs were far more likely than men to work part-time or be self-employed. More than one in ten women are out of work voluntarily, compared to a fraction of men. Other statistics show that more women than men are starting their own businesses, but aren't growing them as fast because they prefer to keep their work hours down.

"Corinne Berman is a woman whose life was turned upside down with the arrival of her children. Before, she was intently focused on her career. A top student, she graduated in 1991 with an MBA from the Richard Ivey School of

GREEN DRAGON PRESS

Business at the University of Western Ontario in London, and within a few years was a senior vice-president at a multinational insurance company, overseeing about 60 people. She was passionate about her work, toiled long hours and made good money. "It was a big adrenalin rush. We were having a blast; working the long hours has a huge benefit." And then Haley, the first of three children, was born. When the baby was 3 1/2 months old, Berman returned to work part-time; when she was 8 months she went back to "the regular full-time swing and grind." She left the house at 7 each morning and tried to be back by 6:30. "I was naïve about children," she now says. Five days a week was too much, and she wangled a four-day workweek. "It was a good deal for the company because you end up packing five days into four," she says. "But you do it because you want the fifth day to do grocery shopping and all the running around so your weekends aren't hell."... In 1999, when she was pregnant with her second child, she was laid off, the casualty of corporate restructuring. "I went out and did interviews and kept coming up against this road block. I wanted to be a senior executive but I didn't want to work five days a week."... After her third child she made the decision not to return to the corporate world. Her husband makes enough money that she can afford not to work full-time for a few years. Last year, she was hired by a community college to teach economics. "I'm not sure the corporate world would take me back," she says. "This isn't' Utopia, but it's close."... (Kids vs Career by Katherine Macklem *Maclean's*, March 15, 2004, volume 117, #11.)

Clearly the workplace suffers. As women continue to prove themselves as major contributors to the success of the work place, their absence has an effect on the labour force. The issue still lies in trying to accommodate mothering into the traditional five day a week workweek. Clearly we need to develop new options. The author ends with a story about a new mother, who is also a traveling executive, experiencing security challenges, when she carries breast milk in her briefcase.

The women's movement may have opened the doors to higher education, work and power but the "messiness" and demands of motherhood are still challenges the next generation will have to accommodate. Kathleen Macklem ends her article with a comment by consultant Nora Spinks, president of Work-Life Harmony Enterprises;

"The number of women who become discouraged or frustrated, or who don't have the opportunity to get back into the paid labour force, is a loss to everybody. What we've failed to do is welcome them and make the necessary adaptations to make it as effective as possible. "

Macklem adds: " It is one thing to allow women into the corridors of power. Motherhood, and its messiness, is more difficult to fathom-and to accommodate."

The article includes the following statistical information:

> 28% of working women are part-time workers, many because they are taking care of families.
> 75% of female executives believe commitment to family hinders advancement, 41% delayed or skipped having children.
> The average working Mother spends 91 minutes daily on childcare compared to 45 minutes for men.
> (Statistics Canada)

KIDS VS CAREER by Katherine Macklem
Maclean's, March 15, 2004, volume 117, #11.

GREEN DRAGON PRESS

Young Women and the Internet

"The increasingly corporate nature of the internet and its use as a marketing tool is becoming a challenge to girls and young women looking for empowering opportunities or resources online that are meant for girls their own age."

Brandi L. Bell

Some facts from www.womenspace.ca

- In Canada, 15 to 19 year olds represent the age group with the most Internet users;
- Men tend to use the Internet more than women in each age group, but the gap is smaller among youth;
- Access to computers and the Internet is not equal among all young women: family composition, level of parents' education, income, language, and geographical location all affect access;
- Even with the high level of availability of computers in schools, there are still differences between the sexes, with girls being less likely to use school-based computers than boys;
- Boys are generally more comfortable with computers and use them out of interest, developing more confidence in using them than girls do;
- Women often would prefer to take classroom-based courses, but choose to take online courses because it is the only way they can fit education into their home and work lives;
- Experiences of online sexism, racism, censorship, and homophobia continue to make young women feel unwelcome or uncomfortable in online environments. Young women are more likely to receive unwanted sexual comments when online.

Sources: Statistics Canada; Dryburgh, H. *Changing our ways: Why and how Canadians use the Internet*. Ottawa, 2001; Environics Research Group. *Young Canadians in a wired world: the students' view*. Ottawa, 2001; Kramarae, C. *The Third Shift: Women learning online*. Washington: American Association of University Women Educational Foundation, 2001.

GREEN DRAGON PRESS

How Does She Do It?

Wendy Mesley's five-year old daughter started kindergarten last fall. The nanny she and her husband, Liam McQuade, share with another family, says the co-host of CBC's Marketplace, "is a huge reason for my sanity. The only time my daughter ever had a high, high fever, I was away for the first time since she was born. She was six months old. You talk about heartache-there was an actual physical ache. I cancelled the last shoot. My life is almost manageable now. With Marketplace, the trips aren't so long. I'm usually just getting to my guilt limit when it's time to come home. Working is part of what makes me me. I can't imagine staying home full-time. I would love to have a half-job, but all the really good jobs in journalism require a fair commitment. I think she understands her parents love her. That's what's most important."

Three weeks into the job, Dr. Sheela Basrur, Ontario's new chief medical officer of health, is still figuring out her hours. They won't, however, hold a candle to the grueling days she put in as head of Toronto's public health system during the SARS outbreak. Her daughter Simone, 13, spends alternate weeks with Basrur and the husband from whom she is separated, who also provides after-school care. "SARS was an extraordinary period of seven days a week and 15 hour days for months on end. I had family support at home and friends who offered to come over and help do the grocery shopping. The one thing Simone has commented on is me answering my cell phone if it goes off when we're together. I have learned to avoid doing that as much as possible."

Every Monday, Christy Clark and her two-year old son, Hamish, leave their Port Moody, B.C. home and travel to Victoria. There, in a makeshift nursery across the hall, a caregiver looks after Hamish and another child. Later in the week, the Minister of Children and Family development and deputy premier, returns home with Hamish, who's in a group childcare program. "Politics is traditionally a male domain. People don't cut you any slack because you're a mom of a little kid. They don't think about the fact that you want to spend your evening with your family when they phone you at 9, when you are putting your kid to bed. To really succeed in politics, you need networking time. You have to give that up if you also want to be an engaged parent. So you don't go out to dinner with colleagues after work, or hang out at the office and have a beer with your deputy-just that casual time when so much work is done and so many relationships get built."

Sue Ferguson in
"KIDS VS CAREER" by Katherine Macklem, *Maclean's*, March 15, 2004, volume 117, #11.
Reprinted with permission.

> • 2004 On August 24th, Justice Minister Irwin Cotler announced the appointments of two women jurists to the Supreme Court of Canada. Rosalie Abella, a human-rights expert who came to Canada as a child refugee, and Louise Charron, a francophone Ontarian from Ottawa were named to fill the two vacancies on the court, bringing the number of women on the nine-member bench to four, the highest in the history of the court, These nominations represent a breakthrough for women in the justice field and brings a gender balance to the bench that is unprecedented not only in Canada but elsewhere in the world.

GREEN DRAGON PRESS

WIFE IS WHAT YOU MAKE IT

"It's a four-letter word regularly uttered in polite society. Though not literally a profanity, it's often spoken as if it were one, especially by women. And it's associated with an array of behaviours. The definition of "wife" isn't easy to pin down. This centuries-old term is teeming with cultural references, a good number of them bordering on the profane. And Toronto journalist *Anne Kingston* digs them all up in The *Meaning of Wife*, deftly weaving them through a discussion of weddings, housework, business, sex, abuse, adultery, divorce and the single life. A little thin analytically, the book does offer an amusing and sometimes shocking appraisal of western ambivalence about wifedom.

Kingston calls that ambivalence the "wife gap." It's produced, she suggests, by a media and industry-driven romantic revival of marriage and domesticity on the one hand, and on the other, a post-feminist backlash that sees more and more women foregoing or reneging on marital vows. A cultural "script" circulates with the gap, encouraging women to believe their happiness hinges on conforming to traditional gender roles. "Women assumed they had been freed from wife," writes Kingston, who's never married, "but wife hadn't been freed from women."

The power of Kingston's message lies in the scope of her research. And she unearths plenty of gems. Consider that a Kinsey Institute index of female sexual satisfaction published last June doesn't include orgasm. Or that in thousands of wedding magazines, the word "wife"appears only a handful of times. Kingston's analysis of the uses and abuses of wifedom is, in places, shrewd. Her dissection of Canada's $3-billion "wedding industrial complex" should be required reading for all brides to be. She also takes to task the likes of Martha Stewart, designer Vera Wang, Disney's Orlando Wedding Pavilion and Mattel's Princess Bride Barbie for foisting their "commercially motivated rules" on women while reducing them to "unreasoning infants" with constant urgings to give into childhood fantasies and spend, spend, spend. It amounts to "an eerie echo of coverture. Except the difference now....is that the bride is not only the consumed but also the consumer."

Kingston peppers the text with wry observations and snappy one-liners: feminism, she notes, has "gone to the mall"; sex for married women "has become the new housework."...

The wife gap, Kingston informs, is beginning to be bridged. At the vanguard of this "revolution" are the women (and men) who chip away at traditional scripts. Aside from noting a growing, if equivocal, social acceptance of the househusband, she returns to a realm of pop culture-including a spate of recent books and movies about wives of important men or husbands who act like wives-to make her point. The trouble is that she spends 266 pages showing us that for every progressive shift in the meaning of wife, there's an equal assertion of its conservative definition. The book however, does give readers a panoramic view of the wife gap's vast - and forbidding - dimensions."

Sue Ferguson, quoted in:
"KIDS VS CAREER" by Katherine Macklem, *Maclean's*, March 15, 2004, volume 117, #11.
Reprinted with permission.

GREEN DRAGON PRESS

Statistics Canada

1. Annual detergent sales in Canada: 557 million dollars;
2. Canadian women who say they are responsible for laundry: 80 per cent;
3. 33 per cent of Canadians spend 2-4 hours per week doing laundry and 24 per cent spend more than 6 hours;
4. There were 9.38 million automatic washing machines in Canada in the year 2000.

Laundry in the year 2000

Unlike women in the early years of the 20th century, women today find doing laundry a fairly easy activity. At the turn of the century, laundry was one of the most labour intensive chores and so women only laundered when absolutely necessary. Laundry was a back breaking, time-consuming chore, when women and their children had to haul and boil huge quantities of water, wash, rinse and wring heavy clothes (most clothing was made out of wool and heavy cotton) and then drag their clothes outside to dry or hang them inside on clothes lines near the hearth. Early wringer washers were only a slight improvement. Automatic washers didn't become standard equipment until the early 1960s. Today, we stick in a pile of laundry, add detergent and press the start button. Once the washer is done, we put the pile into the dryer, add a softening sheet, and press another button. Many of us put on laundry and go out. The only concern about laundry these days is whether the fine fabrics we purchase should have special treatment. No problem for modern day women and men, as they change detergents, or set their machines to different settings. In response, the laundry industry in Canada is producing new products all the time: 52 in 1999, 91 in 2000 and 84 in 2001. With all these new products, the new focus for laundry seems to be an obsession with cleanliness. Although keeping our clothes clean is now a matter of pushing buttons, we must be careful to use appropriate products in order to produce perfect laundry. As well, studies indicate that laundry is still performed predominately by women. Statistics Canada reported that in 1996, 27% of women said that they do laundry on a typical day compared to 4% of men. Statistics Canada adds that women spend on average nearly 17 minutes a day on laundry while men spend a mere 2.4 minutes. Despite the new labour saving devices laundry is still the domain of women. New technology has not removed women from their dominant role in domestic chores. But if modern women spend approximately 6 hours a week, or the equivalent 3 days per month trying to produce perfect laundry, how much better are our lives compared to the "good old days" when we spent one day a month? The improvements will be clear not when we invent new machines or additional products but when laundry becomes the responsibility of those who wear the clothes.

Statistics cited in *Toronto Star*, June 1, 2002, based on Statistics Canada data from Whirlpool Canada, Soap and Detergent Association, Proctor and Gamble, Unilever Canada and Canada Science and Technology Museum.

Gender Stereotypes

Feminists of the Third Wave, Fashion and Mass Culture.

In an article in the *Toronto Star*, March 6, 2004 Daphne Gordon asks the following question: Is breaking the bank to be beautiful truly empowering women in the long term? The article examines how young women feel empowered today to wear whatever they choose, even if it is pink and low-cut, and are willing to max-out their credit cards to achieve this goal. Third wave women (first wave was the late 19th century, second wave was the late 1960s and 1970s) claim that women can be both feminists and fashionistas. A modern feminist icon, Sarah Jessica Parker, for example, from the TV show Sex and the City portrayed a very powerful and outspoken women who also liked to dress in a very pretty and feminine style. She spent an enormous amount of time shopping, looking for just the right pair of shoes. The author suggests that modern women need to find a balance between their love of fashion and looking good, with other interests that will empower them in the long term. She points out that while many young men are busy learning about investments and starting businesses, their female friends are spending most of their lunchtime putting their names on the waiting list for the latest handbag.

But being a feminist is more than having the right to wear whatever you want. Although most young women agree that wearing short skirts, pink frilly tops and push up bras has little to do with female empowerment, few will admit to the impact mass culture has on these decisions. On the one hand, more women have become professionals, scientists, doctors and lawyers, on the other; they seem focused on maintaining their youth, beauty and sex appeal. Music videos and popular magazines are examples of how sexually co-modified women have become

to sell their product. It seems standard now for women to sing or dance half-naked in order to be cool.

Naomi Wolf, in her best-selling book: *The Beauty Myth*, states that patriarchal mass culture uses beauty ideals to control female behaviours and psychology. Clearly the winners these days are the cosmetic manufactures, the pharmaceutical companies and the plastic surgeons. Young and younger women are maxing out these expensive options in order to achieve their beauty choices.

It seems clear that traditional female achievements do not have the same impact. Young women no longer are impressed with the achievements of great women. In Canada a woman heads the Supreme Court, four other females are Supreme Court Justices; we have women in politics, outstanding female performers in the arts, star athletes and women who run their own companies. Young women are overwhelmed with famous and successful women role models. They have many more choices than ever before and clearly feel the pressure to be successful on many levels. It is a challenge for all women to fight to maintain human rights and at the same time, find a balance in their lives between the expectations of society, their family and friends and their own dreams.

GREEN DRAGON PRESS

Another author asks the question:

"So, why did the woman really cross the road?

And she answers:

"Well, to get a haircut, to grab a sandwich before the trial at which she is presiding, to buy socks for her children on her lunch hour, to meet a friend, to pick up her kids at day care, to take her father to the doctor, to pick out a wedding ring, to consult a divorce lawyer, to apply for a promotion, to take a maternity leave, to buy her husband a present, to take her kids to the museum, to get to the shelter for abused women, to pick up her prescription, to run around the track, to find a jar of sauce for a spaghetti supper. Oh, and just maybe to get to the other side."

"What's a Girl to Do? It's the 21st century now-do women know what their stereotypes are up to?" by Judith Timson: *Maclean's* Magazine Sept. 3, 2001.

June Callwood
Photo: Linda Rapson

Knowing the effort that is required not just to create new rights but to keep the ones she successfully campaigned for, journalist and social justice activist June Callwood is worried that the next generation of activists may not be up to the task, because they may be driven primarily by environmental issues.

Food for thought indeed, for Third Wave Feminists, who already have a clear sense of their own empowerment.

GREEN DRAGON PRESS

Second and Third Wave Feminism:
A Generation Gap?

Third Wave feminism is generally defined as a movement of women in their 20s and 30s, who, although building upon the legacy of Second Wave feminist achievements, are struggling to define feminism in today's global context. Third Wave feminists feel that their goal is to celebrate their diversity, to embrace their femininity. They seek to include those who were previously marginalized due to race, class or sexual orientation. The authors of *Manifesta: Young Women, Feminism and the Future*, Jennifer Baumgardner and Amy Richards, advocate "Grrrl Power." Feminists today may have a traditional wedding, stay single, stay home, embrace and flaunt their sexuality.

The concerns of the Second Wave feminists:

"We have produced a generation of uppity women who feel entitled," (Erica Jong)

At a recent conference of Veteran Feminists of America, the division between the second and third wave generations became all too apparently clear. "I don't hear strong, clear feminist voices today...I don't see women coming up with new theories," stated one woman. Many second wave feminists expressed their concern at this conference that the young feminists of today are too "entitled," while many unresolved issues still abound, such as childcare and economic disparity.

The response of the Third Wave

"I think that the impact of the feminist movement was in helping women to achieve a voice...Now we are articulating that voice..." (Kalpana Krishnamurthy)

Third wavers at the conference expressed frustration at the women of the second wave for not making an attempt to understand or appreciate the new struggles and new broadened definition of feminism. Many young women feel that the traditional image of feminism is exactly what alienates girls today. www.manifesta.net/

On Being a Feminist 2004 - Young Women Speak

A feminist is someone (a man or a woman) who believes that men and women are equals, and therefore, they deserve equal chances to pursue their individual goals. A feminist chooses not to tolerate sexism in any shape or form. I myself, being a feminist, would like to show the world a community where children are raised as equals, I would very much like to see such a community today. I'm not saying I favour an Amazon-like society (i.e. simply role reversal) equality is the ultimate goal here. I remember being asked once which "side" I was on (men or women). To this I answered: "I wasn't aware that there were sides." I had the pleasure of saying this to a male surfing instructor who responded with a taken aback expression; perhaps it made him think about this possibility. I'd say it's about time!

Olivia Palloch, 17

GREEN DRAGON PRESS

My generation of women has grown up in a society that is constantly changing. Technology and society are evolving every day. Views of women are also changing. Even though women are still admired and needed for their contribution to society, a sense of feminism is still necessary. The fight for equality is still being fought and it is important that we do not let down our guard. I find myself, even in today's society, defending myself against discrimination, and still having to prove my worth and ability as a woman.

Erin Munro, 16

I believe that feminism is awesome. Without feminism women would be nothing but slaves in our own houses. We would have no say in who would run the country, and frankly, without the say of women, what kind of Canada would we have? Because feminism gives women the same social, political and economic rights as men we have the confidence to accomplish great things in our lives. Because of feminism, men HAVE to listen to what we say. Before feminism, women were too afraid to speak out; afraid of the repercussions and backlash from men who ran our lives. Now, the principle that women should have the same rights as men, means that women don't have to be afraid anymore. We can stand up and speak out. We can accomplish great things. Feminism rocks!

Laura Staton-Mei 16

In the 21st century, being a feminist is completely different from being a feminist in the 19th century. Today, in the world of technology, mass media and communication, the word feminist means something completely different. Feminists fight for women's rights, and for the equality of the sexes. Feminists are women who speak out for women, especially for women who can't. They are women who want equality. Being a woman today in the 21st century does not mean that everything is perfect. We have more say, we can vote but there are still some obstacles that hold us back. Feminists today are trying to eliminate these obstacles. They are strong, brave, courageous and determined to achieve equality.

Elizabeth Tran, 17

A feminist believes in equal rights and equal opportunities for both sexes. They believe that women are just as comfortable in positions of power as they are in more modest circumstances and that women are capable of achieving anything a man can achieve. Feminists value the importance of having the choice to be a businesswoman, a traveler, a housewife, a scientist, an athlete, or all of the above.

Kristen Dobbin, 18

GREEN DRAGON PRESS

Canadian Women's Olympic Hockey Team 2002

"Hockey is about pressure. I knew from Day One what to expect from the US. It was a matter of playing 60 minutes." Danièle Sauvageau

By the final week of the Olympics, the rivalry between the Canadian and the American Women's hockey teams was becoming more and more evident. Canada and the United States have dominated for as long as women's hockey has been played internationally. Canada had won seven straight world championships, which was overshadowed by their devastating defeat in Nagano in 1998. The Canadians went into the Olympics with a 0-8 record against the US, but were determined and "eager to show that they were in no way scared of the US." They began preparing by working on ways to slow down the Americans' power play. Danièle Sauvageau said, "We had played them enough to know what was coming. We started to narrow our focus in practice." Both the US and Canada played through the preliminary round without any major problems or competition. The gold medal game began at 5pm on February 21st, where the cheers of the crowds, in favour of the Americans could be heard. The Canadians kept the words of figure skaters Jamie Salé and David Pelletier, fellow Canadian Olympic athletes in mind; who told them to pretend the cheers were for them. They knew what they had to do, "The plan was to score first, and after that we felt we had them on their heels." They held on throughout the game and played it out to the end, winning the gold medal with a 3-2 lead over the American team. Their dedication to their sport, their perseverance and their unwillingness to give in when winning seemed nearly impossible is what makes each and every woman on this team not only deserving of this gold medal but of the respect and admiration of women everywhere.

Melissa Duff 2002

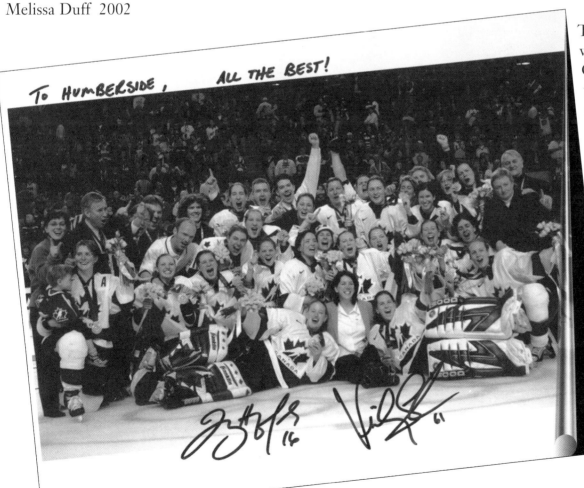

TO HUMBERSIDE, ALL THE BEST!

The Canadian women's gold medal Olympic hockey team and their coaches and assistants pose for a group photo following their 3-2 victory over the United States, Thursday, February 21st, 2002 at the Salt Lake City Winter Olympics.

Photo: Hockey Canada/AP Photo/Kevork Djansezian.

GREEN DRAGON PRESS

Notable Women of the Future

Susan Aglukark
Photo: EMI/Karen Levy

Susan Aglukark

Singer and songwriter Susan Aglukark was born in Churchill, Manitoba and grew up in the western Arctic community of Arivat, now part of Nunavut. Her album, *This Child* made her a well-known throughout Canada in 1995, both as an artist but also as a role model and a spokesperson for the Aboriginal community.

Fiona Sampson

Fiona is a lawyer who has worked for the Ontario Human Rights Commission, the Equality Committee of DAWN (DisAbled Women's Network), taught at Trent University in the Women's Studies Department and at Osgoode Hall Law School. Fiona is currently Director of Litigation, Women's Legal Education and Action Fund (LEAF). She is responsible for the management of all litigation and other legal work undertaken by LEAF.

Perdita Felicien

Named Canadian Press Female Athelete of the Year after winning the l00 metre hurdles in Paris in 2003 and winner of the 60-meter hurdle event at the 2004 World indoor track and field championships. Felicien's trip to the top of the podium was a first - no other Canadian women had ever won gold at the world championships.

GREEN DRAGON PRESS

Irshad Manji

Irshad Manji is a best selling author, TV personality, media entrepreneur and activist. Born in East Africa, Ms. Manji studied at the University of British Columbia where she became the first humanities student to win the Governor General's Gold medal for top graduate. She now promotes innovative thinking in Toronto where she is a leader in various youth movements. She is the author of the book *The Trouble with Islam* which explores the Muslim world today. Risking Utopia: *On the Edge of a New Democracy*, published in 1997, chronicles how young people are getting more involved with their rights as citizens and has inspired school courses and book clubs throughout the world. Manji has received a number of awards including *MS* magazine "Feminist for the 21st Century" and the Simon Wiesenthal Award for Valor.

Irshad Manji
Photo: Big Ideas

Chantal Peticlerc

An accident when she was 13 left Chantal a paraplegic but instead of letting the injury limit her life, her courage, spirit and hard work have enabled her to become one of the greatest wheel chair athletes in the world, winning the gold medal in the women's wheelchair 800 meters at the Athens Parallel Olympics, August 22, 2004.

Severn Cullis-Suzuki

Environmental concerns run in Severn's family. She began early, making a speech at age 12 at the 1992 United Nations Earth Summit. While studying evolutionary biology and ecology at Yale, Severn started the Skyfish project, an on-line forum for debate about how to effect change in environmental policy; the group is moving toward hands-on projects.

GREEN DRAGON PRESS

Activities
2000 and beyond

ILLUSTRATED TIME LINE

Using a roll of shelf paper create an illustrated time line for the twentieth century that includes major historical events and milestones for women.

ACROSS THE CENTURY

Stage a meeting between two women, one from the early 20th century and a contemporary woman. Have them discuss their work, the status of women then and now, including women's roles and their economic and legal status.

INTERVIEW A NOTABLE WOMAN

In pairs, conduct an imaginary interview with one of the notable women listed at the end of each chapter.

Resources

Anderson, Kim and Bonita Lawrence, eds. *Strong Women Stories: Native Vision and Community Survival.* Toronto: Sumach Press, 2003.

Backhouse, Constance. *Colour Coded: A Legal History of Radicalism in Canada.* Toronto: University of Toronto Press, 2004.A

Baumgardner, Jennifer and Amy Richards. *Manifesta: Young Women, Feminism & the Future,* New York: Farrar Strauss & Giroux, 2002.

Canadian Woman Studies/les cahiers de la femme, "Women and the Black Diaspora," Vol. 23, #2, Winter, 2004.

Epp, Marlene, Franca Iacovetta, & Frances Swyripa, eds. *Sisters or Strangers? Immigrant, Ethnic, and Racialized Women in Canadian History,* Toronto: U of T Press, 2004.

HERIZONS: Women's News & Feminist Views

Holmlund, Mona & Gail Youngbird, eds. *Inspiring Women: A Celebration of Herstory,* Regina: Coteau Books, 2003.

Labaton, Vivien & Dawn Lundy Martin, eds. *The Fire This Time: Young Activists and the New Feminism,* New York: Anchor Books, 2004.

Palmer, Alexandra. *Fashion: A Canadian Perspective,* Toronto: U of T Press, 2004.

Richardson, Karen & Stephen Green, eds. *T-Dot Griots: An Anthology of Toronto's Black Storytellers,* Victoria BC: Trafford Publishing, 2004.

www.cwhn.ca	Canadian Women's Health Network
www.mediawatch.ca/	Media Watch
www.nawl.ca	National Association of Women and the Law
www.coolwomen.org	Canadian Women in History
www.swc-cfc.gc.ca	Status of Women Canada
www.womenspace.ca	Womenspace
www.dawncanada.net	DisAbled Women's Network (DAWN) Ca
www.niagara.com/~merrwill/	Women in Canadian History
www3.sympatico.ca/equity.greendragonpress	Green Dragon Press Publishers
www.franco.ca/fnfcf	Fédération nationale des femmes Canadiennes-francaises (FNFCF)www.franco.ca/fnfcf

GREEN DRAGON PRESS

Green Dragon Press

2267 Lake Shore Blvd. West, #1009
Toronto, Ontario, Canada M8V 3X2

Tel: 416-251-6366 Fax: 416-251-6365 www3.sympatico.ca/equity.greendragonpress

History

A New Life in Canada (13.50) & **Starting Life Again** (12.25) 2 video set. Grade 7-12, Adult.

For most of the women Canada was unknown, & some came reluctantly. Many spoke neither English nor French; the customs were alien to them. Some found unexpected opportunities & unlooked-for successes: others met disappointments, prejudice and racism & became discouraged & homesick. No two stories are alike but there are commonalities.
$40. + $5. p&h + GST Total $48.15

I've Something to Tell You: Stories of Immigrant Women. Joyce Scane. Grade 7-12, Adult.

The experiences, both happy and sad, of a diverse group of women who came to Canada seeking a new life.
$20. + $4. p&h + GST Total $25.68

Black Women in Canada: Past and Present. Compiled by Marguerite Alfred & Pat Staton. Grade 7-12, Adult.
Articles, illustrations, archival materials, classroom activities, bibliography to support the integration of the history of Black women in Canada into the curriculum, revised 2004.
$30. + $5. P &h + GST Total $37.45

Canadian Women in History: A Chronology. Compiled by Moira Armour. Grade 9-12, Adult.
A terrific resource for the library and classroom. 2,500 brief entry items about Canadian women, their achievements and issues, listed chronologically and cross-indexed by name and theme. Sources included.
$30. + $5. p&h + GST Total $37.45

Forbidden Voice: Reflections of a Mohawk Indian.
Alma Greene, descended from Mohawk chieftains was recognized from early childhood as a natural healer. She wrote about her people's past and contemporary events she witnessed. Beautifully illustrated.
$30. + $5. p&h + GST Total $37.45

Working Light: The Wandering Life of Photographer Edith S. Watson. Frances Rooney.
Edith Watson traveled across Canada from the 1890s, documenting the lives of rural people, frequently women, at work. She photographed women working fish flakes in Newfoundland and Nova Scotia, making soap, weaving and spinning in Quebec and across the Prairies and into British Columbia. She spent three summers among the Doukhobors in Alberta and BC. The photographs are both valuable as social history and beautifully composed.
$30. + $5. p&h + GST Total $37.45

NEW 2004

Unfolding Power: Documents in 20th Century Canadian Women's History. Gr. 9-12. Adult

An exciting collection of primary documents (diaries, letters, advertisements, essays, photographs) that can be easily integrated into any Canadian history program. Organized chronologically, documenting the decades of the 20th century. Incorporates major themes that defined and impacted on women's lives. End of chapter activities and selected resources.
$63. + $5. p&h + GST Total $72.75

Forthcoming: Spring 2005. It Was Their War Too: Canadian Women in World War 1.
A Resource Collection. Includes diaries, letters, documents, essays and illustrations. Gr. 7-12.

Equity Issues

Are You a Boy or a Girl?
Karleen Pendleton Jimenez. Elementary. Kids spend a lot of time debating with each other over what makes a boy a boy and a girl a girl. It's a time of choices. It's a time of creating themselves. It could be a time for blending and embracing the many ways they express themselves. But is too often a time of narrowing the possibilities of who they can be Are a Boy or a Girl? enters into this conversation and opens it up. It is the story of a child thinking through who she is, learning through her mother's love how to be both strong and soft.
$8.95 + $3. + GST Total $12.85

Harassment Hurts: Sex-Role Stereotyping, Sexism and Sexual Harassment.

Pat Staton & June Larkin. Elementary school resource materials, facilitator's guide, class activities, print and visual resources. Revised 2004.

$25 + $5. p& + GST Total $32.10

Count Me In: Gender Equity in the Primary Classroom.

Judy Kwasnica Mullen. A useful resource for primary teachers, Count Me In combines gender equity theory with practical strategies and resource. The introduction explains such topics as socialization of gender roles, children's conception of gender, school climate and equity issues. Over 200 strategies on how to incorporate gender equity into the classroom. 260 title annotated bibliography of children's books.

$20. + $5. p&h + GST Total $26.75

High School Education Kit on Sexual Harassment.

Originated by the OISE/UT Caucus on Sexual Harassment; revised 1997 by June Larkin & Pat Staton. This kit includes: activities related to understanding what sexual harassment is and how to deal with it; facilitators guide, sample workshop and a bibliography.

$25. + $5. p&h + GST Total $32.10

Embodying Equity: Body Image as an Equity Issue. Carla Rice & Vanessa Russell. Grade 7-12, Adult.

NEW. 148p. A manual for educators and service providers. A creative and innovative practical resource addressing the intersections of body image, identity, prejudice and equity. A blend of theory and almost 50 inter-active exercises, this key resource will help teachers, administrators and service providers address body-related discriminations and exclusions in their populations and settings, providing tools to support individuals and institutions toward change.

$43.50 + $5. p&h + GST Total $51.40

Canadian Women Studies: An Introductory Reader.

A compilation of articles previously published in Canadian Woman Studies, offering a unique and historical perspective on feminism and feminist thought in Canada in the areas of work, public policy, race, class and gender, violence/harassment, media stereotypes, education, health, religion/spirituality. An excellent introductory text for women's studies classes.

$30. + $5. p&h + GST Total $37.45

Weaving Connections: Educating for Peace, Social and Environmental Justice.

Edited by Tara Goldstein & David Selby (Sumach Press). A collection of essays by Canadian educators, which document education philosophies and approaches, developed over the past 30 years directed towards equity, justice, peacefulness and earth awareness. They also challenge some of the current directions in Canadian school reform.

$30. + $5. p&h + GST Total $37.45

Posters

Women's History Posters:

1.Canadian Women in History. **2.** HERstory of Work: Recognizing Women's Contributions. **3.**Women and Education. **4.**Women and the Arts: A Cultural Heritage. **5.** Women in Science and Technology. **6.** Canadian Women in Sports. **7.** Canadian Women and the Law: the Search for Justice.   **8.** Women of Canada Our Century. **9.**Women of Canada: Invent~Discover~Explore. **10.** Celebrating Immigrant Women in Canada. **11.** Canadian Women Writers: Speaking out for Social Justice. **12.** Native Women in the Arts. **13.** International Women's Day. **$7. each + $3. p&h + GST Total $10.70   Any 7 of the above 13 posters: $50. including p&h & GST.**
We Can Do It! Full colour reproduction of WWII Rosie the Riveter showing her muscle.
$20. + $5 p&h +GST Total $26.75

Celebrating Diversity Posters:

1. African Heritage: Piecing Our History Together.
2. Celebrating African Heritage: Origins of Black History Month in Canada.
3. Early African Civilizations.
4. Asian Heritage: Celebrating Textile Art.
5. Welcome to Turtle Island (Aboriginal)
6. Rosemary Brown: Daring to Dream the Impossible.
$7. each + $3. p&h + GST Total $10.70

GREEN DRAGON PRESS